Energy Audit for Professionals

Energy Audit for Professionals

— *Editors* —
Suresh Kumar Dhungel
G. Krishnakumar

CENTRE FOR SCIENCE & TECHNOLOGY OF THE NON-ALIGNED AND OTHER DEVELOPING COUNTRIES (NAM S&T CENTRE)

2013
DAYA PUBLISHING HOUSE®
A Division of
ASTRAL INTERNATIONAL PVT. LTD.
New Delhi – 110 002

ISBN 978-81-7035-805-3

Centre for Science and Technology of the Non-Aligned and Other Developing Countries (NAM S&T Centre)
Core-6A, 2nd Floor, India Habitat Centre, Lodhi Road,
New Delhi-110 003 (India)
Phone: +91-11-24644974, 24645134, Fax: +91-11-24644973
E-mail: namstct@gmail.com
Website: www.namstct.org

Published by : **Daya Publishing House®**
A Division of
Astral International Pvt. Ltd.
81, Darya Ganj, Near Hindi Park,
Delhi Medical Association Road,
New Delhi - 110 002
Phone: 011-4354 9197, 2327 8134
Fax: +91-11-2324 3060
E-mail: info@astralint.com
Website: www.astralint.com

Laser Typesetting : **Classic Computer Services**
Delhi - 110 035

Printed at : **Salasar Imaging Systems**
Delhi - 110 035

PRINTED IN INDIA

Foreword

Provision of adequate energy services is a pre-condition for a decent quality of life, and is consequently an important goal for every developing country. However, at the same time, the availability and pricing of energy resources is becoming ever more challenging, with both availability constraints as well as large price volatility. Energy efficiency therefore becomes an essential ingredient of the energy strategy of every developing country as a means of balancing the energy service needs with energy supply constraints.

We do see, in almost every country of the world, a progressive decline in the energy intensity of economy reflecting, amongst other things, an increasing efficiency of energy use. However, in all countries, there are also many unexploited opportunities for energy conservation and the efficient use of energy. These unexploited opportunities occur in a wide variety of sectors, including in equipment and appliances, buildings, and in industry, especially in small industry. Identifying these opportunities, and addressing them through cost effective measures is an important element in the move towards a more energy-efficient economy.

Energy audit forms the basis of the identification of opportunities and of cost effective interventions to address them. Over the years, energy audit has developed into a rigorous discipline, with well-established methodologies and practices. In India, we have also moved towards the professionalization of energy audits by certifying energy auditors through a national examination. The experiences of energy audits in different sectors and different countries have resulted in important lessons relating to the conduct of energy audits. It is important that these lessons are shared amongst energy efficiency professionals in various countries, and put into practice.

I am extremely happy that the NAM S&T Centre, the Society of Energy Engineers and Managers (SEEM), and the Centre for Energy Studies & Policy Analysis organized the International Hands-on Training for Energy Audit Professionals in Developing Countries, with participation from 17 countries in May 2011. The papers from this programme have now been compiled and edited into this volume. This is of relevance to energy professionals in all countries, and especially in developing countries, and would serve as a useful document to initiate energy conservation activities in countries, industries and buildings.

Ajay Mathur, Ph.D.
Director General,
Bureau of Energy Efficiency (B.E.E.)

Preface

Energy is a basic need of any society or nation to provide for its citizens respectable livelihood. Energy only helps nations to climb the ladder of development. The correlation between energy consumption and gross domestic product of a nation is already well established. In the current world, which is sandwiched between major global problems such as energy crisis and climate change, conservation of energy has emerged as important element of energy management as it aims at reducing energy consumption and demand per capita. Hence it is very significant for each nation to assess its energy potential, consumption needs and establish sound energy security policies. This entails study of existing renewable and non renewable energy sources, estimate reasonably the energy requirement for coming years taking into consideration the growth needs of future generations, which is mainly driven by population explosion and evolution of technology. Energy conservation also paves the way to replace non-renewable energy resources with renewable ones through which sustainable development for future can be ensured. Energy Audit is a quantitative process of assessing the energy consumption pattern in any installation as a result which a practicable energy consumption strategy could be recommended. This study has to dovetail into same the environmental impacts of each of the sources of energy, to develop a future proof energy plan for the nation. It is in the context of future proofing the energy plan, the importance of energy efficiency and deployment of renewable energy assumes humongous proportion. This discussion is all the more relevant in the context of developing nations.

This book consists of a total of fourteen articles that were presented during the *International Hands-On Training on Energy Audit for Energy Professionals in Developing Countries* held in Mumbai, India in May 2011. Nine articles from the authors of Botswana, Cambodia, Malaysia, Mauritius, Nepal, Nigeria and Togo are country status papers, four articles from the authors of Malawi, Sri Lanka and Uganda are research articles whereas the rest one article of the author from India reflects the fundamentals of energy conservation. The compendium of articles discussing these very issues of a clutch of developing nations will be providing many a clue to the policy makers, researchers and students of energy economics. Some of the success stories related to energy conservation measures mentioned in the some articles are expected to encourage the readers of the other countries.

As editors of this book we have tried our best to maintain the beauty of diversified patterns of article composition adopted by the authors. We sincerely thank all the contributors of the articles for their kind cooperation in our work. We are highly grateful to Prof. Arun Prakash Kulshreshtha, Director of The Centre for Science and Technology of the Non-aligned and Other Developing Countries (NAM S&T Centre) for having entrusted us for this crucial task and his leadership in bringing out the book in this form. Roles of the NAM S&T Centre, Society of Energy Engineers and Managers (SEEM), Jawaharlal Nehru Port Trust(JNPT) have been instrumental in facilitating to create a platform where the professionals from different nations could present these papers for which our special thanks are due to Mr. Radhakrishnan IAS, Chairman, JNPT. Last but not the least; we thank Dr. V.P. Kharbanda, Dr Gurjeet Kaur and Mr. Yasir Abbas of NAM S&T Centre, New Delhi, India for their tireless effort in bringing out this book in this form.

Dr. Suresh Kumar Dhungel
Mr. G. Krishnakumar

Introduction

Energy is the basic need of life and for its production the most abundant and unlimited resource on earth is available in the form of renewable sources of energy which can be adapted to applications from powering laptop computers to vehicles to running municipal power plants with no harmful by-products and practically no emissions. Versatile, energy efficient and non-polluting sources of energy have the potential to revolutionise the way the countries can power themselves and prepare for the future. However, despite many benefits offered by it, the renewable energy technologies must overcome several barriers to achieve success for their commercial use. In making the renewable sources a practical and feasible option, cost is the greatest challenge and the price of production remains high for such sources of energy like solar cells and hydro-power. Therefore, technical issues need be resolved and new materials and improved designs are required to make these sources durable and feasible. Utility can also play a significant role in increasing public acceptance of renewable sources by becoming more technologically feasible.

Besides its production, there is also an urgent need to curtail energy wastage in all spheres of our lives for a sustainable development and environment as well as for a better tomorrow not only for us but also as for the generations to come. The individuals and organisations that are direct consumers of energy need to conserve energy to reduce energy costs and promote economic security. Energy conservation is an important element of energy planning and policy as it is aimed at per capita reduction in energy consumption and demand and offsetting the increase in energy supply needed to keep up with the increasing energy demands of the growing population. This strategy also reduces the rise in energy costs and the need for energy imports by developing suitable modern energy saving technologies. The reduced energy demand can provide more flexibility to choose the most preferred methods of energy production. Energy conservation facilitates the replacement of non-renewable resources with renewable energy. It is often the most economical solution to energy shortages, and is a more environmentally benign alternative to increasing the energy production.

Energy conservation represents a cost-effective approach with the development of suitable technologies to raising profitability, enhancing competitiveness and improving environmental performance and sustainability. The possibilities range from relatively simple and low-cost process modifications to sophisticated and more costly investments in pollution prevention technologies.

In order to deliberate on the above issues, the Centre for Science and Technology of the Non-aligned and Other Developing Countries (NAM S&T Centre) in association with the Centre for Energy Studies and Policy Analysis (CESPA), Trivandrum, India and the Society of Energy Engineers and Managers (SEEM), India organised a 11-days 'International Hands-On Training on Energy Audit For Energy Professionals in Developing Countries' during 4-14 May 2011 at Jawaharlal Nehru Port Trust (JNPT), Navi Mumbai, India. Eminent knowledge partners and supporting organisations such as the International Copper Promotion Council of India (ICPCI), Indian Society of Lighting Engineers (ISLE); Indian Society of Heating, Refrigerating and Air Conditioning Engineers (ISHRAE); Petroleum Conservation Research Association (PCRA), India; Maharashtra Energy Development Agency (MEDA); Synergy Consultants Pvt. Ltd.; See-Tech Solutions Pvt. Ltd.; and Kirlosker group played a key role in the overall execution of this training programme.

This Hands-On Training was attended by ~40 trainee participants from 17 countries, namely, Botswana, Brunei, Cambodia, Egypt, India, Indonesia, Iraq, Malawi, Malaysia, Mauritius, Myanmar, Nepal, Nigeria, Sri Lanka, Tanzania, Togo and Uganda. 21 resource persons and trainers for the training programme were from India, but more knowledge exchanges on Energy Audit were made possible through the individual country status reports presented by the foreign participants. During the Training, lectures were delivered by eminent Indian experts and professionals from organisations like SEEM, Energy Management Centre (Kerala), Indian Society of Lighting Engineers (ISLE), International Copper Promotion Council of India (ICPCI), Certification Engineers International Ltd., Senergy Consultant (P) Ltd., Energetic Consulting Pvt. Ltd., Amtech Electronics (India) Ltd., Kirloskar Brothers Ltd., Siemens Ltd., Sioux Power Solutions, Reliance Industries, Sams Elecons and See-Tech Solutions Pvt. Ltd. The overseas participants presented their country/institutional status reports and research papers in the Country Presentation sessions.

In the concluding session, a special Participants' Interactive Forum was organised, which followed the adoption of a set of recommendations titled 'Mumbai Resolution on Energy Management in Developing Countries'.

The present publication comprises 14 technical and review papers that are primarily based on the deliberations of the above Hands-On Training Workshop, and the adopted Recommendations on Energy Management. I would like to express my deepest gratitude to Mr. Suresh Dhungel, Senior Technical Officer, Nepal Academy of Science and Technology (NAST), Kathmandu and Mr. Krishnakumar, Chief Operating Officer, SEEM India for reviewing and editing the manuscripts and giving their valuable comments to make it a high quality publication. I am also indebted to Dr. Ajay Mathur, DG BEE for sparing his valuable time in writing the 'Foreword' for this book. It was highly gracious of Mr. Luxman Radhakrishnan, IAS, Chairman, Jawaharlal Nehru Port

Trust (JNPT) to have offered JNPT for conducting case studies on Energy Audit, without which the Training Workshop would have been totally incomplete and I am personally indebted to him for the wonderful gesture. Last but not the least, the valuable services rendered by the entire team of the NAM S&T Centre, particularly by Mr. M. Bandyopadhyay, Dr. V.P. Kharbanda, Ms. Isha Parmar, Mr. Yasir Abbas and Mr. Pankaj Buttan in compiling the presented papers, liaising with the authors and editors and for giving a final shape to this volume are highly appreciated.

I sincerely trust that this publication will serve as a priceless reference material not only for the developing countries but also for other countries as well and pave way for promotion of South-South and North-South cooperation in the area of Energy Audit.

Prof. Dr. Arun P. Kulshreshtha
Director and Executive Head,
NAM S&T Centre

Contents

Chapter 1

Electrical Energy Challenges in Southern Africa: A Case of Botswana

James Jakoba Molenga

Botswana Technology Centre,
Gaborone, Botswana
E-mail: jmolenga@yahoo.co.uk, jmolenga@botec.bw

ABSTRACT

One of the primary concerns today in Botswana is that the country's power station can only generate 20 per cent of electricity required in the country. Botswana is far from self sufficiency in electricity as 80 per cent of its supply is imported from its neighboring member countries of the Southern African Power Pool (SAPP) of which Botswana is also a member. The country has opted to signing long and short term electrical contracts with some members of the SAPP. Since most of the members of SAPP do not meet their own power demand, the supply to the countries importing electricity is reduced in most of the cases when the contracts are renewed. As a result the power exporting countries supply the power to Botswana only when they have excess power. Consequently, the country has faced the problem of electrical power shortage, which needs to be addressed as a matter of urgency.

This paper provides the status of electricity in Botswana and also provides an overview of the challenges lying ahead for energy supply in the country. The status of electrical power in the members of the SAPP versus that of Botswana is kept in perspective and analyses of how SAPP members can benefit from each other. Methods of Demand Side Management and Energy Efficiency that are used to improve the energy supply in Botswana are discussed in this article.

Keywords: *Compact fluorescent lamps, Energy efficiency, Energy audit, Demand side management, Smart meters, Load shedding, Reserve margin.*

1. Introduction

1.1 Economic Sector Review

Botswana is a land locked country in Southern Africa and had an estimated population of 2. 038 228 million people in August 2011 population census. According to the Central Statistics Office Bulletin of October 2011[5], annual population growth rate between 2001 and 2011 was 1.9 per cent.

Botswana's economy was dependent almost entirely on livestock production until the 1970s, when it became an important exporter of diamonds and other minerals. After the discovery of diamonds more than three decades ago Botswana's economy, fuelled by diamond revenue, experienced a rapid growth such that the GDP was classified amongst the highest in Africa as opposed to the classification amongst the world's poorest countries at independence when agriculture was the main-stay of the economy. The economy which is predominantly dependent on the mining of diamonds constitutes about 80 per cent of the country's exports and 35 per cent of its GDP.

Driven in large part by the expenditure of mineral revenues, but also by private sector investment in a relatively favourable investment climate, the Botswana economy grew extremely fast. In the 42 years up to 2007/08, the real growth of GDP averaged 8.7 percent per annum. As stated in the National Development Plan (NDP) 10, Botswana is currently classified amongst the middle income countries because of its high GDP of USD7800 in 2008. Much of the diamond revenue was invested in infrastructure development and in education. However, despite the numerous achievements, by the year 1998 the country still experienced numerous challenges which included (1) low productivity in non-mining sectors, (2) poverty in most of rural Botswana, which contributed to urban migration, (3) high unemployment rate, (4) instability in the country's currency (Pula) value, mainly affecting the revenue from diamonds and, (6) the impact of HIV/AIDS.

On a global scale according to UNDP (2005) Botswana belongs to a large group of countries that are considered to be neither involved in Science, Technology and Innovation (STI) nor its diffusion at any significant level. Botswana does not have a strong tradition of technical research and development that can be used as a basis for developing "home grown" technology. According to the World Economic Forum competitiveness groupings, Botswana is in transition between stage 1 (factor driven economies who are still focusing on basic requirements such as infrastructure development, health and primary education and macroeconomic stability) and stage 2 (efficiency driven economies that are focusing on efficiency enhancers such as higher education and training, labour market efficiency, goods market efficiency). An innovation driven economy is in stage 3, where most of the developed countries fall, and it focuses on innovation and sophistication factors. Therefore, the quest to have a coherent explicit and implicit policy environment which will create opportunities for strengthening STI activities in Botswana necessitates the need to assess Botswana's innovation policy environment. Effective and efficient STI policies are regarded as the catalyst for the development of fairly strong S&T infrastructure to ensure that technological capacities are translated into knowledge-intensive, value-added goods and services across all the sectors of the economy.

1.2 Energy Sector Review

In Botswana, the Botswana Power Corporation (BPC) is the sole entity that generates, transmits and distributes electricity within the country. The BPC is a government controlled Public Utility Company, which has four coal powered thermal power generators in the town called Palapye. It is situated at about 300 Km far from the capital city, Gaborone. Each generator at the Power Station has a maximum power capacity of 30 MW. As a result the total power capacity of the four generators is 120 MW whereas the estimated demand, as mentioned in the BPC annual report for the year 2008/2009, was 530 MW [9]. Due to the high demand in electricity which was 496 MW in 2007, the country resorted to import of electricity from neighbouring countries.

Currently, the country imports about 80 per cent of electricity from neighboring countries, the bulk of which comes from ESKOM in South Africa and Electricidade de Mozambique (EDM) of Mozambique. ESKOM, which supplies about 60 per cent [3] has a 5 year Power Purchase Agreement (PPA) with BPC for the period 2008 -2012. The previous Power Purchase Agreement (PPA) that BPC had with ESKOM expired in 2007. At the time of renewal of the contract, import of electricity to Botswana was reduced because of electricity shortages in South Africa. With the renewed PPA the ESKOM reduced the supply of power to Botswana from 400 MW to 180 MW.

The shortfall in power requirements forced BPC to look for supplementary imports from Nampower in Namibia and EDM of Mozambique. Botswana had to sign short term contracts with EDM and Nampower in order to meet deficit supply from ESKOM. The shortfall that was expected to be covered by supply from Nampower and EDM, however, it was not adequate and as a result the country faced electricity shortage from the years 2007/08 to date. The country had to resort to load shedding and the schedule for load shedding was introduced under which power supplies to the customers was to be cut off at different times of a day at different locations. As mentioned above, in the fiscal year 2008/9 the maximum power demand of the system was 530 MW, an increase of 2.1 per cent from previous year's maximum demand. The increase in the demand was due to more connections of rural communities to electricity grid, as shown in Figure 1.1.

The total number of new connections of the year under review (2008/9) was 17, 480, whereas in the previous year it was 14,474 customers only. This increase was due to BPC's rural electrification schemes that resulted in the expansion of the grid. Figure 1.1 shows percentages of new connections in the ten districts of Botswana, excluding major towns and cities. The total number of customers base increased by 9.7 per cent, from 181,125 to 196,615 by the year under review [3].

During the National Development Plan 9 [8](government's 5 year development infrastructure plan *i.e.* NDP 9), there has been an increase in access to electricity in rural areas from about 25 per cent in 2004 to 43 per cent in 2008, as shown in Figure 1.2. The increase in the connection of electricity in rural areas was the result of the

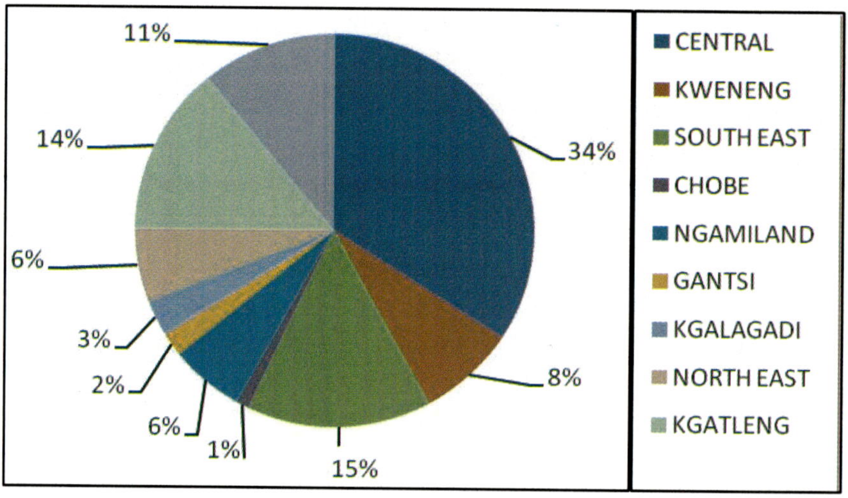

Figure 1.1: New Customer Connections by Districts in the Rural Areas [3]

introduction of rural electrification scheme under which the government wanted to increase access to electricity in rural areas and enhance rural livelihoods. According to the BPC's annual report of 2009, there were 118,798 domestic/residential customers connected during the year compared to 6,245, which were in other categories that included the business category as well.

The growing demand of electricity aggravates the scenario of energy supply shortage from ESKOM and other SAPP countries that supply electricity to Botswana. A number of demand supply management and demand side management techniques have been introduced, and are expected to address the problem of supply gap emanating from inadequate generation capacity in Botswana and the Southern African region for the period 2008 – 2012.

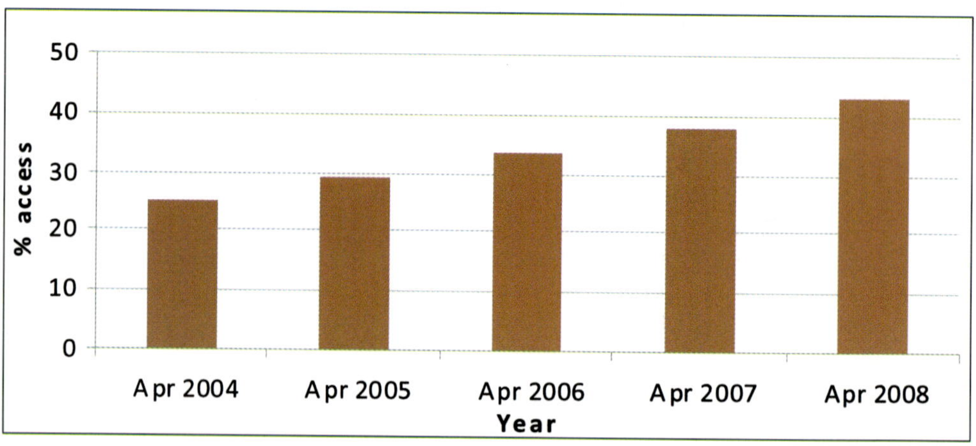

Figure 1.2: Access to Electricity in Rural Areas [2]

1.3 Challenges Facing Electricity Suppply in Botswana

Some of the major electricity supply challenges facing electrical supply services can be summarized as follows:

- ✰ Increase in the price of coal
- ✰ Delay in obtaining approval for tariff increase
- ✰ Increase in the price of power/energy imports
- ✰ Shortage for materials for construction
- ✰ Prolonged outages of the generator(s) at the Power Station
- ✰ Increase in operating cost
- ✰ Weakening of the Pula against the South African currency after the Pula was devaluated in February 2004 as most of the materials are purchased from South Africa.
- ✰ Demand – Supply gap of Electricity as supply is 80 per cent lower than demand in on average

2. The Southern African Power Pool (SAPP)

The Southern African Power Pool (SAPP) is a cooperation of the national electricity companies in Southern Africa under the auspecies of the Southern African Development Community (SADC). Most of the members of the SAPP, especially those sharing borders, have created common power grid between their countries and a common market for electricity in the SADC region. SAPP was founded in 1995. The SAPP was created with the primary aim of providing reliable and economical electricity supply to the consumer of each of the SAPP members, consistent with reasonable utilisation of natural resources.

Co-operation in the electricity sector is not a new phenomenon in the Southern African region as it has taken place at policy, planning and operational levels and involved governments, power utilities and financial agencies over a period of several decades. To formalise this interaction, several of the utilities in the region came together under the auspices of SADC to formulate the SAPP. The members of the SAPP have undertaken to create a common market for electricity in the SADC region and to let their customers benefit from the advantages associated with this market. The member countries of SAPP are Angola, Botswana, Democratic Republic of Congo, Lesotho, Malawi, Mozambique, Namibia, South Africa, Swaziland, Tanzania, Zambia and Zimbabwe. Even with the existence of the SAPP, electricity shortage is still a major challenge, as shown in Figure 1.3.

The Figure 1.3, shows in percentage what the SAPP countries are planning to achieve in the generation plans or target reserve margin and what the actual reserve margin is for the period 2008 to 2013. The figure shows that the shortage of electricity within the SAPP members will exist until the year 2013. In the year 2013, the planned generated electricity, which is targeted by the SAPP countries, will then exceed the actual reserve margin. In 2013 the planned generation capacity will exceed the actual

SAPP Generation Capacity Reserve

Target vs Actual Reserve, per cent

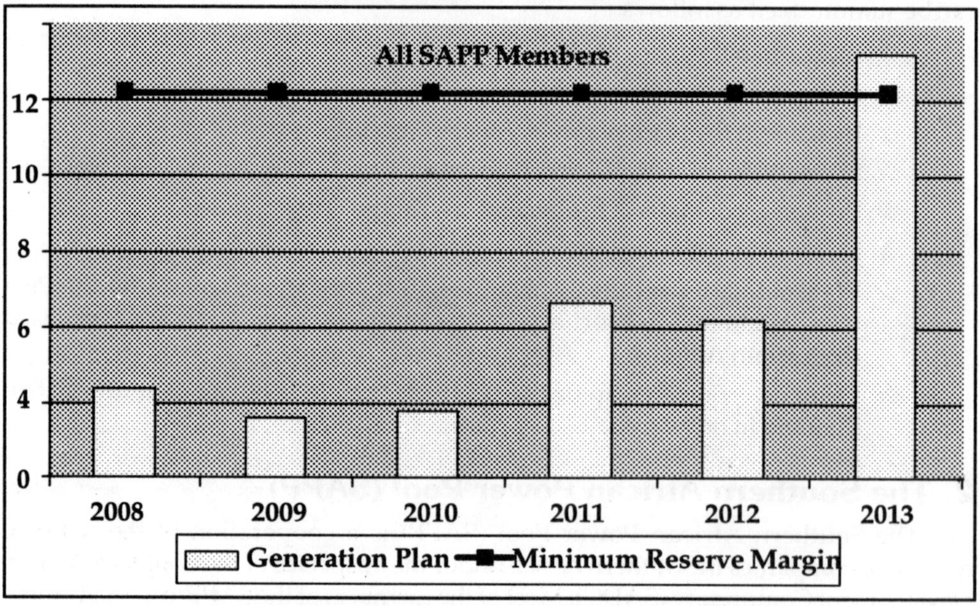

Figure 1.3: Planned Electricity Generation Plans Versus all SAPP Members' Actual Reserve Margin [10]

reserve. This will only happen if most of the projects that are planned for construction are undertaken and completed well on time. In Botswana, a 600 MW coal fired thermal power station is being constructed.

Apart from purchasing electricity from the SAPP member states, two diesel powered generators were built by BPC in order to combat electricity shortage. These diesel generators are only operated during peak times of energy requirements. Electricity deregulation has also been finalized and it is expected that private companies will apply to generate electricity locally to compete with BPC. Private companies will be encouraged to produce electricity from renewable energy sources and currently the government is working on finalization of the renewable energy feed in tariffs (REFIT). In order to address the problem of electricity shortage, the Botswana Power Corporation has introduced the demand side management that includes:

- ✰ Replacement of all incandescent bulbs used for domestic purposes with compact fluorescent lamps (CFLs)
- ✰ Introduction of the usage of smart meters in major towns and cities
- ✰ Introduction of the load shedding schedule

3. Energy Demand in the Country

3.1 Energy Sectors

The Technical Report on National Energy Policy for Botswana (March 2009) shows that when all energy sources are considered, the household takes the largest share of energy use. However, it should be mentioned that if fuelwood is excluded then transport takes the lead. This analogy shows that a lot of people in Botswana use firewood in their homes and it also show that petroleum is most used energy in the country. This information is backed by the fact that only 43 per cent of the rural communities had access to electricity in 2008. The information is summarised in Tables 1.1 and 1.2 which was adapted from the Technical Report on National Energy Policy for Botswana (March 2009). The primary energy sources that formed part of the discussion are; petroleum, electricity, coal, firewood and solar. The total primary energy sources are shown in Figure 1.4.

Table 1.1: Energy Demand–All Energy Sources

Sub-sector	*Per cent*
Transport	38.0
Mining	31.2
Government	9.5
Trade and Hotels	7.3
Manufacturing	7.0
Household	5.5
Agriculture	1.5
Total	100

Table 1.2: Energy Demand–(Excluding fuelwood) [6]

Sub-sector	*Per cent*
Household	42.0
Transport	23.3
Mining	19.10
Government	5.8
Trade and Hotels	4.5
Manufacturing	4.3
Total	100

3.2 Total Primary Energy Supply

It is clear from Figure 1.4 that the dominating primary energies are fuelwood, coal, and petroleum. Solar energy contributes about 1 per cent of the total primary energy even though Botswana has abundant solar energy resources, receiving over 3,200 hours of sunshine per year, with an average insolation on the horizontal surface of 21 MJ/m^2 as shown in the National Development Plan 10 Report. This is one of the highest insolations in the world. The wind energy has a low potential in the country with the average wind speeds of about 5 m/sec.

The bulk of petroleum is mainly used in the transport sector, and coal is used for water heating and in thermal power generation. It really shows that the renewably energy uptake within the country is very low. In order to address energy disparity, all options for power generation should be exploited.

4. Energy Efficiency Using Compact Fluorescent Lamps

BPC is a sole entity that is responsible for generation, transmission and distribution of electricity in the country. BPC has come up with methods for reducing

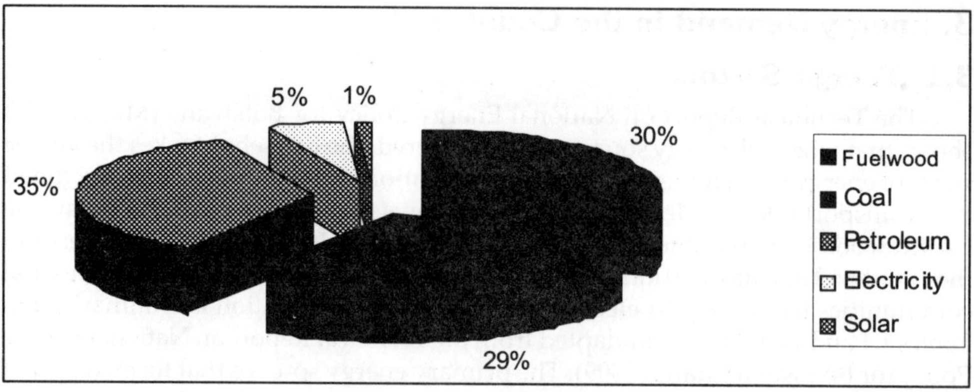

Figure 1.4: Total Primary Energy Sectors in Botswana in 2001 [7]

electricity demand that is increasing, by addressing energy demand on the customer side. All household incandescent bulbs in the country were replaced with compact fluorescent lamps (CFL) distributed by BPC free of charge. Customers were required to exchange CFLs with the incandescent bulbs. The major benefits of using CFL are that it reduces the energy requirements of the consumer, has a longer life and it also reduces the energy bill, as they use 80 per cent energy less than incandescent bulbs. The Corporation has planned to swap ordinary incandescent bulbs with Compact fluorescent lamps (CFL) across the country. This exercise is expected to save approximately 30 MW of power. The CFL program covered the entire country. One of the benefits of rolling out the program was that it resulted in reduction of load shedding.

5. Demand Side Management Using Smart Meters

In November 2009, BPC launched the Hot Water Load Control (HWLC) pilot project, where 466 smart meters were installed in the city of Gaborone, and that paved the way for a major rollout of the effort to major cities in the African nation. The smart meters load control project is expected to be rolled to other towns and cities, and it is estimated to shove off 40 MW of electrical consumption once it is used in the targeted areas. The way they operate is that once the electricity demand increases the BPC control centre is able to disconnect the electrical geysers from the power supply, hence reducing power load shedding to the entire operations in the homesteads. The BPC will start disconnecting a certain area, and target other areas if the supply and demand does not match.

6. Energy Audit and Demand Side Management

Botswana and other Southern African countries are facing severe shortage of power as shown in Figure 1.3, due to increased demand and insufficient supply. Although there is shortage of electricity in the country, little has been done on energy audits so that efficiency measures could be put in place. Up to now only six energy audits have been done in public institutions. Botswana Technology Center (BOTEC) was involved in one of the audits. More can be done in the industry and commercial areas so that the results from the energy audits can be used to address the problem of the high electricity demand. Also, the energy efficient building design guidelines have not been enforced although they were developed in 2008.

7. Discussion

This article shows that Botswana has depended on electricity that it purchased from neighboring countries in Southern Africa for over thirty years, most of which comes from South Africa. The reason why Botswana had to depend on imports from South Africa was that it was cheaper to purchase electricity from South Africa than to build additional power plants in Botswana. With the shortage of electricity in South Africa and the entire region, Botswana had to grapple with the problem of electricity shortage, which forced the country to implement load shedding that was more prevalent in the fiscal years 2008/9 and 2009/10.

Botswana was then forced to build two diesel power generators that only operated during peak demand hours so that the situation of power blackouts is alleviated. Given the gravity of the situation, BPC had to implement the demand side management measures that were expected to reduce the burden on the only ailing BPC grid. These measures include the roll out of CFLs to all households and encourage them to use smart meters to reduce the load by disconnecting electric geysers when electricity demand exceeds the supply. The decline in power import from South Africa has forced BPC to build a 600 MW coal fired thermal power station in order to have adequate security in terms of local produced electricity. It is very unfortunate that the solar energy contributes very little in the total primary energy supply, even though the country has the highest solar insolation of about 21 MJ/m^2.

As a member of SAPP, Botswana benefitted a lot from the integrated grid supply in the region because the country is able to purchase electricity if other countries have excess electricity. However, most of the SAPP members do not have enough reserve margins as shown in Figure 1.3. In order to improve electricity security supply most of the members of the SAPP are planning to build more power stations as shown in Appendix 1.

8. Conclusion

Botswana has a shortage of electricity supply for which it depends on the import of electricity from the neighbouring African Countries. Large section of the rural community is still not connected to electricity grid. Energy efficiency can be used to reduce the electricity demand from the network. It has been shown that with the roll out of the CFL in the country, about 30 MW can be saved and BPC is likely to reduce the demand of electricity in the whole country by 40 MW if the areas that are targeted with smart meters are connected. Very few activities have been carried out in energy audit even though applying the results from the audit can reduce the burden on the energy supply. Several challenges have to be tackled that affect the energy demand management such as lack of manpower to undertake energy audits and implementation of energy audit measures. There is also lack of policy to enforce building energy efficiency guidelines of 2008. Renewable energy source such as solar energy needs to be exploited in order to provide access to electricity for its larger population.

References

1. A. Maramwidze. Mmegi Newspaper. January 12, 2010 http://www.thebusinessdiary.co.bw/p=331 (accessed 17 Mar. 2011)
2. Botswana Energy Draft Policy: 2009. Gaborone. Botswana
3. Botswana Power Corporation Annual Report 2008/09. Gaborone. Botswana
4. C. Kiravu et al. 2008. Towards Sustainable Energy Management in Botswana. http://active.cput.ac.za/energy/web/DUE/DOCS/291/Paper%20-%20Kiravu%20C.pdf (accessed 14 Mar. 2011)
5. Central Statistics Newsletter, October 2011. Gaborone. Botswana.
6. C.T. Mzezewa. 2009. National Energy Policy for Botswana, Final Draft Report. Gaborone. Botswana
7. Department of Energy, Energy Statistics Pamphlet (2001). Gaborone. Botswana.
8. National Development Plan 9. Gaborone. Botswana
9. National Development Plan 10. Gaborone. Botswana
10. Southern African Power Pool Annual Report 2008

APPENDIX 1: Future Power Generation Plants by SAPP [10]

Sl.No.	Country	Project Name	Capacity [MW]	Expected Date	Estimated Project Cost USD [M]	Secured Funding
		LONG TERM GENERATION PROJECTS: (2009-2013)				
1.	Mozambique	Massingir	40	2009	55	N
2.	Mozambique	Temane Gas	750	2011	370	N
3.	Malawi	Fufu	100	2012	141	N
4.	Mozambique	Benga Coal fired	450	2012	800	N
5.	Mozambique	Lurio	183	2012	340	N
6.	Tanzania	Kinyerezi	200	2012	190	N
7.	Zimbabwe	Lupane	300	2012	368	N
8.	Zimbabwe	Hwange Expansion	600	2012	500	N
9.	Zimbabwe	Kariba South Extension	300	2012	200	N
10.	Zambia	Kafue Gorge Lower	750	2012	600	N
11.	Zambia	Kabompo	34	2012		N
12.	Botswana	Morupule Expansion (Phase 2)	600	2013	900	N
13.	Botswana	Mmamabula Phase 1	2,400	2013	8000	N
14.	DRC	Busanga	240	2013	300	N
15.	DRC	Nzilo 2	110	2013	180	N
16.	Namibia	Walvis Bay	400	2013	700	N
17.	Namibia	Baynes	360	2013	640	N
18.	Swaziland	Lubombo	1,000	2013		N
	TOTAL		**8,817**		**13,584**	
		LONG TERM GENERATION PROJECTS: (2014 -2015)				
19.	Zambia	Maamba coal fired	500	2014	192	N
20.	DRC	Inga 3	4,300	2015	3,600	N
21.	Lesotho	Oxbow	80	2015	155	N
22.	Lesotho	Muela Phase-2	110	2015		N
23.	Mozambique	Mphanda Nkuwa (Phase I)	1,500	2015	2,000	N
24.	Mozambique	Moatize	1,500	2015	2,700	N
25.	Mozambique	HCB North Bank	850	2015	771	N
26.	Namibia	Kudu	800	2015	640	N
27.	Tanzania	Ruhudji	358	2015	611	N
28.	Zimbabwe	Batoka	800	2015	2,500	N
29.	Zimbabwe	Gokwe North	1,400	2015	1,357	N
	TOTAL		**12,198**		**14,526**	

Chapter 2

Energy Sector in Cambodia

Khlaing Amradararith

Ministry of Industry, Mines and Energy,
Department of Energy Technique,
#45, Norodom Blvd, Daun Penh, Phnom Penh, Cambodia
E-mail: mimedet@forum.org.kh

ABSTRACT

Kingdom of Combodia, is a country in Indo-China peninsula, with a population of about 15 millions. Seventy percent of the rural population of Cambodia lacks access to electricity. The national energy policy and the strategies envisioned in the same aim at securing economical access to energy, to the deprived. The mix of plans and programs seeks to address various barriers through policy initiatives and also deploy various appropriate technologies to achieve the above objective.

Keywords: *Cambodia, Electricity, Energy, Rural electrification fund (REF), Renewable energy (RE).*

1. Introduction and Country Profile

The Kingdom of Cambodia is a country located in the southern portion of the Indo–China Peninsula in south-east Asia, in the lower Mekong region. It is bordered by Thailand on the north-west, Vietnam on the east and south, and Lao PDR on the North. It has got a land area of 1,81,035 km^2. Cambodia has a population of 14.8 million with a per capita GDP of US$286. Its annual growth rate is 5.8 per cent.

Seventy percent of the rural population of Cambodia lacks access to electricity. Kerosene is predominantly used for domestic lighting. Car batteries are deployed by some for lighting and TV. Grid electricity may not be available to a majority of the Cambodian population for many years to come. This necessitates massive deployment

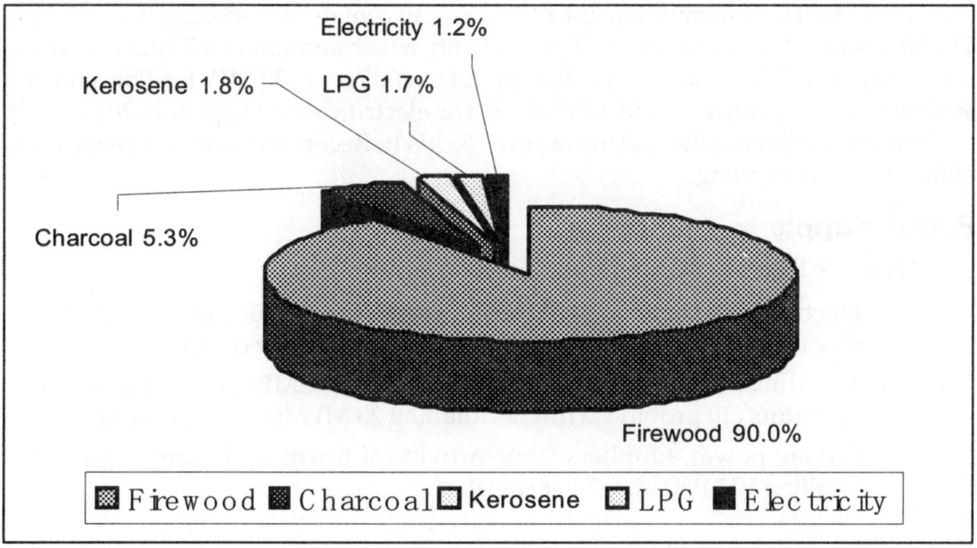

Figure 2.1

of alternatives to supply electricity to the deprived population. Solar photovoltaics (PV), being a mature technology, will find a range of possible applications in Cambodia.

2. An Overview of the Electric Power Scenario in Cambodia

Cambodia's National Energy Policy was formulated in 1994. The overall framework of the policy is centred on the theme of providing adequate supply of low-cost energy to homes throughout Cambodia. This in turn has to be ensured by reliable and secure electricity supply at prices which will encourage investment in Cambodia and also promote its economic development. The policy also provides for encouragement of exploring environmentally and socially acceptable development of energy resources needed to supply power to all sectors of the Cambodian economy. It also seeks to encourage efficient use of energy and to minimize the harmful environmental effects resulting from energy supply and use.

Cambodia's Energy Strategy

Under the National Energy Policy, an energy strategy with several components is envisaged. This strategy centers on extra power generation in Phnom Penh and Siem Reap, and diesel generation in eight regional centres. Another significant component of the strategy is to import power from Vietnam and Thailand. Five huge hydel projects and a gas-based generation station at Kompong Soam also form part of this strategy. Cambodia will also pin its hopes on the ASEAN power grid and a backbone grid.

Energy Demand in Cambodia

The energy demand in Cambodia can be understood from the following facts: Presently, 24 small isolated power systems cater to Cambodia's electricity requirements. The transmission link between load centers is practically non-existent. The largest system is in the capital Phnom Penh, which accounts for 75 per cent of the whole country's demand. The peak demand in 2009 was 120 MW for Phnom Penh and 40 MW for all other provincial centers. The electrification rate is only 20 per cent, with an annual per capita consumption of 55 kWh. Reconstruction and revamping of the system is ongoing.

Power Supply in Cambodia

There are three main groups of power supply utilities:

- Electricité du Cambodge (EDC) – a public sector utility (Phnom Penh and six other large towns, totalling 155 MW (*i.e.*, ~85 per cent))
- The Ministry of Industry, Mines and Energy (MIME) provincial electricity operators (10 provincial towns, totalling 20 MW (*i.e.*, ~10 per cent))
- Private power suppliers (four provincial towns and many rural areas totalling 10 MW (*i.e.*, ~5 per cent))

3. Goals and Targets

Renewable Energy (RE) Market Opportunity

According to the MIME estimates, the total capacity of the market for RE is expected to be approximately 300 MWp.

Cambodia's National Policy on Renewable Energy-Based Rural Electrification

The following principles and objectives are inbuilt in Cambodia's national policy on renewable energy-based rural electrification. This policy endeavours to provide access to reliable, safe and environmentally clean electricity services to rural areas, at an affordable cost to the national community. It is expected to act as a market enabler and encourages private sector participation in providing rural renewable electricity services. It seeks to provide an effective legal and regulatory framework to support its objective of enabling access to reliable, safe and clean electricity services in rural areas, at an affordable cost. Provisions are made in the policy to encourage the most efficient systems for generation, transmission and distribution of electricity from clean and renewable energy sources, to enable a rational electricity tariff policy through the promotion of differentiated tariffs based on cost recovery principles. It also addresses the need to promote renewable electricity systems for rural applications as part of a national portfolio of grid and off-grid technologies, provided they are the least-cost options for the local communities. It is expected to ensure adequate resources and appropriate institutional mechanisms to empower the poor, particularly those in rural areas.

Strategy on Renewable Energy

Various strategies are envisaged for the widespread adoption of renewable energy. These include wide expansion of the access of electricity services to the rural population through the development of appropriate programmes and action plans to promote renewable energy technologies (RETs). Private entrepreneurs will be motivated and encouraged to participate in providing efficient and cost-effective services benefiting the whole community, at the same time expanding the supply base for RE services. Another strategic measure will be the creation of a comprehensive legal and regulatory framework to enable effective participation of government, private and community-based entities in providing electricity services to the rural consumers and to facilitate systematic market and institutional development in the RE sector. Development of an appropriate tariff policy and the institution of a rational tariff regime is expected to ensure wide and equitable access of electricity services to all sections of the population, especially the rural. Environmentally sustainable distributed generation technologies, including RETs in the on-grid and off-grid modes, will be promoted to increase the access to and affordability of electricity services to the rural consumers. The RE systems shall also contribute to the empowerment of the rural poor by creating economic opportunities and uplifting the standard of living through electricity services, and also by involving them in the planning, and operation, maintenance and management (OM&M) of the programmes providing those services.

Cambodia's Renewable Energy Targets

- ☆ The overall goal of the Royal Government of Cambodia (RGC) is to achieve 70 per cent electrification coverage in grid-quality electricity to rural households by the year 2030 from the current level of 20 per cent.
- ☆ The current overall RE target determined for the World Bank-supported Rural Electrification and Transmission (RE&T) project is 45,000 new electricity services by rural electricity entrepreneurs (REEs), which include RETs.

Rural Electrification Fund (REF)

REF has been created by the Royal Government of Cambodia and the World Bank, with the goal of encouraging private sector investment in electricity supply to the rural population, through smart subsidies and smart credit schemes, for reasons of social equity. The electricity selling price to the rural population would be such that the rural entrepreneurs will still make profit. Funding for such investment will come by way of grants and loans at low interest rates and with long-term repayment periods, from various credit and financing institutions.

Cambodia's REF Targets

- ☆ REF will achieve
  - Three hydropower mini-grid projects (up to 6 MW)
  - 10,000 solar home systems
  - Three viable renewable energy businesses
  - 50–100 trained renewable energy personnel
- ☆ The RE projects shall be PV, mini-hydro, diesel mini-grids or grid extension with existing standards.

Solar REF

Solar REF is expected to ensure supply of electricity to rural public facilities such as healthcare centres, training centres, schools, pagodas, bridges and streetlighting. Sources of funding can include philanthropic donations by individuals, companies and institutions.

Case Study

Project Site Selection Criteria

The area selected for the project has the following characteristics:

- ☆ A high willingness to pay for electricity
- ☆ A relatively well-built infrastructure such as roads and railroads
- ☆ A relatively high and stable income and standard of living
- ☆ Moves towards social and economic transformation with regional development plans
- ☆ Location of many REEs in the area; REEs' cooperation is necessary for project implementation

Selection of the Target Sector

- ☆ *Target Sector*: general households
- ☆ *Reason for selection*: Public facilities, including schools, clinics and pagodas, are generally facing chronic financial difficulties. Moreover, though the electrification of such facilities is necessary, it is difficult to make it a viable project, as the number of target facilities is quite less than expected. Therefore, households are selected as the target sector.

Selection of Target Communes/Villages

- ☆ Communes/villages connected by main roads (National Route 5 and other main roads)
- ☆ Communes/villages with existing REEs, except in the case of a mini-grid built commune centre
- ☆ Households with a willingness to pay over $4 (baseline criterion of willingness to pay set at $4). Currently non-electrified households that are willing to pay at least $4 or more are included.

4. Barriers

There are several barriers that hinder the smooth progress towards achieving the above-mentioned goals and targets in the rural electrification/renewable energy sectors, some of which are listed below:

Policy Barrier

Thanks to three decades of very destructive wars, the lack of efficient human resources in both the government and the private sector is by far the most important barrier that blocks the development of the country in general, and of the renewable energy sector in particular.

Financial Barrier

Low income coupled with a high level of illiteracy in general, particularly among the people in rural areas, is another barrier that hampers the development of RETs. The high investment cost of the renewable energy equipment, without a substantial and judiciously granted subsidy and without proper education and training (on OM&M) of personnel, is not compatible with such a rural environment.

Institutional Barrier

Due to organizational and managerial barriers and also due to the lack of means, Cambodia cannot yet properly address its population's basic needs.

Social Barrier

Lack of basic socio-economic and technical data concerning the RETs, such as the meteorological data on the wind and the rainfall for potential regions, poses another barrier for RE development.

Managerial Barrier

Low awareness due to lack of information, which, in turn, is due to the lack of means for the creation and distribution of educational materials, for the organization of workshops, for the installation of demonstrations centres, and for the dissemination and support of potential RETs forms yet another barrier in the RE sector.

Technical Barrier

Weakness in financing, banking and credit systems is also a barrier for the development of the RE sector. For example, practically, private funds are not yet available for renewable energy users' access, and there are no plans for offering credit to PV users.

5. Conclusions

Rural electrification, along with other socio-economic infrastructure development, is a main component of the poverty alleviation policy of the Royal Government of Cambodia. And rural electrification using renewable energy, such as solar energy systems, can be an elegant solution to address both utilization of the national resources and global environmental issues.

Solar energy systems can help accelerate the penetration rate of electricity to remote areas, where other technologies cannot economically address issues such as absence of wind and micro hydro, and the very high cost for connection to the grid. Thus, thanks to solar electricity, remote health and vocational training centres, pagodas, schools, water pumping stations and so on can make available to the rural population vital services that would help address its basic needs such as vaccination, clean water, education, lighting and implementation of information and communication technologies.

In view of effective diffusion of RETs, more dissemination works and adaptive research are needed. All such works would help guiding the MIME and the RGC in their efforts in rural development, by accelerating the electricity penetration rate using the cheapest and the most adaptive source of energy, like the solar energy, for example.

Along this line of thinking, we appeal to the international community of donors and NGOs to institute more renewable energy demonstration centres, with the aim of disseminating the RETs and at the same time acting as training centres for the OM&M of the systems.

Chapter 3

Pollution Due to Lights and Measures for its Reduction

Prakash Barjatia

Ex-Director,
MIT School of Energy and Lighting, Pune, India
E-mail : dr.prakash.b@hotmail.com

ABSTRACT

Almost everybody is aware of pollution due to industries or due to automobiles. However, very few are aware of pollution due to lights. In recent years, specifically in the developing world, awareness about pollution due to lights has gained much significance. The main cause of pollution due to lights is over-illumination and the use of inefficient light sources. It has got a significant effect on the health of not only human beings, but also animals and plants. This is one of the main reasons why many countries have decided to ban the manufacture, sale and use of incandescent bulbs. The electric bulb developed by Edison converts only 10 per cent of the energy consumed to illumination or light; the remaining 90 per cent causes heating of the atmosphere. The main cause of pollution due to lights is the ignorance of the users regarding the right type of light sources for the right application. Thus, there is an urgent need for creating awareness by spreading the knowledge of light sources through academic courses, seminars, conferences and debate among the public. In this paper, an effort has been made to highlight the different sources of light pollution and also the measures to control the same by the use of appropriate types of light sources and luminaires.

Keywords: *Light, Pollution, Illumination, Glare, Measures.*

1. Light Pollution

Light pollution (also known as photo pollution, luminous pollution) refers to light that is considered annoying, wasteful or harmful. It also causes damage to the environment and health, as do other forms of pollution such as air pollution, noise pollution, water pollution and soil contamination.

Light pollution is a broad term that refers to multiple problems, all of which are caused by inefficient, unappealing or avoidable use of artificial light. Specific categories of light pollution include light trespass, over-illumination, glare, clutter and sky glow. A single offending light source often falls into more than one of these categories.

Light pollution is excess or obtrusive light created by humans. Among other effects, it disrupts ecosystems, can cause adverse health effects, obscures the stars for city dwellers, interferes with the functioning of astronomical observatories and wastes energy. Light pollution can be construed to have two main forms: (a) annoying light that intrudes on an otherwise natural or low-light setting and (b) excessive light, generally indoors, that leads to worker discomfort and adverse health effects.

2. Causes of Light Pollution

Light pollution is fallout of the industrialized civilization. Its sources include lighting of building exteriors and interiors, advertising, commercial properties, offices, factories, streetlights and illuminated sporting venues. It is most severe in the highly industrialized and densely populated areas of North America, Europe and Japan, but even relatively smaller amounts of light can become noticeable and create problems. In India, it is visible in the commercial areas of the metro cities, namely, Mumbai, Kolkata, Chennai and Delhi.

Generally, people wish to reduce light pollution. However, it is unrealistic to expect the populations to significantly reduce their use of light, and light pollution in turn, given the industrial society's economic reliance on artificial lighting. Detractors posit that light pollution is a problem similar to other traditional forms of pollution. Energy conservation advocates contend that light pollution must be addressed by changing the habits of society, so that lighting is used more efficiently, with less wastage and less creation of unwanted or unneeded illumination. The case against light pollution is strengthened by a range of studies its health effects, suggesting that excess light may induce loss in visual acuity, hypertension, headaches and increased incidence of carcinoma. Since not everyone is irritated by the same lighting sources, it is common for what one person perceives as light "pollution" to be light that is desirable for another. One example of this is found in advertising, where an advertiser wishes particular lights to be bright and visible even though others find them annoying. Other types of light pollution are more certain. For instance, light that accidentally crosses a property boundary and annoys a neighbor is generally wasted and polluting light.

2.1 Light Trespass

Light trespass occurs when unwanted light enters one's property, for instance, by shining over a neighbor's fence as shown in Figure 3.1. A common light trespass problem occurs when strong light enters the window of one's home from outside, causing problems such as sleep deprivation or blocking of an evening view.

Figure 3.1: Light Trespass

Light trespass is particularly problematic for amateur astronomers, whose ability to observe the night sky from their property is likely to be inhibited by any stray light from nearby sources. Mostly, major optical astronomical observatories are surrounded by zones of strictly enforced restrictions on light emissions.

2.2 Over-Illumination

Over-illumination is the excessive use of light as shown in the Figure 3.2. It is observed that over 30 per cent of all energy consumed by the commercial, industrial and residential sectors is used for lighting. Energy audits of existing buildings demonstrate that the lighting component of residential, commercial and industrial energy usage accounts for about 20 to 40 per cent. Again, energy audit data demonstrate that about 30 to 60 per cent of the energy consumed for lighting goes wasted.

Causes of Over-Illumination

- ☆ Not using timers, occupancy sensors or other controls to extinguish lighting when not needed.
- ☆ Improper design, especially of workplace spaces, specifying higher levels of light than needed for a given task.
- ☆ Incorrect choice of fixtures or light bulbs, which do not direct light into areas as needed.
- ☆ Improper selection of hardware that consumes more energy than needed to accomplish the lighting task.
- ☆ Insufficient training of building managers and occupants to use lighting systems efficiently.

Figure 3.2: Lightning Levels Over Twice Recommended Levels

- Inadequate lighting maintenance resulting in increased stray light and energy costs.

2.3 Glare

Glare is often the result of excessive contrast between bright and dark areas in the field of view. For example, glare can be associated with directly viewing the filament of an unshielded or badly shielded light. Light shining into the eyes of pedestrians and drivers can obscure night vision for up to an hour after exposure. Caused by high contrast between light and dark areas, glare can also make it difficult for the human eye to adjust to the differences in brightness. Glare is particularly an issue in road safety, as bright and/or badly shielded lights along the roads may partially blind drivers or pedestrians unexpectedly and thus contribute to accidents.

Glare can be categorized into different types:

- *Blinding Glare,* which describes effects such as that caused by staring into the sun. It is completely blinding and leaves temporary or permanent vision deficiencies.
- *Disability Glare,* which describes effects such as being blinded by lights from oncoming vehicles or light scattering in fog or in the eye, which reduces contrast, as well as reflections from print and other dark areas that render them bright, causing a significant reduction in vision capabilities.
- *Discomfort Glare,* which does not typically cause a dangerous situation in itself, but is annoying and irritating at worst. It can potentially cause fatigue if experienced over extended periods.

2.4 Sky Glow

Sky glow refers to the glow effect that can be seen over densely populated areas. It is a combination of the light reflected from what it has illuminated and all the badly directed light in that area being refracted by the surrounding atmosphere. Rayleigh scattering, which makes the sky appear blue during daytime, also affects the light that comes from the earth into the sky, which is then redirected to become sky glow, seen from the ground as shown in Figure 3.3. As a result, blue light contributes significantly more to sky glow than an equal amount of yellow light. Sky glow is particularly irritating for astronomers, because it reduces contrast in the night sky to the extent where it may become impossible to see even the brightest stars.

Figure 3.3: Sky Glow Over City

2.5 Ignorance

Among several things that are taken for granted, lighting is one. Providing illumination by providing fixtures and light sources is considered to be the simplest of tasks. Quite often no scientific study is carried out before any such projects, causing some or the other effects enumerated above. Being a neglected topic, in majority of the countries there are no legislations curbing the present practices leading to pollution due to lighting.

3. Measurement of Light Pollution

Measuring the effect of sky glow on a global scale is a complex procedure. The natural atmosphere is not completely dark, even in the absence of terrestrial sources of light. This is caused by two main sources: air glow and scattered light.

At high altitudes, primarily above the mesosphere, UV radiation from the sun is so intense that ionization occurs. When these ions collide with electrically neutral particles they recombine and emit photons in the process, causing air glow. The degree of ionization is sufficiently large to allow a constant emission of radiation even during the night when the upper atmosphere is in the earth's shadow.

Apart from emitting light, the sky also scatters incoming light primarily from distant stars and the Milky Way, but also sunlight that is reflected and backscattered from interplanetary dust particles (the so-called Zodiacal light).

To precisely measure how bright the sky gets, night time satellite imagery of the earth is used as raw input for the number and intensity of light sources. These are put into a physical model of scattering due to air molecules and aerosoles to calculate the cumulative sky brightness. Maps that show enhanced sky brightness have been prepared for the entire world.

4. Effects of Light Pollution

4.1 Energy Wastage

Lighting is responsible for one-fourth of all the energy consumed worldwide, and case studies have shown that several forms of over-illumination constitute energy wastage, including non-beneficial upward direction of night time lighting.

4.2 Effects on Human Health and Psychology

Medical research on the effects of excessive light on human body suggests that a variety of adverse health effects may be caused by light pollution or excessive light exposure, and some lighting design textbooks use human health as an explicit criterion for proper interior lighting. Health effects of over-illumination or improper spectral composition of light may include increased incidence of headaches, worker fatigue, medically defined stress, decrease in sexual function and increase in anxiety.

Common levels of fluorescent lighting in offices are sufficient to elevate blood pressure by about eight points. There is some evidence that lengthy daily exposure to moderately high lighting leads to diminished sexual performance. Specifically in the USA, there is evidence that levels of light in most office environments lead to increased stress as well as increased worker errors.

Several published studies also suggest a link between exposure to light at night and the risk of breast cancer, due to suppression of the normal nocturnal production of melatonin.

4.3 Disruption of Ecosystems

Life exists with natural patterns of light and shade, so disruption of those patterns influences many aspects of animal behaviour. Light pollution can confuse animal navigation, alter competitive interactions and influence animal physiology.

Light pollution may also affect ecosystems in other ways. For example, lepidopterists and entomologists have documented that night time light may interfere with the ability of moths and other nocturnal insects to navigate. Night-blooming flowers that depend on moths for pollination may be affected by night lighting, as there is no replacement pollinator that would not be affected by the artificial light.

This can lead to species decline of plants that are unable to reproduce and change an area's long-term ecology.

Migrating birds can be disoriented by the lights on tall structures/towers. The number of birds killed after being attracted to tall towers range from 4 to 5 million per year or even more.

Other well-known casualties of light pollution include sea turtle hatchlings emerging from nests on beaches.

Nocturnal frogs and salamanders are also affected by light pollution. Since they are nocturnal, they wake up when there is no light. Light pollution may cause salamanders to emerge from concealment later than normal, giving them less time to mate and reproduce.

4.4 Diminution of Safety

It is generally agreed that many people require light to feel safe at night, but campaigners for the reduction of light pollution often claim that badly or inappropriately installed lighting can lead to a reduction in safety if measured objectively, and that, at the very least, it is wrong to assume that simply increasing the nighttime lighting will lead to improved safety.

The International Dark Sky Association claims that there are no good scientific studies that convincingly show a relationship between lighting and crime. Furthermore, the association claims that badly installed artificial lights can create a deeper contrast of shadows in which criminals might hide. The New England Light Pollution Advisory Group claims that some light emitted by some fixtures can be a significant hazard to motorists, pedestrians and bicyclists due to scattering of light and glare.

4.5 Effect on Astronomy

Sky glow reduces the contrast between stars and galaxies in the sky and the sky itself, making it more difficult to detect fainter objects.

5. Measures for Reducing Light Pollution

5.1 Possible Solutions

Reducing light pollution implies many things, such as reducing sky glow, reducing glare and reducing light trespass. The method for best reducing light pollution, therefore, depends on exactly what the problem is in any given instance. Possible solutions include

- ☆ Utilizing light sources of the minimum intensity necessary to accomplish the light's purpose.
- ☆ Turning lights off using a timer or an occupancy sensor, or manually when not needed.
- ☆ Improving lighting fixtures, so that they direct their light more accurately towards where it is needed, and with less side effects.

- Adjusting the type of lights used, so that the light waves emitted are those that are less likely to cause severe light pollution problems.
- Evaluating the existing lighting plans and re-designing some or all of the plans depending on whether the existing amount of lighting is actually needed.

5.2 Improving Lighting Fixtures

A flat-lens luminaire, which is a full-cutoff fixture, may be effective in reducing light pollution. It ensures that light is only directed below the horizontal, which means less light is wasted through directing it outwards and upwards.

The use of full-cutoff lighting fixtures, as much as possible, is advocated by most campaigners for the reduction of light pollution. It is also commonly recommended that lights be spaced appropriately for maximum efficiency and that lamps within the fixtures not be over-rated. The use of full-cutoff fixtures may help to reduce sky glow by preventing light from spreading in unwanted directions. Full cutoff typically reduces the visibility of the lamp and reflector within a luminaire, so the effects of glare may also be reduced. The use of full-cutoff fixtures may allow for lower-wattage lamps to be used in fixtures, producing the same or sometimes a better effect, on account of being more carefully controlled.

5.3 Use of Appropriate Energy-Efficient Light Sources

Several types of light sources exist, each having different properties that determine its appropriateness for certain tasks, particularly efficiency and spectral power distribution. It is often the case that inappropriate light sources have been selected for a task, either due to ignorance or because more sophisticated light sources were unavailable at the time of installation. Badly chosen light sources often contribute to light pollution unnecessarily. Some types of light sources, in the order of their energy efficiency are listed in Table 3.1.

Table 3.1: Properties of Light Sources

Type of Light Source	*Colour*	*Efficiency (Lumens per watt)*
Low-pressure sodium	Yellow	80–200
High-pressure sodium	Pink/Amber-white	90–130
Metal Halide	Bluish white/White	60–120
Mercury Vapour	Blue-greenish White	13–48
Incandescent	Yellow/White	8–25
LED (Light Emitting Diode)	Close to daylight	80 - 100
CFL (Compact Fluorescent Lamp)	Close to daylight	45 - 60
Low Pressure Sodium	Yellow	80 - 200
High Pressure Sodium	Pink/Amber-white	90 - 130
Metal Halide	Bluish-white/White	60 -120
Mercury Vapour	Blue-greenish White	13 - 48
Incandescent	Yellow/White	8 - 25

5.4 Awareness Programmes

To create awareness among users, designers, architects, consultants, law makers and manufacturers, there is a need for arranging educative programmes by NGOs.

6. Conclusion

The issue of pollution due to lighting is integral with energy conservation. Energy conservation advocates contend that light pollution must be addressed by changing the habits of society, so that lighting is used more efficiently, with less wastage and less creation of unwanted or unneeded illumination. The case against light pollution is strengthened by a range of studies on health effects, suggesting that excess light may induce loss in visual acuity, hypertension, headaches and increased incidence of carcinoma. All these issues are linked with ignorance of the users and the lighting providers. The only solution appears to be to spread the message through awareness programmes in urban/rural areas, in schools/colleges, for users and manufacturers alike, which will be having a long-term socio-economic impact.

The long-lasting success of all such initiatives and projects for Saving of Electricity-n-Environment (SEE) lies in creating awareness. It is therefore suggested to spread the message of light pollution prevention in the following ways:

1. Spreading the message of light pollution prevention through lighting education by different type/level of educational/awareness programmes
2. Creating awareness about the cost–benefit analysis of the use of energy-efficient light sources
3. Removing ignorance of the users about the benefits of switching over to such energy-efficient light sources
4. Encouraging NGOs/institutes to embark upon such educational/awareness programmes on lighting for the benefit of society

The above measures shall result in the following benefits:

1. Saving of a precious source of energy, namely, electricity
2. Saving in energy bill for the common man, and thus improving his economic status
3. Saving the environment from light pollution due to the use of inefficient light sources
4. Saving the mankind from the harmful effects of global warming
5. On the employment front, such awareness will generate employment opportunities, thus improving the socio-economic status of individuals.
6. Increase in the number of such programmes will motivate individuals to opt for teaching profession in lighting, thus also improving employment opportunity.
7. Companies/manufacturers will be able to expand their business because of the easy availability of competent, educated manpower, thus improving the economy of the country.
8. It will help the government to frame policies about different types of educational/awareness programmes on lighting.

Chapter 4

Effect of Installing Thermosiphon Solar Water Heating System on Total Energy Bill at Mzuzu University

Lameck K. Nkhonjera[1] *and Precious Chaponda*[2]

[1]*University of Malawi-The Polytechnic, Physics and Biochemical Sciences, P/Bag 303, BT 3, Malawi*
E-mail: lnkhonjera@poly.ac.mw
[2]*Mzuzu University, Energy Studies Department, P/Bag 201, Mzuzu 2, Malawi*
E-mail: preciouschaponda@yahoo.com

ABSTRACT

Mzuzu University (MZUNI), one of the public universities in Malawi, has a student population of about 1800, out of which 23 per cent is accommodated in the university's student dormitories, while the rest are housed either in the university's apartments or in their own off-campus accommodation. MZUNI uses energy for lighting, cooking and water heating (electric water geysers in students' dormitories), as well as for powering equipment (laboratory equipment and other teaching gadgets). Water heating and cooking are the two major activities that contribute substantially to the energy consumption. Electricity being high-grade energy, its use for heating is regarded wasteful. Replacement of electric cooking and water heating by alternate methods would save utility energy, thereby mitigating the problem of electricity outage resulting from insufficient generation capacity. A wise option would be the replacement of electric water heaters by solar heaters. But, would the installation of solar water heaters bring about positive savings on the total energy bill? This study systematically determines the average monthly energy bill at MZUNI and the students' daily hot water demand. Subsequently, the thermosiphon solar water heating system (TSWHS) is sized and simulated. Finally, the system's life cycle cost (LCC) analysis is conducted. The results show that 76 per cent of the time in a year, the energy consumption of the TSWHS would be met by solar energy; even with the incorporation of auxiliary electric heating, electric water heating bill would be reduced from 9 per cent to 0.8 per cent of the total annual energy bill; 107 MWh of utility energy can be saved annually; and the system's payback period of 9 years can be realized with a 10 per cent rate of return on investment. It can therefore be concluded that installation of a TSWHS at MZUNI is both economically viable and saves utility energy.

Keywords: *Thermosiphon solar water heating system, TRNSYS, Energy bill, Life cycle cost.*

1. Introduction

Malawi, lying between 9° and 18° latitude and 32° and 36° longitude, is one of the least electrified nations in the world, with a mere 7.6 per cent of her population connected to the grid (Millennium Challenge Account, 2010). Small as this percentage may be, its peak power demand is higher than its 284 MW generation capacity, and consequently the country experiences frequent power outages due to load shedding. However, this problem can be mitigated if consumers follow energy conservation practices.

In line with this, the government is promoting the use of compact fluorescent lamps (CFL) instead of incandescent bulbs, and in the 2010–11 national budget money was allocated for free distribution of CFL to selected households. This scheme is expected to roll out in 2011. By sector, industry consumes a high proportion of the generated electricity (46 per cent), followed by the service sector, which consumes 11 per cent (MARGE, 2009). If these sectors engage in serious energy conservation measures, then the peak demand can be lowered so much so that periods of power cut are shortened if not completely eliminated. For instance, energy savings in universities, which are grouped under the service sector, can contribute to a reduction of the peak demand. Mzuzu University (MZUNI) is one of the universities in Malawi where this potential exists.

MZUNI has about 1800 enrolled students pursuing different undergraduate and postgraduate studies in different disciplines under five faculties. Energy at MZUNI is used for cooking, lighting, air-conditioning, powering educational equipment, water heating and transportation. Energy source of the aforementioned uses, except transportation, is grid electricity, which is backed up by diesel power generation. Energy for transportation comes from fuel used in running the fleet of university vehicles, and, in the context of this paper, the total energy bill excludes cost of transportation energy. Electricity is high-grade energy, and is supposed to be used where other primary sources of energy cannot meet the purpose. For instance, electric heating is counter-conservative if primary energy sources like solar, biomass or natural gas can be used to achieve the same purpose. Therefore, replacing the electric cooking pots and electric water geysers at MZUNI would be of paramount importance as far as saving grid power is concerned. However, selection of the alternative primary source should not compromise environment protection. With an increasing rate of deforestation in Malawi, use of fuel wood for cooking and water heating at MZUNI would not be environmentally friendly. On the other hand, use of natural gas (not available in the country) would not be economically viable. The solar cookers developed in the country are meant for small-scale application and are limited to use in direct sunshine with cooking times 50–100 per cent longer than that of conventional cooking methods (Vetter, 2006), and therefore are not suitable for bigger institutions like MZUNI. Nevertheless, according to Ascough (Ascough, 1999), domestic solar water heating technology has worked well in institutions and resulted in a reduction of electricity bill. In Cot' Devour, the performance of thermosiphon solar water heater has been analysed, and found to have an efficiency of more than 50 per cent (Koffi, et al., 2007).

Out of the MZUNI student community, 425 students are accommodated in on-campus dormitories. There are 35 hostels (22 for male and 13 for female) of 7-bed capacity (7 rooms with 1 bed per room) and 9 hostels (5 for male and 4 for female) of 20-bed capacity (10 rooms with 2 beds per room) all of which are provided with electric water geysers (not all are currently functional), basically for showering. Against this background, it is hypothetically taken that replacement of the existing electric geysers with thermosiphon solar water heating systems (TSWHS) would be technically feasible and economically viable. However, performance of solar technology is site-dependent; hence, this study aimed at finding out whether the installation of TSWHS at MZUNI would be cost-effective. This was achieved by precisely establishing the monthly total energy bill, establishing the students' hot water demand, sizing and simulating the TSWHS, and carrying out a life cycle cost (LCC) analysis of the designed system.

2. Methods

In order to come up with the measurable effect of installing a TSWHS on total energy bill at MZUNI, it was decided to determine the monthly energy cost of MZUNI, establish the students' daily hot water demand profile, size and simulate the TSWHS and carry out LCC analysis. The monthly energy bill was calculated as the sum of the monthly electricity bill and the expenditure on diesel for the stand-by generator. Procedurally, the data for 2006–10 electric bills and expenditure on stand-by generators were sourced from the Electricity Supply Commission of Malawi's (ESCOM's) and the university's records, respectively. Then the respective monthly average of the collected data was calculated, and the sum of the two averages gave the monthly energy bill.

When establishing the students' hot water demand profile, it was assumed that hot water would exclusively be used for showering. Therefore, a survey on the students' showering habits was conducted and a structured questionnaire was used to collect seasonal data on students' preference of cold to hot shower, times of the day when shower is normally taken (two different times in a day implied taking shower twice a day) and the time taken per shower. In each hostel, a questionnaire was administered to the occupants of every fourth room from the previously sampled room; thus, 2 rooms (2 people) were sampled in a 7-room-7-bed hostel, and 3 rooms (6 people) in a 10-room-20-bed hostel, totalling to a sample size of 124 (74 males and 50 females). In addition, in every hostel, the time taken for a shower to fill a 20-litre bucket was recorded and the average time was calculated, which when divided into 20 litres gave the average shower flow rate (Q) in litres/minute. From the survey data, the average shower time in minutes per student ($\bar{t}$) can be calculated and the number of hot showers (N_s) taken in each hour of the day can be established. Subsequently, the daily hot water demand profile for each season is drawn, from the hourly hot water demand (W_h) given by equation (1).

$$W_h = N_s Q\bar{t} \text{(litres)} \tag{1}$$

The standard thermosiphon solar water heaters are classified according to their water storage capacity, and since there are 44 separate dormitories with different bed capacities, each dormitory is supposed to be installed with a solar heater with enough water storage capacity for the occupying students. If the number of students in each dormitory is N_{sd}, then the minimum storage tank capacity required is given by

$$S = N_{sd} \times Q \times \bar{t} \text{(litres)} \tag{2}$$

Therefore, each dormitory is sized to have been installed with a thermosiphon solar water heater of around S litres.

The sized system is simulated using the version 16 of Transient System (TRNSYS 16) simulation studio. As shown in Figure 4.1, the simulation model comprises a weather data reader (type 109-user), a thermosiphon collector with integrated storage (type 45a), the load profile (type 14), a tempering valve (type 11b), a tee piece (type 11h), an online plotter (type 65a) and an LCC calculator (type 29a). Description of the

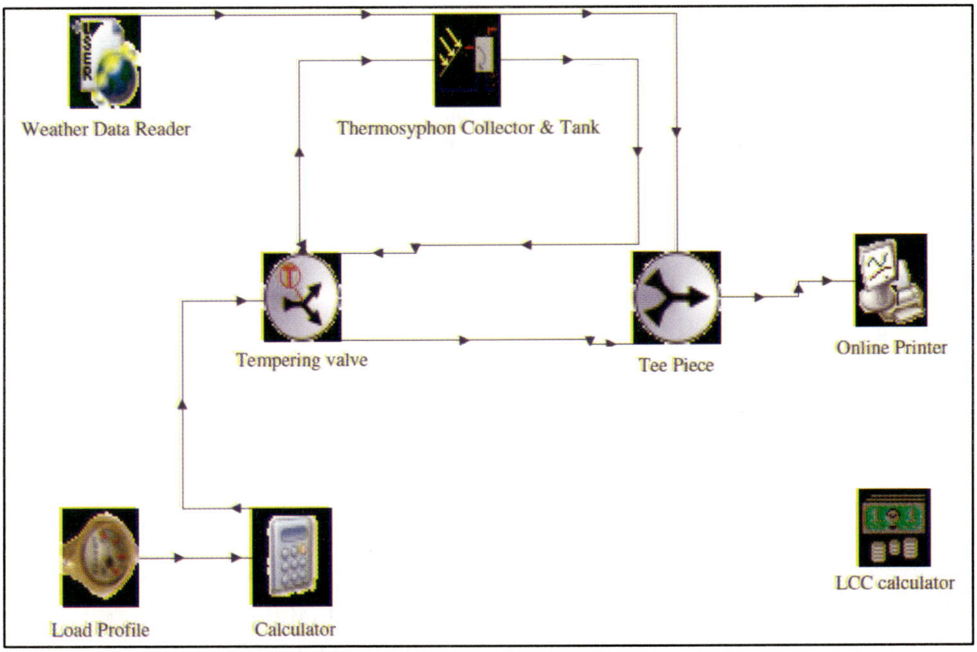

Figure 4.1: Simulation Model in TRNSYS Simulation Studio Showing Connection of Components

mathematical models used in these components can be found in the Component Mathematical Reference of TRNSYS 16 Documentation.

Performance of the collector depends on the ambient temperature, incident solar radiation and incident angle. These variables are obtained from the weather data reader. For a thorough performance analysis of the solar collector, replacement temperature and load flow rate are of much importance and these are obtained from the tempering valve. The load profile provides the hourly water requirement from the shower head. The average hot shower temperature (T_{avg}) for a normal person is about 42°C, meaning that water from the storage tank at temperatures higher than 42°C requires cooling by cold water mixing. The amount of hot water leaving the top of the storage tank is assumed to be equally replaced by cold water entering at the bottom. With this assumption, the hourly demanded shower water, obtained from the load profile, can be taken as cold, because part of it enters the bottom of the tank and part of it is used for cooling purpose. If the temperature (T_h) of hot water leaving the tank is higher than T_{avg}, then it is mixed with cold water to cool it to T_{avg}. In the model, this mixing is done at the tee piece and diversion of the incoming cold water is done by the tempering valve. The tempering valve controls the diversion by checking the temperature of water leaving the top of the storage tank. If it is higher than T_{avg}, then cold water is proportionally diverted so that when mixed at the tee piece, the output water is at 42°C. If $\dot{m}$ is the mass flow rate obtained from the load profile at a temperature T_i, then the proportion of $\dot{m}$ sent for cooling is given by

$$\gamma = \begin{cases} \dfrac{T_{avg-T_i}}{T_{h-T_i}} & \text{for } T_h > T_{avg} \\ 0 & \text{for } T_h > T_{avg} \end{cases} \tag{3}$$

The outlet temperature and flow rate are plotted online and printed to a file using the online printer. The TRX thermosiphon solar water heater (Figure 4.2) was thus simulated, and the simulation parameters were both obtained from manufacture's data sheet and calculated.

Finally, LCC analysis was performed in the LCC calculator, and its results sent to an external printer.

3. Results

From the past 5-year electricity and diesel bills, the average monthly bill in Malawi Kwacha (MWK) is found to be MWK 1,426,445 (1 USD = MWK 180), with the diesel bill contribution being 5 per cent. Analysis of the survey results shows that 95 per cent of the students, regardless of the season, prefer hot shower whenever it is available. Of the respondents, 99 per cent indicated that, in a day, they take a shower between 05:00 and 08:00, with 48 per cent taking a second shower between 18:00 and 21:00. The average time taken to fill a 20-litre bucket was found to be 4.6 min; thus $Q = 4.3$ l/min, and $\bar{t}$ was found to be 5 min. Consequently, evaluation of equation (1) gives 3015 Kg/hr as water mass rate between 05:00 and 08:00, 1447 kg/hr between 18:00

Figure 4.2: TRX Thermosiphon Type Solar Water Heater

and 21:00, and zero mass rate for the rest of the day, as depicted in Figure 4.3. There was no substantial difference between the load profile patterns in cold and hot seasons. As a result, the profile in Figure 4.3 was taken to be true for the whole year.

As mentioned above, there are 44 hostels, out which 9 have 20-bed capacity and the rest have 7-bed capacity. The 20-bed hostels were sized to have two numbers of the 200L TRX thermosiphon solar water heaters (Figure 4.2), while the latter hostels were sized with one similar heater, totalling to 53 heaters. Simulation of these heaters shows that temperatures below the set average shower temperature of 42°C concentrated during the months of April to June as shown in Figure 4.4. However, it is shown in Table 4.1 that 76 per cent of the time the hot shower would be available and it further shows that even on days of very low insolation, the water temperature could not fall below 25°C; it is maintained at a temperature at least 5°C higher than its initial temperature of 20°C.

In order to make the system available year-round, auxiliary heating is required. Therefore, for any temperature below 42°C, the energy required to raise the temperature to 42°C was calculated. The sum of these energies was regarded as the ideal auxiliary heat required. Figure 4.5 presents the percentagewise monthly solar and auxiliary

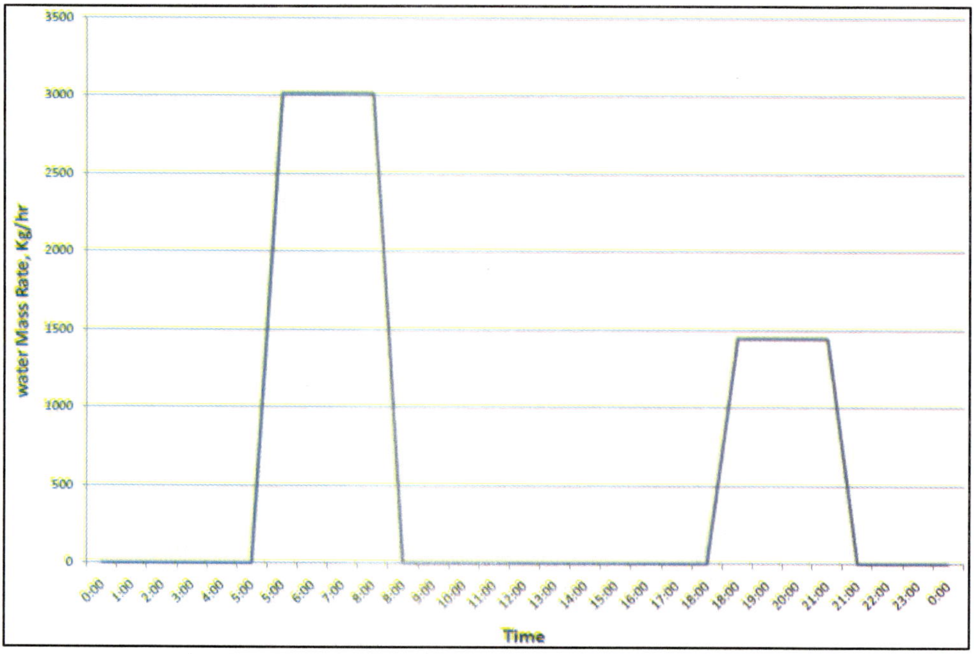

Figure 4.3: Hot Shower Water Demand Profile

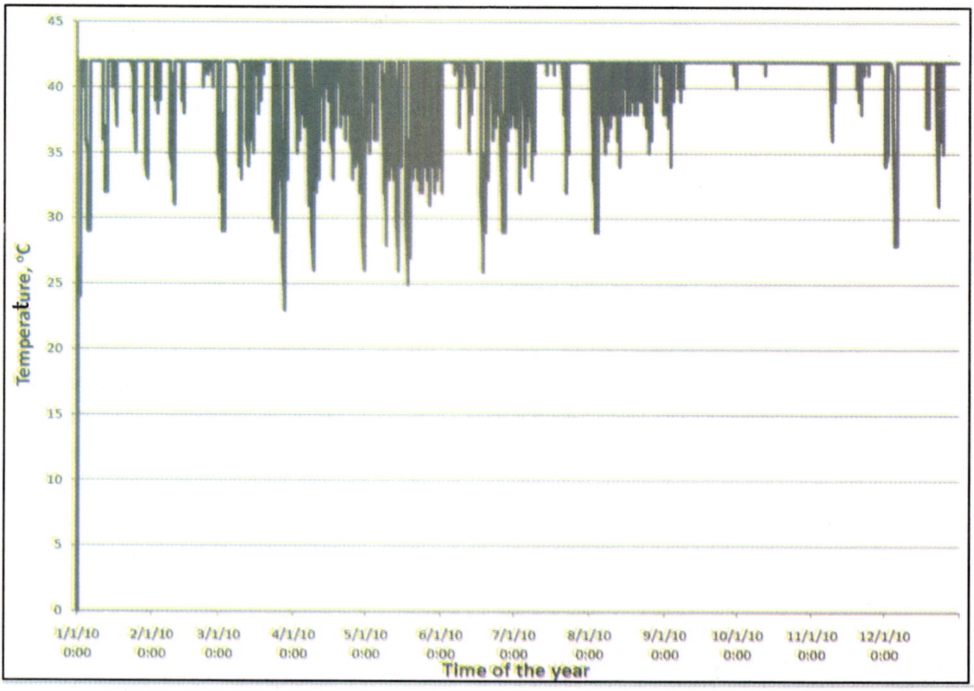

Figure 4.4: The Plot of Temperature of Shower Water Against Time

Table 4.1: Percentage Distribution of Temperature of Shower Water

Temperature Range (ºC)	*Percentage*
20–25	0
26–30	3
31–35	8
36–40	13
40–42	76

heating contribution. In agreement to Figure 4.4, auxiliary heating is much required between March and June. Besides, in October and November the solar fraction is almost unity. Overall, auxiliary heating contributes 9 per cent of the total water heating required in the year.

For a detailed LCC analysis, it was required to determine the amount of auxiliary heating required, which would, apart from maintenance cost, turn to be the major component of operation cost. From the relevant 5-year data of the National Bank of Malawi (National Bank of Malawi, 2011), the average inflation rate was found to be 9 per cent and the market discount rate was taken as 7 per cent. In Malawi, the cost of a 200L thermosiphon solar water heater of evacuated-tube type is currently about MWK 330,000 (installation cost inclusive). Thus, the capital cost was calculated as MWK 17,662,000. Considering that TSWHS needs low maintenance, its cost was estimated at 0.2 per cent of the capital investment; thus, the operation cost in the first year is MWK 18,000, which is the sum of the annual auxiliary heating bill and maintenance cost. The results of the simulated LCC analysis show that the rate of return of investment is 10 per cent, with a payback period of 9 years. See Table 4.2 for detailed yearly cash flow for the 20-years life span.

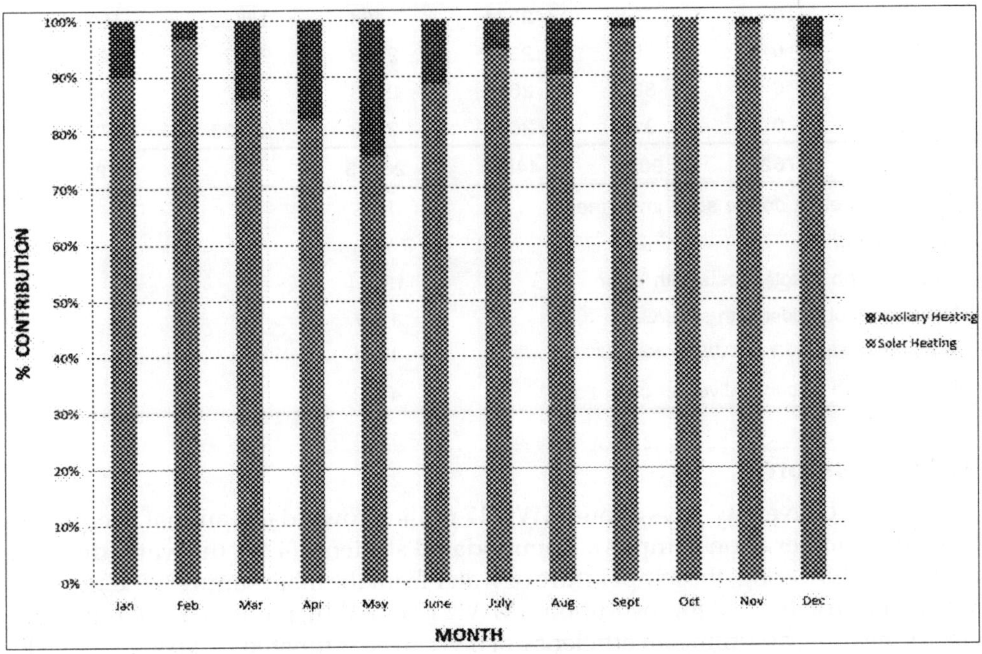

Figure 4.5: Contribution of Solar and Auxiliary Heating

Table 4.2: Results of Economic Analysis (Amounts in '000 MWK)

Yr	*Capital Investment*	*Operation Cost*	*Fuel Bill Saved*	*Net Cash Flow*		
				Annual	*Cumulalive*	*Present Worth*
0	17622	0	0	–17622	–17622	–17622
1	0	18	1846	1828	–15794	1709
2	0	19	1883	1863	–13931	1628
3	0	21	1920	1899	–12031	1551
4	0	23	1959	1936	–10095	1477
5	0	25	1998	1973	–8122	1407
6	0	27	2038	2011	–6112	1340
7	0	30	2079	2049	–4063	1276
8	0	32	2120	2088	–1975	1215
9	0	35	2163	2127	153	1157
10	0	38	2206	2232	2320	1102
11	0	42	2250	2208	4528	1049
12	0	46	2295	2249	6778	999
13	0	50	2341	2291	9069	951
14	0	54	2388	2285	11403	905
15	0	59	2435	2377	13780	861
16	0	64	2484	2420	16199	820
17	0	70	2534	2464	18663	780
18	0	76	2584	2508	21171	742
19	0	83	2636	2553	23724	706
20	0	91	2689	2598	26323	671
Totals	**17622**	**902**	**44846**	**26323**		**4722**
The rate of return on the solar investment				10%		
Pay Back Period				9 years		
Present worth of total costs with solar				19671		
Annualized total cost with solar/GJ				1597		
Annualized energy cost W/O solar/GJ				1981		
Present worth of cumulative net cash flow				4722		

4. Discussion

Mzuzu University pays about MWK 17 million towards its annual energy bill. From the number of on-campus accommodated students (425), the water demand profile for showering, the temperature of water from the main supply (20°C) and the Malawi electricity tariff for institutions (MWK 13.6/KWh), the annual bill purely for electric heating, assuming an efficiency of 0.9, can be estimated as MWK 1,846,000, representing about 10 per cent of the total bill. Therefore, there is a potential for electricity bill saving if solar water heaters are installed, which requires only about 9 per cent of auxiliary heating. The computation of the auxiliary heating bill shows that it contributes only 0.8 per cent of the total energy bill. In addition, solar radiation is favourable, leading to 76 per cent system availability, justifying the payback of the high investment cost within 9 years. Further, the 24 per cent system unavailability is attributed to low insolation, which is concentrated in the months of April to July in Malawi. Nevertheless, even during the days of very low insolation, solar heating is able to raise the temperature of incoming cold water from 20°C to at least 25°C. This is attributed to the capability of TSWHS to utilize diffuse radiation. The hot season in Malawi spans from September to April. The high insolation is, however, between September and November, which is why the solar factor in these months is high, as can be seen in Figure 4.4. From December to March, rains prevail leading to a low clearness index, hence low insolation. From the results of the study, TSWHS is viable at MZUNI and it offers positive savings on total energy bill over the life span of the system. This implies that implementation of such a project would save 107 MWh of utility energy annually. The saved energy would, to some extent, ease the problem of load shedding resulting from low generation capacity. Besides, installation of solar heaters would promote the use of the technology, which, if used as replacement to the electric water geysers in the country, can tremendously reduce, if not eliminate, the load shedding problem. It should be noted that optimization analysis was not done in this study, and thus it is envisaged that further utility energy savings may be possible. Several studies (Nahar, *et al.*, 1995; Joudi, 1999; Kalogivou, *et al.*, 1999; Karaghouli and Alnasser, 2001) have demonstrated differences in the performance of solar water heaters due to different designs, manufacturing materials and weather conditions. Therefore these variables are to be considered in the optimization of TSWHS to identify the best saving option.

5. Conclusions

From the results of this study, the following conclusions can be drawn:

1. Installation of a TSWHS at Mzuzu University dormitories will bring about a reduction in the university's energy bill. It can reduce the water heating energy bill from 10 per cent of the total energy bill to a mere 0.8 per cent.
2. It is economically viable to install thermosiphon solar water heaters at Mzuzu University dormitories, as the investment cost would be paid back within 9 years out of the 20-year life span of the system, and by the end of the 20 years, savings of MWK 4,722,000 (present worth) could be realized.
3. Annually, 107 MWh of utility energy can be saved, thereby narrowing the gap between demand and supply which results into frequent power outage.

References

Ascough, J., 1999. An Overview of Solar and Solar-Related Technologies in Zimbabwe. *The Zimbabwe Science News*, 33(1), pp. 26–32.

Joudi, K. A., 1999. Computer Simulation of a two phase thermosiphon solar domestic hot water heating system. *Energy Conversion Manager*, 42(1), pp. 775–793.

Kalogivou, A., Dentsoras, A. and Sofia, A., 1999. Modelling of Solar Domestic Water Heating Systems. *Solar Energy*, 65(1), pp. 335–342.

Karaghouli, A. and Alnasser, W., 2001. Experimental Study of Thermosiphon Solar Water Heater in Bahrain. *Renewable Energy*, 24(1), pp. 389–396.

Koffi, E. P., Gbaha, P., Sako, M., N'guessan, Y., Sangare, M., Konani, M. and Ado, G., 2007. Experimental Thermal Performance Study on a Thermosiphon Solar Water Heater, With Internal Exchanger, in Cote D'ivoire. *Global Journal of Pure and Applied Sciences*, 13(4), pp. 557–561.

MARGE, 2009. *Malawi Biomass Strategy*. Malawi Government, Lilongwe, Malawi.

Millennium Challenge Account, 2010. Compact Program for the Government of the Republic of Malawi (2011 - 2016): Concept Paper for the Energy Sector. Millennium Challenge Account – Malawi Country Office Secretariat, Lilongwe, Malawi.

Nahar N., Marshall, R. and Brinkworth, B., 1995. Investigation of Flat-Plate Collectors Using Transparent Insulation Materials. *International Journal of Solar Energy*, 17(1), pp. 117–134.

National Bank of Malawi, 2011. Inflation Rates. http://www.natbank.co.mw/index.php?pagename=inflation_rates (accessed 28 April, 2011).

Vetter, H., 2006. Solar Cooking in Madagascar: Solar Cooker Project of ADES. *Madagascar Conservation and Development*, 1(1), pp. 22–24.

Chapter 5

Energy Efficiency Initiatives in Malaysia

C.S. Tan[1], *Endang Jati Mat Sahid*[2] *and Y.P. Leong*[3]

Institute of Energy Policy and Research (IEPRe),
Universiti Tenaga Nasional (UNITEN), Malaysia
E-mail: [1]*chingsin@uniten.edu.my;* [2]*endang@uniten.edu.my,*
[3]*ypleong@uniten.edu.my*

ABSTRACT

Development of energy sector in Malaysia is guided by three principal objectives of the National Energy Policy which was introduced in 1979, that is supply objective, utilization objective and environmental objective. The aim of the utilization objective is to promote an efficient utilization of energy and to discourage wasteful and non-productive patterns of energy consumption.

The Malaysia government's approach towards realizing this objective is to focus on improving energy efficiency in industry sector and to encourage efficiency in energy production, transportation, conversion, utilization as well as consumption through various awareness programmes.

In order to reduce inefficiency and wasteful use of energy in industrial facilities there is a need for the Government to work with the industry and promote energy efficiency in industrial facilities. Along these lines, a number of industrial energy efficiency initiatives are being planned and this includes the energy auditing programme, energy services companies support programme and technologies demonstration programme.

This paper will look into the key issues and challenges of EE development, action plans and implementations taken in Malaysia and identify broad strategies which can be catalyst for EE initiatives in Malaysia.

Keywords: *Energy efficiency, Green building index, Energy labeling, Energy policy.*

1. Status of Energy Supply and Demand: Past and Current

The main sources of commercial energy supply in Malaysia in 1980 were derived from crude oil and petroleum products (75 per cent) followed by natural gas (21 per cent), hydro (3.5 per cent) and coal and coke (0.5 per cent). In the period from 1990 to 2008, the share of crude oil and petroleum products in the total primary energy supply has declined, while that of natural gas and coal and coke has increased indicating a successful reduction in the overall dependence on crude oil and petroleum products as shown in Figure 5.1.

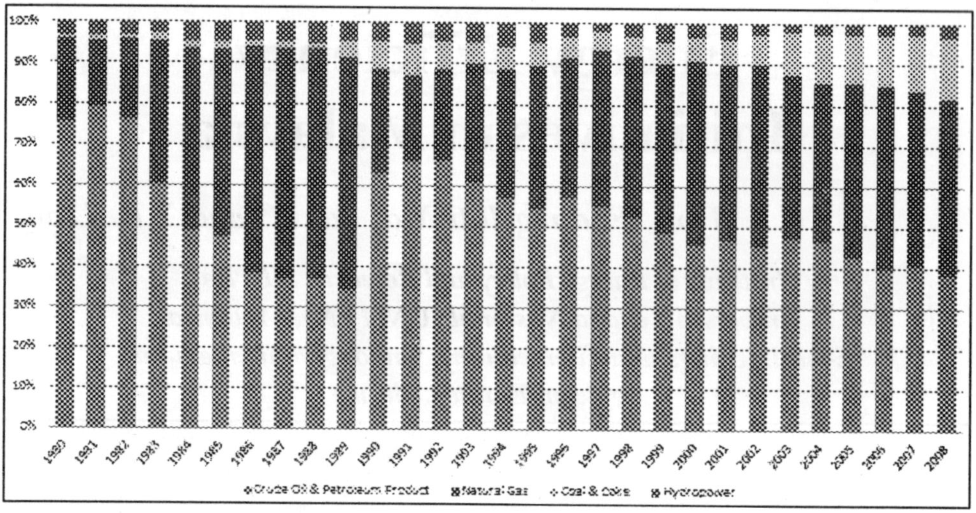

Figure 5.1: Share of Energy Input in Commercial Energy Supply (1980-2008)
***Source*: National Energy Balance**

The commercial energy use and supply in Malaysia from year 1980-2008 is illustrated in Figure 5.2. It shows that the commercial energy supply has increased almost six times from 10,927 ktoe in 1980 to 64,040 ktoe in 2008, driven largely by crude oil and natural gas supply. Natural gas dominates this composition with almost 27,800 ktoe in 2008 followed by crude oil and petroleum products at 24,494 ktoe, and coal and coke and hydropower with 9,782 ktoe and 1,964 ktoe respectively.

On the other hand, commercial energy use has increased seven times, from 6,385 ktoe in 1980 to 44,901 ktoe in 2008, driven largely by the industry and transport sectors' demand. If this trend continues, there could be a potential scenario where Malaysia will use energy inefficiently.

In 2008, approximately 6,205 thousand tonnes of oil equivalent (ktoe) of commercial energy was consumed in the residential and commercial sector as compared to 826 ktoe and 3868 ktoe in 1980 and 2000 respectively. Figure 5.3 represents the trend in energy consumption of the sector. The share of this sector in the total energy consumption has remained between 12 and 14 per cent in the past three decades.

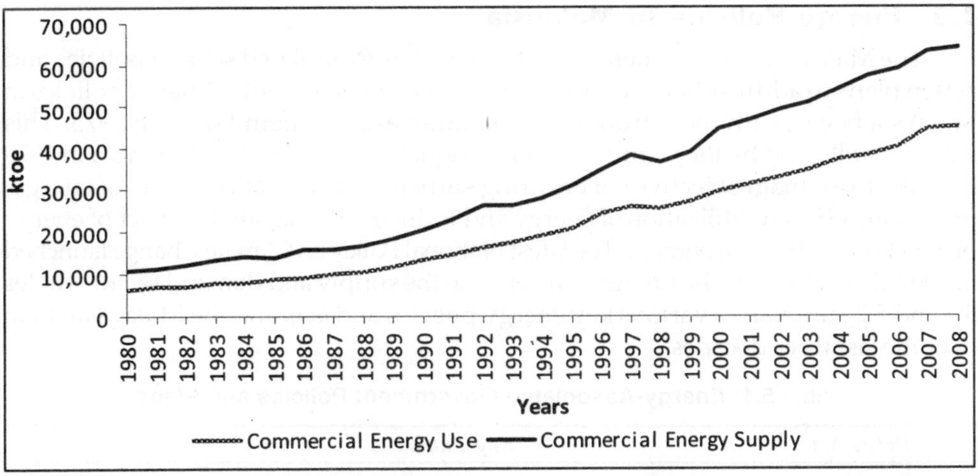

Figure 5.2: Commercial Energy Use and Commercial Energy Supply (1980-2008)
***Source*: National Energy Balance**

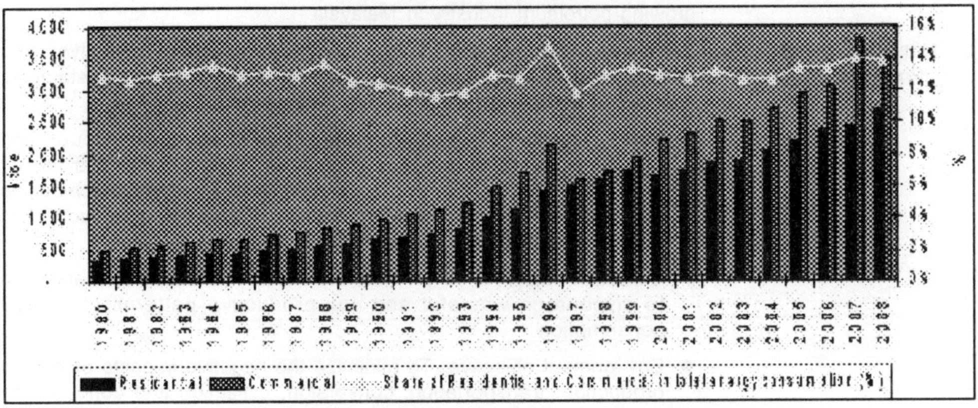

Figure 5.3: Share of Residential and Commercial Sector in Total Energy Consumption in Malaysia
***Source*: National Energy Balance**

To enhance the level of achievement of the utilization objective, it is believed that the market approach needs to be supplemented by the regulatory approach. The National Energy Efficiency Master plan (NEEMP) is currently being formulated and will focus on the designation of large consumers by appointing energy managers and labeling of equipments. This policy will help in reducing of Greenhouse Gas emission in Malaysia that the Honorable Prime Minister of Malaysia has pledged at the Climate Change Conference COP-15 in Copenhagen in December 2009 to voluntarily reduce 40 per cent CO_2 emission intensity of GDP by year 2020 as compared to 2005 with condition on receiving the transfer of technology and finance of adequate and effective levels from Annex 1 countries.

1.1 Energy Policies in Malaysia

The Malaysian government over the years has formulated several policies and action plans to address her energy concerns. The development of energy policies in Malaysia began with the introduction of National Petroleum Policy in 1975. This was then followed by the formulation of National Energy Policy of Malaysia in 1979 with the three main objectives of ensuring sufficient and reliable supply of energy, promoting efficient utilization of energy and reducing the negative impact of energy production on the environment. The latest National Policy on Climate Change launched in 2009 also highlights the Energy Efficiency in the supply and demand sector. Tables 5.1 and 5.2 summarize various key energy policies and acts and the Malaysian Plan over the last three decades.

Table 5.1: Energy-Associated Government Policies and Plans

Policy/Act	*Key Emphasis*
National Petroleum Policy (1975)	✩ Introduced to ensure optimal use of petroleum resources and regulation of ownership, management and operation, and economic, social, and environmental safeguards in the exploitation of petroleum due to fast growing petroleum industry in Malaysia
National Energy Policy (1979)	✩ Formulated with broad guidelines on long-term energy objectives and strategies to ensure efficient, secure and environmentally sustainable supplies of energy. It has three main objectives: ● Supply objective: To ensure the provision of adequate, secure, and cost-effective energy supplies through developing indigenous energy resources both non-renewable and renewable energy resources using the least cost options and diversification of supply sources both from within and outside the country ● Utilization objective: To promote the efficient utilization of energy and to discourage wasteful and non-productive patterns of energy consumption ● Environment objective: To minimize the negative impacts of energy production, transportation, conversion, utilization and consumption on the environment
National Depletion Policy (1980)	✩ Introduced to safeguard against over exploitation of oil and gas reserves. Thus, it is production control policy
Four Fuel Diversification Policy (1981)	✩ Fuel diversification was designed to avoid over-dependence on oil as main energy supply and aimed at placing increased emphasis on gas, hydro and coal in the energy mix
Electricity Supply Act (1990)	✩ Regulates the licensing of electricity generation, transmission and distribution
Gas Supply Act (1993)	✩ Regulates the licensing of the supply of gas to consumers through pipelines, prices, the control of gas supply pipelines, installations and appliances as well as safety
Five Fuel Diversification Policy (2001)	✩ Introduced in recognition of the potential of biomass, biogas, municipal waste, solar and mini hydro as potential renewable energy resources for electricity generation, SREP

Contd...

Table 5.1–*Contd...*

Policy/Act	*Key Emphasis*
Energy Commission Act (2001)	☆ The Energy Commission (or Suruhanjaya Tenaga) was established to provide technical and performance regulation for the electricity and piped gas supply industries, as the safety regulator for electricity and piped gas and to advise the government on matters relating to electricity and piped gas supply including energy efficiency and renewable energy issues. ☆ The Electricity Supply Act 1990 and Gas Supply Act 1993 have both been amended to allow the Energy Commission to take over these responsibilities
National Biofuel Policy (2006)	☆ Supports the five fuels diversification policy. Aimed at reducing the country's dependence on depleting fossil fuels, ☆ Promoting the demand for palm oil. Five key thrusts: transport, industry, technologies, export and cleaner environment. Highlights: ☆ Producing a biodiesel fuel blend of 5 per cent processed palm oil with 95 per cent petroleum diesel ☆ Encouraging the use of biofuel by giving incentives for providing biodiesel pumps at fuelling stations ☆ Establishing industry standard for biodiesel quality under Standards and Industrial Research Institute of Malaysia (SIRIM) ☆ Setting up of a palm oil biodiesel plant
The National Green Technology Policy (2009)	☆ Intensification of Green Technology research and innovation towards commercialization. ☆ Strong promotion and public awareness of Green Technology. ☆ Promotion of Green Building Index ☆ Promotion of application of RE in commercial and residential buildings such as PV, rainwater harvesting, phasing out of incandescent lights
National Policy on Climate Change (2009)	☆ ST5-P2: Consolidate the energy policy incorporating management practices that enhances renewable energy (RE) and energy efficiency (EE). ☆ KA19 - ST5 : Promote RE and EE for power generation through: • Burden sharing between government and power producers; • Establishment of EE and RE targets/standards; • Inclusion of RE in generation mix by power producers; and • Promotion of RE generation by small and independent developers including local communities.

1.2 Regulatory and Institutional Frameworks

The Ministry of Energy, Green Technology and Water (MEGTW) is the main agency responsible for the planning, formulation and implementation of policies, formulation and enforcement of Acts and regulations in the energy, green technology and water sectors. However, there are many other organizations which are responsible for planning and operation on the overall energy sector in Malaysia at different levels. The key stakeholders in the Malaysian energy sector and their respective functions are briefly outlined in Table 5.3.

Table 5.2: Malaysia's Key Emphasis from 7MP to 10MP for Energy Development

Malaysia Plan	*Key Emphasis*
Tenth Malaysia Plan (2011–2015)	Short term goals vested in National Green Technology Policy: ✰ Increased public awareness and commitment for the adoption and application of green technology through advocacy programmes ✰ Widespread availability and recognition of green technology in terms of products, appliances, equipment and systems in the local market through standards, rating and labeling programmes ✰ Increased foreign and domestic direct investments (FDIs and DDIs) in green technology manufacturing and services sector ✰ Expansion of local research institutes and institutions of higher learning to expand research, development and innovation activities on green technology towards commercialization through appropriate mechanisms ✰ New RE act and FiT mechanism to be launched ✰ Accelerating the implementation of energy efficiency initiatives in the industrial, commercial, residential and transport sectors;
Ninth Malaysia Plan (2006–2010)	✰ Emphasis on strengthening initiatives for EE especially in transport, commercial and industrial sectors, and in government buildings ✰ Encourage better utilization of RE through diversify fuel sources ✰ Intensify efforts to further reduce the dependency on petroleum provides for more efforts to integrate alternative fuels ✰ Incentives in promoting RE and EE are further enhanced
Eighth Malaysia Plan (2001–2005)	✰ Emphasis on the sustainable development of energy resources, both depletable and renewable. The energy mix includes five fuels: oil, gas, coal, hydro and RE ✰ Intensify efforts on ensuring adequacy, quality and security of energy supply ✰ Greater emphasis on EE: encourage efficient utilization of gas and RE as well as provide adequate electricity generating capacity ✰ Supports the development of industries in production of energy-related products and services. Highlights in promoting RE and EE: • Incentives for EE. • Incentives for the use of RE resources. • Incentives to maintain quality of power supply
Seventh Malaysia Plan (1996–2000)	✰ Emphasis on the sustainable development of depletable resources and the diversification of energy sources· Ensuring adequacy of generating capacity as well as expanding and upgrading the transmission and distribution infrastructure ✰ Encouraged the use of new and alternative energy sources as well as efficient utilization of energy

2. Barriers to Energy Efficiency

The main barriers to implement energy efficiency (EE) among others include:

1. Limited knowledge or awareness of EE techniques and their economic benefits.

Table 5.3: Key Stakeholders in the Energy Sector

Stakeholders	*Functions*
Energy Unit of Economic Planning Unit (EPU)	☆ The EPU provides the general direction and strategies and determines the level of implementation.
The Ministry of Energy, Green Technology and Water (MEGTW)	☆ The role of MEGTW is to formulate energy appropriate policy, in coordination with the EPU. ☆ To administer and manage the nation's energy, green technology and water functions
The Energy Commission or Suruhanjaya Tenaga (ST)	☆ EC was established in 2001, replacing the Department of Electricity and Gas Supply (DEGS) ☆ The EC is the regulatory agency for the electricity and piped gas supply industry. ☆ The Commission's main tasks are to provide technical and performance regulation for the electricity and piped gas supply industry, as the safety regulator for electricity and piped gas and to advise the Minister on all matters relating to electricity and piped gas supply including energy efficiency and renewable energy issues.
Malaysia Green Technology Cooperation (MGTC)	☆ Malaysia Green Technology Cooperation (MGTC) has been restructured in 2010 to replace PTM which was established in 1997. ☆ It undertakes the development and coordination of energy research. The aim of MGTC is to be the focal point on energy implementation and catalyst for linkages with universities, research institutions, industry, and domestic and international energy organizations ☆ The major functions including: • Promoter of National EE and RE programmes related to green technology policy, and • Coordinator and lead manager in energy research and development, and demonstration projects.
Petroleum National Berhad (Petronas)	☆ Responsible for exploration, development, refining, and marketing and distribution of petroleum product
Tenaga National Berhad(TNB)	☆ Responsible for generation, transmission and distribution of electricity in Peninsular Malaysia.
Sarawak Energy Berhad (SEB)/Sabah Electricity Sdn. Bhd. (SESB)	☆ Responsible for generation, transmission and distribution of electricity in East Malaysia.

2. Limited access to information and benchmarks for EE technologies.
3. An unwillingness to incur what are perceived to be the 'high-cost/high-risk' transaction.
4. Preference for industries to focus on investments in production rather than on efficiency.
5. Lack of financier prepared to finance EE investments.
6. Insufficient stringency of regulations on EE standards and inadequacy in their implementation.
7. Few EE technology demonstration projects by industry or government.

8. Inadequate local energy support services and lack of trained industry and financial sector personnel in energy management.
9. Large multinational corporations with production facilities in the country often feature state of art energy efficient designs, but domestic industries, particularly the medium and small companies are less enterprising. Energy users are often reluctant to try out innovative solutions unless they are confident that claimed benefits are achievable. They may also have little need to use less energy if they can easily pass energy costs on to their customers.

Several action plans and measures have been taken by Government of Malaysia to promote and improve energy efficiency in the industrial, commercial and residential buildings. Information on Energy Efficiency has been disseminated through mass media, newspapers, conferences, seminars, workshops and publication. The following sections highlight the energy efficiency development in Malaysia.

3. Action Planks for Promoting Energy Efficiency

Major Initiatives taken to improve Energy Efficiency can be categorized into three sectors namely, Industry, Commercial and Residential.

3.1 Industry

In the industry sector, several initiatives have been carried out to promote and improve energy efficiency. This can be seen in the Malaysian Industrial Energy Efficiency Improvement Project (MIEEIP). This Project was funded by United Nation Development Program (UNDP), Global Environmental Facility (GEF), private sector and Government of Malaysia. It was initiated in mid 1999 and was implemented between 2000 and 2007.

The implementation of MIEEIP was one of the Government's efforts in promoting efficient use of energy in the industrial sector. The objective of MIEEIP is to improve EE in Malaysia's industrial sector by identifying and reducing barriers to efficient industrial energy use and encouraging implementation of EE improvement projects in industries, promoting capacity building of local EE experts and consultants and prepare groundwork for authorities to develop a legal basis for improving EE.

Eight (8) energy intensive industrial sub sectors have been identified in MIEEIP programme there are Iron and Steel, Cement, Wood, Food, Glass, Pulp and Paper, Ceramics and Rubber. However, additional manufacturing sub-sectors are also identified during this program. These include Plastic, Chemical and Textile. Eight (8) MIEEP programmes have been identified to promote efficient use of energy in industrial sector as outlined in Table 5.4.

Publication of *The Energy Efficiency and Conservation Guidelines for Malaysian Industries Part 1: Electrical Energy-use Equipment*. The guidelines encourage industries to adopt energy efficiency practices as well as manage and improve their energy utilization and environmental management covering a number of commonly-used equipments such as fans, motors, pumps, chillers, transformers and air-compressors.

Table 5.4: MIEEIP Components (UNDP, 2006)

No.	MIEEIP Component Programme	Description
1	Energy-use Benchmarking Programme	Creation of data collection and database system for energy benchmarking set up. Benchmarking will help to educate industries on energy use reporting and awareness for continuous improvement.
2	Energy Audits Programme	Assessing current practice in energy auditing and to develop standardized energy audit tools and procedures. By 2007, 54 factories from various sub-sectors of industries have been audited.
3	Energy Rating Programme	Dissemination of information to increase awareness and encourage the use of energy efficient equipment through energy rating programmes such as on refrigerator, fan, etc
4	EE Promotion Programme	Provision of user-friendly mechanisms to access and retrieve relevant information. A collection of techniques and technologies applications database on the successful EE applications in their energy saving efforts are being documented and disseminated to encourage participation through the Federation of Malaysian Manufacturers (FMM). Newsletter, conferences, workshops, seminars and website will be used as a medium of dissemination of information.
5	Energy Service Companies (ESCOs) Support Programme	Educating ESCOs in the identification of feasible project, technical know-how and increase more full-time professional energy auditors.
6	Energy Technology Demonstration Programme	Several demonstrations projects with proven technologies can be developed, implemented and monitored in selected sub-sectors of industry. Substantial benefits can be shown by demonstrating actual application and not necessarily costly. These involving feasibility studies of the system, the engineering design, installation, operation, monitoring and evaluation
7	Local Energy Efficient Equipment Manufacturing Support Programme	Provision of training, technical assistance and financial incentives to encourage and assist local equipment manufacturers to the selected manufacturers production such as fans, blowers, boilers, motor rewinding and industrial kilns
8	Financial Institutional Participation Programme	Demonstration of the technical and financial viability of energy efficiency measures, energy saving potential and the corresponding potential for GHG emissions reduction will help to train local banking and financial institutions to fund EE projects in industry

Publication of *The Industrial Energy Audit Guidelines*. This is a standard general energy audit guideline that can be used as a reference material by energy consulting firms providing energy audit services to industries. It is prepared based on 54 energy audits in eight industrial sub sectors under Malaysian Industrial Energy Efficiency Improvement Project (MIEEIP)

Enforcement of *The Efficient Management of Electrical Energy Regulations* 2008 under the Electricity Supply Act to ensure that any installation which consumes more than 3 million kWh of electricity over a period of six months will be required to engage an electrical energy manager. The energy manager will be responsible for analyzing the total consumption of electrical energy, to advise on the development and implementation of measures to ensure efficient management of electrical energy as well as to monitor the effectiveness of the measures taken.

3.2 Commercial

The first LEO building of the Ministry of Energy, Green Technology and Water was built in 2004 as a demonstration building on Low Energy Building to create awareness and the Green Energy Office of Malaysia Green Technology Corporation (MGTC) formerly known as Pusat Tenage Nasional (PTM) was built in 2008. These demonstration buildings hope to encourage private builders to construct and design low energy buildings.

A green building rating tool called the Green Building Index (GBI) has been developed to encourage the construction of green buildings. Energy Efficiency requirement under MS 1525:2001 which is the *Code of Practice on the Use of Renewable Energy and Energy Efficiency in Non-Residential Buildings* will be incorporated in the amendments to the Uniform Building By-Laws (UBBL) for all buildings in Malaysia.

A handbook entitled '*Fiscal Incentives for Renewable Energy and Energy Efficiency in Malaysia*' has been published by the Government of Malaysia to offer attractive incentives to encourage the generation of RE and adoption of EE initiatives as well as for improvement of Power Quality (PQ) amongst energy producers and users in Malaysia. The incentives granted including Pioneer Status (PS), Investment Tax Allowance (ITA), Duty Import Exemption and Sales Tax Exemption on machinery, equipment, materials, spare parts and consumables and Tax and Stamp duty exemption for GBI certified property are provided for industrial and commercial companies who take measures to practice energy efficiency in their premises. This handbook does not address fiscal incentives for the transport sector.

3.3 Residential

Appliance 'Star' Labeling was introduced in 2002. The evaluation and rating of the appliances is carried out by Energy Commission. The Energy Star Rating Label indicates a product's energy performance. The more stars there are on the upper part of the label the more energy efficient the product is. 5 stars indicate that it is the most energy efficient model. Figure 5.4 shows the comparative label and endorsement label by Energy Commission. The endorsement label indicates the most energy saving and high quality of a product.

Eight (8) EE appliances are listed in Energy Commission's website. Those EE appliances are Refrigerators, Domestic Electric Fans, Ballast for Fluorescent Lamps, Electric Lamps, Air Conditioners (Split Unit), Televisions, High Efficiency Motors and Insulation Materials. Out of these eight appliances only four (4) appliances have been 'star labelled'. There are televisions, refrigerators, Domestic Electric Fans and Air Conditioners (Split Unit).

3.4 Campaign for Promoting Energy Efficiency

Various campaigns have been launched from 2003-2006 to promote Energy Efficiency:

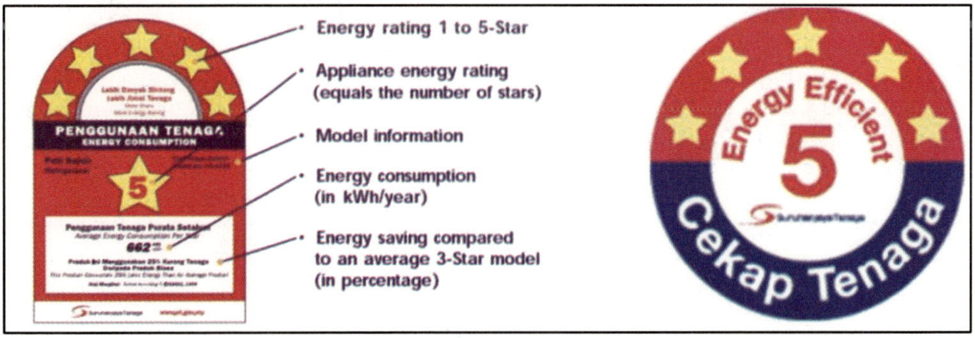

Figure 5.4: Comparative Label (Left), Endorsement Label (Right)

(*a*) Newspaper and Mass Media EE Awareness Campaign

Publication of Energy efficiency guide for households titled 'Your Guide to Energy Efficiency at Home' and 'Be Energy Efficient Guidebook' published by Energy Commission is distributed to the public. Regular TV commercial on energy saving tips at home has been aired through national TV stations.

'Promotion of Awareness and Education in RE and EE among School Children and general public' by Centre for Education and Training in Renewable Energy and Energy Efficiency (CETREE) which is located in the University of Science Malaysia (USM). Mobile van equipped with various education kits brochures and equipment was used to conduct activities in schools. Workshops were also conducted to train teachers to promote RE and EE in schools and this will help in propose a new school syllabus to educate school children on EE (CETREE, 2002). Activities such as seminars and exhibitions on energy efficiency are organized for general public and students.

(*b*) High Efficient Motor Campaign in 2005

A Six months campaign beginning in May 2005 with the aim of encouraging manufacturers to use High Efficiency Motors (HEMs) in their operation. Fiscal incentives have been introduced by the government for efficient electrical equipment and insulation material.

(*c*) Refrigerator Campaign 2006

Energy Commission launched advertising and promotion campaign, featuring Energy Rating Label for Energy Efficient Refrigerators on 11 February 2006. Incentives are given to a 5-STAR rating refrigerators.

4. National Measures taken to Promote Long Term Energy Efficiency

4.1 National Policy in Energy Efficient Lighting in Comparison with Other Economies

Many countries including US, Japan, Korea, Singapore and Europe have planned to phase out incandescent bulbs in stages by using more efficient lighting in buildings.

In Malaysia the incandescent light bulbs will be phased out in stages by year 2014. This policy aims to ensure efficient use of energy among consumers. It also helps in reducing overall global warning by producing less CO_2 emission with the saving of natural resources for powering of energy. Table 5.5 shows the selected government's policy in phasing out incandescent light bulbs.

Table 5.5: Phasing Out of Incandescent Light Bulbs

Economy	*Government Policy in Energy Efficient Lighting*
Taiwan	To replace incandescent light bulb with LED lamp from 2009 in government building. Incandescent lamps are banned from 2012
Australia	Incandescent light bulbs are banned after 2010
European Union	Incandescent light bulbs are banned from production and use after 2009
Korea	Incandescent light bulbs will be phased out by 2012
Japan	Incandescent light bulbs will be phased out by 2012
Canada	Incandescent light bulbs will be phased out by 2012
USA	Incandescent light bulbs will be phased out by 2014
England	Incandescent light bulbs will be phased out gradually by 2012
Malaysia	Incandescent light bulbs will be phased out in stages by 2014

4.2 Green Rating Tools in Selected Economies

Worldwide, there is already a push towards building more energy efficient buildings. It began in the 1990 with BREEAM (UK, 1990) and later LEED (US, 1996) as listed in Table 5.6. The introduction of the green building ratings was the result of the realization that buildings and the built environment contributes significantly to green house gas emissions and thus they needed to be re-designed to reduce their negative impact to the environment. Green rating tools are very much dependent upon location and environment. Most of the Green Rating tools are concentrated within the temperature climate zones such UK's BREEAM, US's LEED, Japan's CASBEE and Australia's GREENSTAR. Their sample logo is illustrated in Figure 5.5.

ASIA countries are also trying to catch up with this trend, by instituting its own standards, modelled after those adopted by other countries, in the late 2000s. Apart from Singapore Government's GREENMARK, Malaysia' Green Building Index (GBI) rating tool is also designed for tropical climate.

Figure 5.5: From Left, GBI Malaysia, Green Mark Singapore, Green Star Australia and LEED US

Table 5.6: Green Rating Tools

Country	*Green Rating Tool*	*Launched*
United Kingdom	Building Research Establishment Environmental Assessment Method (BREEAM)	1990
France	High Quality Environmental standard (HQE)	1992
United States	Leadership in Energy and Environmental Design (LEED) Green Globes	1996
Australia	Green Star	2003
Japan	Comprehensive Assessment System for Building Environmental Efficiency (CASBEE)	2005
Singapore	Green Mark	2005
China	Green Building Assessment System (GBAS)	2006
Malaysia	Green Building Index (GBI)	2009
UAE	Pearl Design System	2010
India	LEED India Green Rating for Integrated Habitat Assessment (GRIHA) by TERI	2004 2009

4.3 GBI Malaysia

GBI Malaysia was introduced on 3rd January 2009 by Pertubuhan Akitek Malaysia (PAM) and the Association of Consulting Engineers Malaysia (ACEM) and officially launched on 21st May 2009 (GBI, 2011).

GBI Malaysia was introduced to promote sustainability in the built environment and raise awareness among developers, architects, engineers, planners, designers, contractors and the public about environmental issues and our responsibility to the future generations.

It provides an opportunity for developers and building owners to design and construct green, sustainable buildings that can provide energy savings, water savings, a healthier indoor environment, better connectivity to public transport and the adoption of recycling and greenery for their projects and reduce impact on the environment.

The GBI Malaysia certification process starts with an assessment of the building design by a certifier appointed by Greenbuildingindex.Sdn.Bhd. The assessment process involves an assessment at design stage leading to the award of the provisional GBI rating. A final award is given one year after the building is first occupied. For buildings recertification, the buildings will also have to be reassessed every three years in order to maintain their GBI rating to ensure they are well-maintained. Points are given for performance above benchmarks and current industry practice. The buildings will be awarded based on four types of ratings, namely certified, silver, gold and platinum depending on the scores achieved. The assessment of Non residential and residential properties under the GBI Rating system is based on six (6) main key criteria as follows:

1. Energy Efficiency (EE)
2. Indoor Environment Quality (EQ)
3. Sustainable Site Planning and Management (SM)
4. Material and Resources (MR)
5. Water Efficiency (WE)
6. Innovation (IN)

The GBI for Non Residential Rating tool evaluates the sustainable aspects of buildings that are commercial, institutional and industrial in nature. This includes factories, offices, hospitals, universities, colleges, hotels and shopping complexes. More emphasis is placed on energy efficiency and indoor environmental quality as these have the greatest impact in the areas of energy use and well-being of the occupants and users of the building. Figures 5.6 to 5.8 demonstrate two successful GBI certified EE projects in Malaysia.

The GBI for Residential Rating tool on the other hand evaluates the sustainable aspects of residential buildings. This includes linked houses, apartments, condominiums, townhouses, semi-detached and bungalows. More emphasis is on sustainable site planning and Management followed by energy efficiency.

These GBI rating tool will help reduce the negative impact to the environment and can lead to a reduce carbon footprint. The GBI Classification is shown in Table 5.7.

Table 5.7: Green Building Index Points and Rating

Points	*GBI Rating*
86+ points	Platinum
76 to 85 points	Gold
66 to 75 points	Silver
50 to 65 points	Certified

Recently a new GBI for Township Rating tool was launched in 29th March 2011 (GBI, 2011). The GBI Township Tool sets out a vision for sustainability within the built environment and provides guidance to assist end users to deliver a sustainable township. Following are the Six (6) core categories that have been identified for the delivery of Sustainable Townships in Malaysia.

1. Climate, Energy and Water
2. Ecology and Environment
3. Community Planning and Design
4. Transportation and Connectivity
5. Building and Resources
6. Business and Innovation

Five (5) township pilot projects were registered under the GBI Township Tool. There are TTDI Alam Impian, Broga Valley, Ken Rimba, Elmina East in Selangor and Karambunai Integrated Resort City in Sabah. More GBI rating tools are set to be launched this year this includes The Industrial Rating Tool, The Data Center Rating Tool, The Mall Rating Tool, The Hotel Rating Tool and The Public Health Rating

Tool. Since its inception in May 2009, GBI Malaysia has received over 160 applications for registration, 38 per cent of which are new residential buildings, 60 per cent are new non-residential buildings and 2 per cent existing non residential buildings.

Figure 5.6: Green Energy Office (GEO) Building, MTGC, Bangi Formerly Known as PTM Malaysia's First GBI Certified Rating Building

Figure 5.7: Low Energy Office (LEO) Building, MEGTW's Building, Putrajaya

Figure 5.8: Energy Efficiency Building, Energy Commission, Putrajaya, Malaysia's GBI Platinum Rating Building

4.4 National Energy Efficiency Master Plan Study (NEEMP)

According to a survey conducted by the International Energy Agency (IEA) for the 1971-2006 periods, Malaysia is ranked fifth among eight ASEAN countries in terms of energy intensity. One of the main barriers to Malaysia's energy efficiency efforts is the Government's policy on giving subsidies on energy prices for the power and non-power sectors.

Realizing the need for Malaysia to set clear goals and targets to use energy more efficiently, Malaysia embarked on an Energy Efficiency Master Plan Study in March 2009. The main objective of the Energy Efficiency Master Plan Study is to develop the Energy Efficiency Policy and Energy Efficiency Action Plan in the industrial, building and Residential Sectors. The Master Plan has clear goals and targets to coordinate and implement energy efficiency and energy conservation programmes in a systematic and holistic manner.

The Energy Efficiency and Conservation Policy Statement as recommended in the EEMP is 'Rational use of energy through Energy Efficiency and Conservation policy instruments to achieve a low-carbon and high income economy for sustainable development and energy security and mitigating climate change'. Nine (9) Policy instruments have been identified to accelerate the pace of EE development in Malaysia'.

1. Enactment of an EE&C Act (EECA)
2. Establishment of an Energy Efficiency and Conservation Agency of Malaysia (EECAM)
3. Financing Mechanisms
4. Funding
5. EE&C Measures
6. Capacity Building, Training, Education and Awareness
7. Standards and Labeling
8. Co-generation
9. Implementation Plan.

Out of the nine policy instruments mentioned above, enactment of the EE&C Acts needs to take priority as well as the establishment of an Energy Efficiency and Conservation Agency. Education alone may not be effective in ensuring the success of EE measures outlined in the EEMP. With the legal instrument in place, it would be easier to steer efforts toward energy efficiency at a greater speed. Penalty should be imposed on inefficiency energy users.

Funding is required for measures such as the establishment of an EE&C revolving fund and tax incentives. Sourcing of funds is a challenge for Malaysia since the Malaysian Government needs to be carefully allocating its budget for other programs as well.

Sufficient funds are required to ensure implementations of all policy instruments are effective. The EEMP Study has estimated that funding of RM4.8 billion is required over a period of 10 years with balance of payment by year 2020 of RM 153 billion. By implementing the action plan on EE, energy saved at year 2020 would be 10,704 ktoe or 26 per cent. Energy intensity would decrease by 26 per cent at year 2020. CO_2 emissions reduction at year 2020 is expected to be 26 per cent or 51,103 $ktCO_2$.

5. Way Forward

Energy efficiency has been extensively studied in Malaysia but the implementation is very slow and patchy. That's why Energy Efficiency in Malaysia is still a long way to go in achieving more efficient utilization of our energy resources. Initiatives on energy efficiency have been carried out but on a fragmented basis. If the same outputs can be achieved using less energy, then the costs of energy infrastructure development will be reduced and benefit the society.

Transportation sector should be including as part of EE program. The EE program should review specifications and standards for motor vehicles and if possible implement mandatory Minimum Energy Performance Standards (MEPs).

Following are some of the brief strategies proposed to improve energy efficiency in the country. The Energy Efficiency and Conservation (EE&C) shall be classified into 4 pillars as shown in Table 5.8.

Table 8: Energy Efficiency and Conservation (EE&C) Strategies

Pillar	*Strategy Approach*
Institutional	☆ Integrate fragmented EE&C programs with a one stop agency supported by a dedicated EE&C legislation
	☆ This agency will regulate, implement, monitor and verify all EE&C Programs, capacity building and serve as an EE&C data bank
Economic	☆ Achieve a low-carbon economy and high income economy through heightened competitiveness with extensive Domestic Direct Investments and Foreign Direct Investments
	☆ Move the economy up the value chain and improve energy security
Social and Human Capacity	☆ Continually and regularly disseminate information on EE&C to the general public via mass media to enhance awareness·Intensified technical capacity building for implementation of EE&C measures through training, examination and certification for Energy Managers, Energy Auditors and ESCOs.
	☆ Build pool of diverse resources consisting of trainers, lecturers, economists, planners, financial and legal practitioners who are conversant with EE&C to support implementation of EE&C policy
	☆ Introduce a curriculum on EE&C at all levels of the education system including at professional level in order to inculcate the sustainable practice of EE&C
Environment	☆ Encourage development of clean and green technologies. This will help to conserve the use of depleting primary energy and reduce final energy demand without affecting GDP growth
	☆ Ensuring the national commitment on the reduction of CO_2 emission intensity by 40 per cent in 2020 against base year 2005 is achieved.

6. Conclusions

Energy efficiency is an important means towards achieving sustainability and reducing the impacts of the energy sector on the environment. The Government of Malaysia recognizes the benefit and importance of EE in the country and several action plans and measures have been taken to ensure economic, energy and environmental sustainability. This includes the drafting of National Energy Efficiency Master Plan which is in progress at the moment of writing this paper. Many programs and facilities have been planned and implemented; however, the response on EE activities was not encouraging mostly due to relatively cheap energy price. These may change if the government decided to reduce or eliminate subsidy and allow energy price to follow the real market price. Such unpopular act may receive resistance at the beginning but in the long run it will create an energy prudent and smart society.

Furthermore, most important, levels of awareness on energy efficiency must be enhanced and a culture of energy conservation must be developed. Government offices, universities, hospitals and schools should be a prime emphasis area to implement and demonstrate the benefits of improved energy productivity. Regular awareness programmes and services for consultation for target groups are important. The existence of Energy Service Companies (ESCOs) to assist industry in evaluating and implementing energy-efficient solutions has been shown to be beneficial.

A practical energy efficiency master plan for transport sector such as fuel economy program, energy efficient transportation system and introduction of alternative fuel cars with lower fuel consumption has to be thoroughly considered and developed. Finally, the provision of technical, commercial and financial services to Energy Efficiency in various sectors are often necessary to facilitate the adoption of efficient use of energy.

References from websites

Ar. Chan Seong Aun, 2004. Energy Efficiency : Designing Low Energy Buildings Using Energy 10, Pertubuhan Arkitek Malaysia (PAM), CPD Seminar 7th August 2004

http://www.pam.org.my/Library/cpd_notes/Energy-Efficiency.pdf (accessed 14 April 2011)

CETREE, 2002, 'Your Guide to Energy Efficiency at Home: Tips on smart use of energy to save money at home', Centre for Education and Training in Renewable Energy and Energy Efficiency (CETREE)

http://www.st.gov.my/eest/eeguide/index.htm (accessed 26 April 2011)

Economic Planning Unit website

http://www.epu.jpm.my (accessed 30 April 2011)

Green Building Index (GBI) website

http://www.greenbuildingindex.org/ (accessed 27 April 2011)

Malaysia Green Building Confederation (MGBC), 2010. 'New Opportunities and New Challenges', Sustainable Buildings South East Asia 2010, Conference E-Booklet, SB10SEA, 2010

http://www.mgbc.org.my/Resources.html (accessed 14 April 2011)

Ministry of Energy, Green Technology and Water website

http://www.kettha.gov.my (accessed 30 April 2011)

United Nations Development Program (UNDP), Malaysia, 'Achieving Industrial Energy Efficiency in Malaysia', ISBN 983-40995-7-6

http://www.undp.org.my/uploads/Achieving_Industrial_Energy_Efficiency_2006.pdf (accessed 14 April 2011)

References from Books

National Energy Balance 2008 Malaysia, Pusat Tenaga Malaysia (PTM), ISSN No. 0128-6323

Chapter 6

Practicing Sustainability in Malaysia

Rosnida Binti Mohd Yusof

Head Deputy Director,
Environment and Energy Branch, Public Works Department, Malaysia
E-mail: Rosnida@jkr.gov.my

ABSTRACT

Malaysia, a developing country in South East Asia has a population of 2.4 millions and an area of 0.33 million square kms. Malaysian Premier reiterated the country's commitment to sustainability, in 2009 United Nations Climate Change Conference 2009 (COP 15), by announcing voluntary cut of 40 per cent in national energy intensity by 2020, from 2005 levels. This task is divided into three major areas of concern: (1) Reduction and management of solid waste, (2) Renewable energy and (3) Energy efficiency. Energy efficiency will have to contribute to reductions to the tune of 9 million tons per year of CO_2 emission for the years 2010 to 2020. Of the above, the Public Works Department(PWD) plays a key role in efforts in the area of energy efficiency. The article gives a perspective of PWD's the strategy and course of implementation of its initiatives in energy efficiency.

Facts on Malaysia

Malaysia is one of the developing countries in South East Asia with two distinct parts: Peninsular Malaysia to the west and East Malaysia to the east. Peninsular Malaysia is located south of Thailand, north of Singapore and east of the Indonesian island of Sumatra. East Malaysia is located on the island of Borneo and shares borders with Brunei and Indonesia.

Malaysia covers an area of 329,847 km^2, with a population of 23,953,136 (July 2005). It is a truly multi-racial country with Malay being the largest ethnic group making up to 50.4 per cent of the population, followed by Chinese 23.7 per cent,

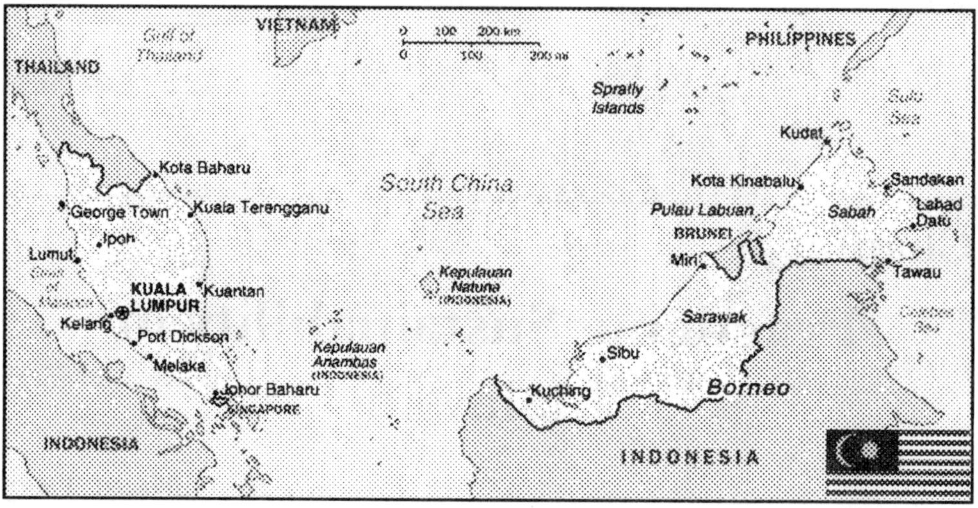

Figure 6.1: Malaysia

Indigenous 11 per cent, Indian 7.1 per cent and others 7.8 per cent. The people embrace many religions such as Islam, Buddhist, Taoist, Hindu, Christian and Sikh; in addition, Shamanism is practiced in East Malaysia. Bahasa Melayu is the official language and English is the second language, while others such as Chinese dialects, Tamil, Telugu, Malayalam, Punjabi and Thai are also spoken; in addition, in East Malaysia several indigenous languages are spoken, the most widely used ones being Iban and Kadazan.

Malaysia is a hot and humid country with two distinct south-west monsoons during the months of April to October and the north-east monsoon during the months of November to January. Natural hazards could occur from flooding during the monsoon season, landslides because of heavy rains, and haze and forest fires especially during the dry season of September to October.

Malaysia, like other developing nations, faces many environment-related issues such as air pollution from industrial and vehicular emissions, water pollution from raw sewage, deforestation, and smoke and haze from forest fires. However, the government is taking active steps to minimize these threats by introducing acts and regulations to control these issues.

Practicing Sustainability

Addressing the United Nations Climate Change Conference 2009 (COP 15) in December 2009, Prime Minister Datuk Seri Najib Tun Razak said Malaysia was committed to doing its best to combat climate change. Malaysia has adopted a voluntary national reduction indicator of up to 40 per cent in terms of GDP emission intensity by 2020, compared with the 2005 levels.

The Natural Resources and Environmental Ministry has identified that Malaysia will have to reduce 50 million tons/year of CO_2 emissions to achieve the aforesaid goal. This figure is further divided into three major areas of concern: (1) Reduction and management of solid waste, (2) Renewable energy and (3) Energy efficiency. Energy efficiency will have to contribute to reductions to the tune of 9 million tons per year of CO_2 emission for the years 2010 to 2020.

In line with the above statements, the Public Works Department (PWD) is striving to contribute to the achievement of the nation's goal, especially in the area of energy efficiency. PWD has already started practicing energy efficiency measures for new and existing buildings under its responsibility. Activities such as implementation of energy-saving measures, energy audits and identification of special projects and national projects are already on the way.

Energy audits have been carried out manually in schools, living quarters, offices and health clinics throughout Malaysia. Also, online energy audits have been carried out in four buildings in the Ministry of Works Complex and three buildings in the Putrajaya Government Complex. This online monitoring was done in collaboration with the Danish Energy Saving Trust (DEST).

A few special projects have been identified to be the model for practicing energy efficiency in new buildings. Although statistics have shown that normal buildings have a building energy index (BEI) between 200 and 300 kWh/m^2 per year, the PWD strives to do better than that. These model buildings, depending on the category they are in, have a targeted BEI of between 100 and 150 kWh/m^2 per year, much lower than the national average.

Energy saving measures have been carried out in the prime minister's office and block F of the PWD headquarters. Saving measures in these two existing buildings were undertaken based on the report of an energy audit done earlier. PWD has only taken 'no-cost' measures for these two buildings, and already significant savings of more than 10 per cent have been achieved.

The Director General of PWD has a special interest in this energy savings programme in block F of the PWD headquarters. A group was identified to form the energy management team to carry out the programme. Setting a baseline from an energy audit, the team was set on a quest to save energy from July 2008. The actions taken include:

1. Taking measurements, via a data logger, of the office lux and temperature levels
2. Conducting awareness programmes for the occupants.
3. Taking air infiltration tests to measure the moisture content that goes into the building and also that which comes from the occupants.
4. Taking measurements of weekend base load and identifying the office equipment still in use after working hours.
5. Activating server hibernation for computers not in use after 7 pm.
6. Doing daylighting simulation to improve lighting in the office
7. Sealing the windows located between the air-conditioned and the non-air conditioned area.
8. Fixing doors and windows to avoid infiltration.

9. Daily monitoring of potential infiltration through open doors and windows.
10. Rescheduling of the air-conditioning hours in the prayer hall.
11. Switching off lamps during lunch hours.
12. Announcing the savings achieved for the week to the occupants.
13. Identifying and getting rid of unnecessary UPSs.
14. Delamping of areas with a lux level of over 350–500 lux.
15. Shutting off the air-conditioner in the canteen while improving air circulation by other means.
16. Preparing of weekly savings report by the facility manager.
17. Holding monthly meetings to discuss the improvement measures taken.

It took a real team effort to implement the above measures; but the PWD has done it and has managed to achieve a significant savings of 16.39 per cent (in terms of kilowatt hour/person) for the period from July 2008 to December 2009, as shown in Figure 6.2.

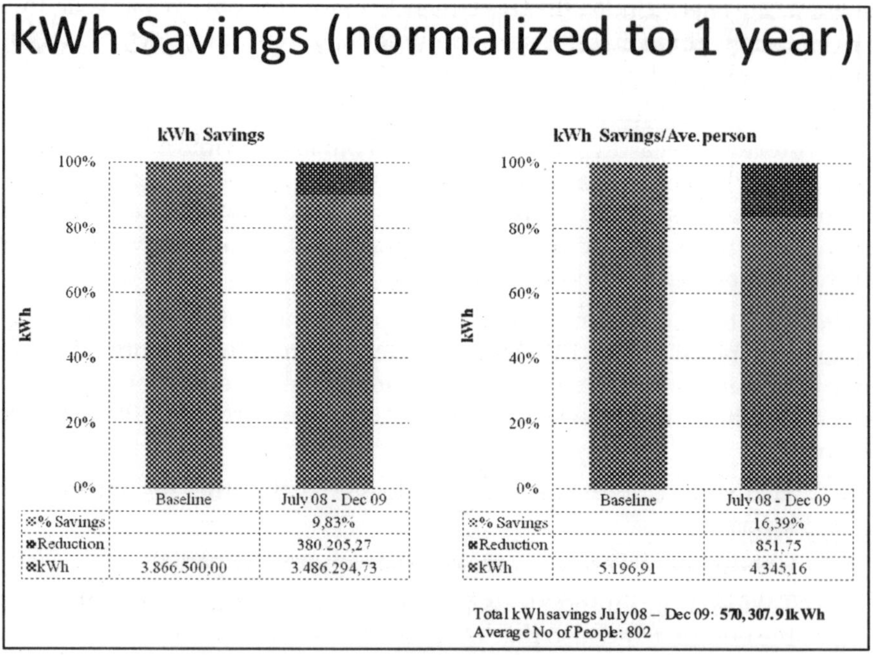

Figure 6.2

The Environmental and Energy Branch (EEB) is directly under the Deputy Director of the expert sector of PWD. It is the responsibility of the EEB to oversee the implementation of all environment- and energy-related issues in government projects in Malaysia. It is a really heavy load for a small branch, but we are working hard towards a greener building-construction industry.

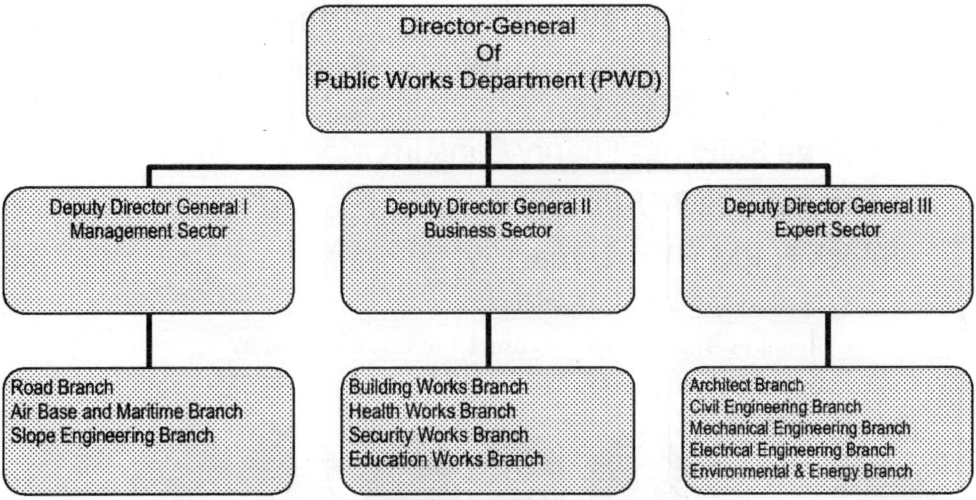

Figure 6.3: Organizational Chart

Existing Laws and Regulations

In the area of building technologies, Malaysia is governed by a few laws such as

1. Uniform Building By-law, UBBL
2. Malaysian Standard MS 1525:2007
3. Electrical Energy Regulations 2008
4. Environmental Management System EMS 14000
5. Quality Manual ISO 9001:2000

The above scenario shows that energy saving measures can be implemented either in an old building that was built when there was no energy efficiency efforts in mind or in a new or quite recently constructed building with energy-efficient equipment in place.

An average office building in Malaysia consumes 75 KWh/m^2/year of energy, which produces 120 kg of CO_2/m^2/year, and it requires six large mature trees to absorb every 120 kg of CO_2. This means that every person in an office (with an area of 14 m^2) requires 84 large mature trees to absorb his CO_2 emission in a year!

PWD has 22,000 existing government buildings under its maintenance responsibility, which converts to about 220 million square metres. If PWD were to target 30 per cent energy savings, which amounts to 60 kWh/m^2/year for government buildings, it will help to reduce CO_2 emission of up to 8.5 million tonnes/year. These numbers are only for government buildings; so just imagine what it would be like if the whole nation takes part in this energy saving programme! However, this exercise does require consolidated efforts and investment to materialize successfully, as described in Figure 6.5.

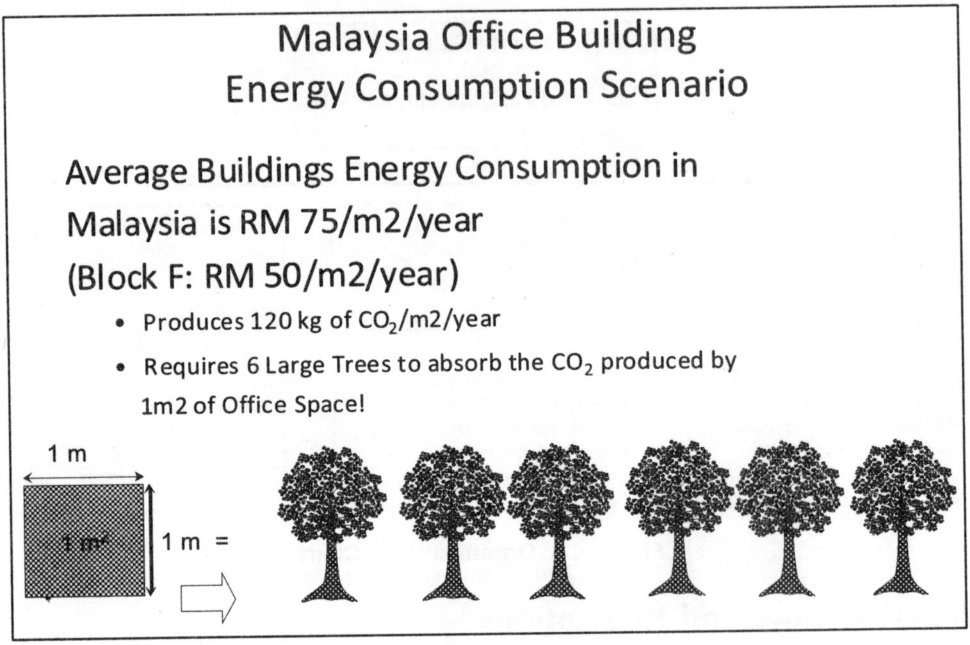

Figure 6.4

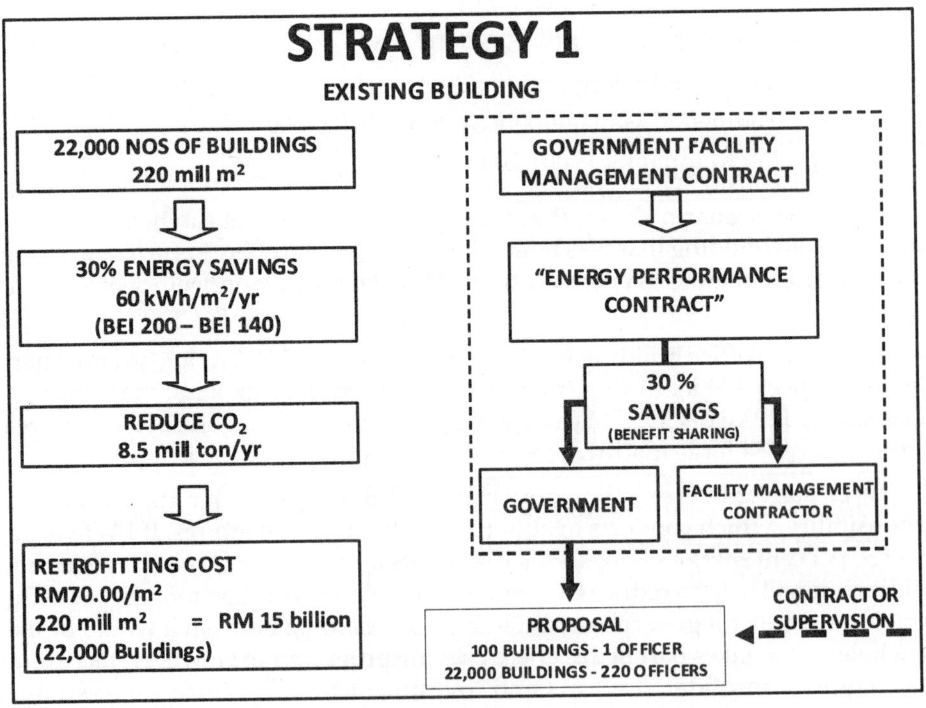

Figure 6.5

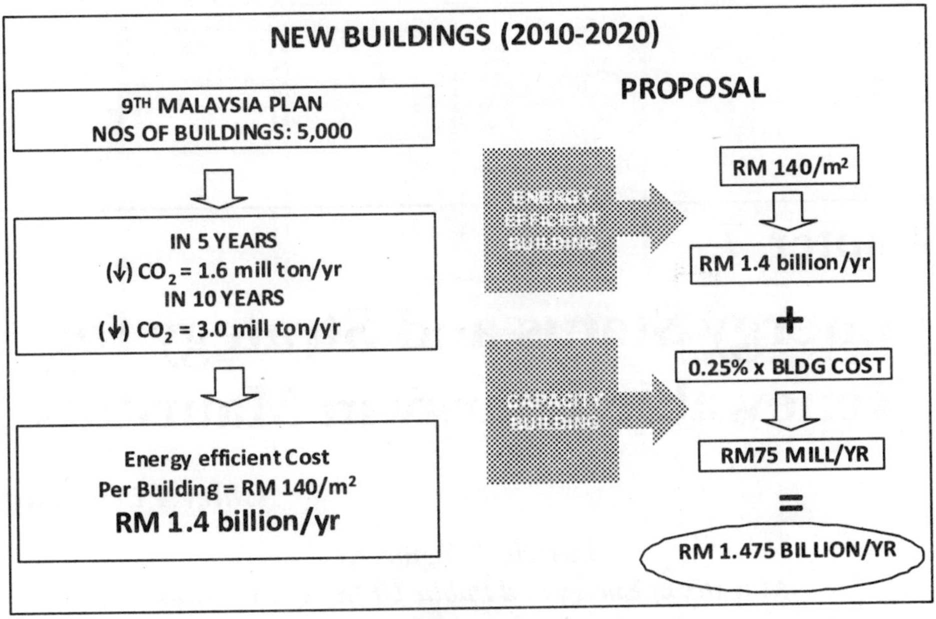

Figure 6.6

Strategies were also devised for new buildings that would be entrusted unto PWD by the government. If PWD were to build 5000 buildings in the 9th Malaysia Plan, a reduction of 1.6 million tonnes/year of CO_2 emission can be achieved in 5 years, and, subsequently, 3 million tonnes/year of CO_2 emission reduction can be realized up to the year 2020. This target can be achieved since PWD has set the BEI for the buildings between 85 and 160 kWh/m^2/year depending on the category of the building. This proposal is further illustrated in Figure 6.6.

PWD strongly believes that it can contribute significantly to the nation's target of reducing CO_2 emissions, given the opportunity to do so as described above. Building energy-efficient buildings and going green are no longer optional, but mandatory. When homes and other buildings require more energy for cooling and lighting, more resources will be needed. It is with the spirit of saving the earth for our future generation that PWD will work together with other agencies towards building the nation for a better future.

Chapter 7

Energy Status and Strategy for Renewable Energy in Mauritius

Ashley Purmanund

Electrical Engineer,
Ministry of Energy and Public Utilities, Mauritius
E-mail: apurmanund@mail.gov.mu

ABSTRACT

Mauritius imports more than 80 per cent of its sources of energy in the form of fossil fuels. As the price of fossil fuel is very volatile, the country is highly motivated to decrease its dependency on fossil fuel and at the same time reduce its greenhouse gas emission.

Moreover, Mauritian demand for energy is rising by 5 per cent yearly. Thus, to meet the new economic challenges and the increase in energy consumption, several aspects of energy production are being reviewed.

Along with the implementation of new wind farms, solar photovoltaic power plants and mini hydro power plants, Mauritius wants to promote small-scale distributed energy production and to create awareness in energy saving among its population. In addition to these measures, the concept of energy efficiency is also being introduced in residential and non-residential buildings. And to finance those new projects, new funding schemes shall be made available to all energy sectors for the implementation of new projects. Thus, the renewable sector is being reviewed and a long-term strategy is being devised such that by 2025 the dependency on fossil fuel shall be reduced to 65 per cent and 35 per cent of the energy production shall be from renewable sources.

Keywords: *Energy, Renewable energy, Economy, Fossil fuel, Strategy.*

1. Introduction

1.1 Geography

Mauritius is situated in the Indian Ocean, slightly over the Tropic of Capricorn, at latitude 20° south and longitude 58° east of Greenwich. It is around 2,000 km from the east coast of Africa and some 850 km east of Madagascar. The island is of volcanic origin, with an area of 1860 km^2 and almost entirely surrounded by coral reefs.

The Republic of Mauritius includes the main islands Mauritius, Rodrigues, Agalega and St Brandon, and has an exclusive economic zone (EEZ) of 1.9 million km^2.

The climate is sub-tropical, with winter prevailing from May to September and summer from October to April. According to official statistics, the population has been increasing at an average rate of 1 per cent per annum for the past 5 years and by December 2010, the population was 1,283,415.

1.2 Economic Overview

The Mauritian economy relies mainly on three sectors: (1) the tourism industry, which is in the process of restructuring in order to meet the objective of attaining 2 million tourists by 2015; (2) the information and communication technology industry, where lots of investments are being made, including human resource development and (3) the textile industry, which has put Mauritius on the world economic map. The sugar industry, which has been for long the backbone of the Mauritian exports, has seen a drastic fall in exports following the new sugar regime of the European Union. Therefore, a restructuring of the sugar industry is now being taken up along with developing the new sector of sea foods.

Mauritius is now classified as a middle-income country, and in the '2010 Global Human Development Report', Mauritius achieved human development indices of 0.701, raking 72th out of 169 countries. The actual gross domestic product growth rate is estimated to be around 4.6 per cent in 2011. In 2010, the GDP was $9.73 billion and the GDP (PPP) per capita was $14,000.

To sustain the economic activity of the country and to align its development with the Kyoto Protocol, the island has to improve on its renewable energy capacity, at the same time reducing its greenhouse gas emission. The renewable energy sector is bound to play a very important part in the future, in the country's quest to continue with its economic progress.

2. The Energy Sector

The Central Electricity Board (CEB), established in 1952, is the sole agency for the transmission, distribution and commercialization of electricity in Mauritius. In 2010, the CEB produced around 40.9 per cent of the country's total power requirements from its four thermal power stations and eight hydroelectric plants; the remaining 59.1 per cent was purchased from independent power producers – mainly sugar industry-owned – who produce electricity from bagasse/coal.

2.1 Electrical Energy Production

In 2010, 2,689 GWh of electricity was generated as compared with 2,577 GWh in 2009, representing an increase of 4.3 per cent. Thermal energy accounted for 96.2 per cent, and hydro/wind 3.8 per cent. The peak electricity demand in 2010 reached 404.1 MW (+3.9 per cent) in the Island of Mauritius, as compared with 388.8 MW in 2009.

Table 7.1: Fuel Input for Electricity Production, 2010

Fuel	*Per cent*
Diesel and Fuel oil	24.6
Kerosene	0.8
Coal	51.2
Bagasse, Hydro, wind	23.4
Total	**100.0**

2.2 Total Primary Power Requirement

Total primary energy requirement, also known as total primary energy supply, is obtained as the sum of indigenous production (fuel wood, hydro, wind and bagasse) and imports (fossil fuel) less re-exports and bunkering, after stock adjustments. Final energy consumption is the total amount of energy consumed by end users as a final product. End users are mainly categorized into five sectors: manufacturing, transport, commercial and distributive trade, households and agriculture.

Table 7.2: Total Power Required in 2010

Fuel	*Tonne*	*ktoe*	*Per cent*
Diesel, Gasoline and Fuel oil	571,573	573.5	40.3
Kerosene (incl. aviation)	126,293	131.3	9.2
LPG	59,292	64.0	4.5
Coal	667,835	414.1	29.0
Bagasse, Hydro, wind	Bag (1,406,371)	241.6	17.0
Total		**1424.5**	**100.0**

It is to be noted that the transport sector used slightly more than 400 ktoe, and this amount is almost certain to increase in the coming years as the number of vehicles and aircraft flights keeps on increasing.

3. Renewable Energy and Long-Term Strategy

Mauritius has no oil, natural gas or coal reserves and therefore depends heavily on imported energy sources. In the 1980s, more than 70 per cent of the electricity requirement was met with oil-based power generation. This made the country very vulnerable, as oil price is highly volatile. At the turn of the century, Mauritius's dependency on fossil fuel continued to increase thanks to the rapid development of the country. However, new strategies are now being developed to reduce this dependency on imported energy sources.

3.1 Hydropower

CEB operates eight hydroelectric stations having a total installed capacity of 59 MW. The full installed capacity can only be exploited during wet periods with heavy rainfall. The amount of energy that can be generated from the hydro power stations varies significantly over the year, from less than 5 GWh in the driest month to some 20 GWh in the wet season. During an average year, some 100 GWh is generated by the eight hydro power plants. The hydropower potential in the country has been almost fully tapped by the eight hydro power plants, and there are other very competitive uses of the existing water resources.

Nevertheless, the government's strategy is to encourage the setting up of mini and micro hydro plants, at potential sites wherever economically viable. In 2010, a 375 kW mini hydro plant was commissioned, and it is expected to generate some 2 GWh per year. In 2012, a similar-size plant will be operational generating and additional 1 GWh per year.

3.2 Wind Energy

The main islands of Mauritius and Rodrigues are for the major part of the year exposed to the south-east trade winds and are, therefore, conducive for wind energy exploitation. A Wind energy resource assessment study financed by the UNDP was carried out in the mid-1980s. The study confirmed that there are potential sites on the two islands for the setting up of wind farms, with some areas having an annual average wind speed of 8.0 m s^{-1} at 30 m above ground level.

However, the pilot projects in Mauritius and Rodrigues implemented in the mid-1980s were not successful, as the wind turbines were damaged by cyclones.

Following the technological improvement in the generation of electricity from wind energy, in Rodrigues, since 2010, a wind farm comprising three 60 kW and four 275 kW wind turbines has successfully been running and contributing more than 10 per cent to the total electricity generation.

The new strategy of the government is to resort to the build–operate–own (BOO) model for the implementation of any future wind farms in Mauritius. Thus, by the end of 2012, the first part of a wind farm situated in the north of the island, with a capacity of 18 MW, will be commissioned. The total energy generated is expected to be around 30 GWh from the 18-MW farm.

A similar project with a capacity of 20–30 MW is already on its way on the high plateau in the centre of the island, and it is expected to start running by the end of 2013.

It is also notable that the CEB is proposing to set up a wind farm comprising four wind turbines of 200—300 kW each, in the centre of the island. The farm is planned to be commissioned by early 2013 and is expected to generate some 2.5 GWh.

3.3 Bagasse Energy

Mauritius produces about 18 per cent of its electricity from renewable resources, namely, hydro and sugar cane bagasse. Mauritius has a very valuable asset in the form of cane biomass. Of all cash crops, sugar cane absorbs solar energy the best, with 55 tonnes of carbon dioxide fixed per 100 tonnes of cane produced per hectare. Thus, each year 6 million tonnes of environment-friendly biomass is produced in the form of sugar cane, cane leaves and cane tops.

The strategy of the government is to use bagasse more efficiently in the future with a view to increase the contribution of bagasse-based electricity in the medium-term, from the present level of 350 GWh to 600 GWh per annum. It is to be noted that research and development in the sector is being accelerated at the African–Caribbean–Pacific (ACP) level, where Mauritius is playing a leading role in developing new varieties of sugar cane with higher biomass production capability.

A new variety of sugar cane that can produce between 15 and 25 per cent more fibre than the current ones was developed by the Mauritius Sugar Industry Research Institute in 2007. Development and use of such varieties of sugarcane can help to increase the amount of electricity produced from bagasse. The long-term strategy of the government is to encourage the use of new varieties of sugar cane with higher biomass content and any other technology that could be commercialized so as to increase the amount of energy generated from bagasse.

3.4 Solar Energy

Mauritius is situated in the tropics and thus benefits from more than 2900 hours of sunlight per year. Yet, the present cost of generating photovoltaic (PV) electricity is relatively high when compared to other conventional and renewable sources, despite the progressive reduction in the cost of the technology in the last decade.

In order to encourage the use of solar energy, whether for water heating or electricity production, incentive schemes have been implemented to enable long-term strategic goals to be achieved. Further incentives shall be worked out in the future following the first phase of solar energy development.

3.4.1 Solar Water Heaters

Since 1992, the Development Bank of Mauritius has been offering a concessionary rate of interest on loans for the purchase of solar water heaters. However, it was estimated in 2008 that only some 25,000 households, out of a total of about 330,000, used solar water heaters for domestic water heating. With the setting up of the Maurice Ile Durable (MID) Fund in July 2008, the solar water heater loan scheme operated by the Development Bank of Mauritius has been revisited with an outright grant of Rs 10,000 from the MID Fund offered for every solar water heater purchased so as to double the number of domestic solar water heaters by the end of 2009. Loan facilities also are provided by the Development Bank of Mauritius, but the grant is not contingent to a loan being availed from the Bank. The outcome of the new scheme has been beyond expectations, with some 49,000 applications received by the Bank. Given the budgetary ceiling of the MID Fund, only some 29,000 households benefitted from the grant scheme as of 31 December 2009. Encouraged by the positive outcome of the scheme, the government is proposing to design and implement another scheme for promoting an even wider use of solar energy for water heating in households and in other sectors of the economy.

3.4.2 Solar Photovoltaic

With a view to promoting clean energy, and in line with the vision to democratizing the electricity grid, the Ministry of Energy and Public Utilities, in collaboration with the CEB, has launched the Small-Scale Distributed Generation project. Through this initiative, small independent power producers (SIPPs) are being given the opportunity to produce their own electricity from renewable energy sources, comprising wind, solar and mini-hydro technologies, and export any excess power generated to the CEB grid. Some 200 applications have been received at the CEB for a total of 2.6 MW while the limit was set at 2.0 MW.

Expressions of interest for the setting up of grid-connected solar photovoltaic energy projects of capacity up to 10 MW in Mauritius by private developers have been invited by the CEB. The plant is planned to be commissioned by the end of 2013.

3.5 Waste-to-Energy Strategy

Waste-to-energy generation is part of the solid-waste management strategy of the government to relieve the existing landfill site. The objective is to incinerate waste, which allows for the generation of electricity as a useful output from the process. The electricity generated from such facilities will be supplied to the national grid.

The setting up of a 3 MW gas-to-energy unit is nearing finalization. The promoter of the plant is expected to generate some 110 GWh over a period of 5 years.

3.6 Geothermal Strategy

An assessment for the geothermal energy potential in Mauritius shall soon be initiated, as the island is situated on the Mascarene plateau, close to the Réunion Island Hotspot. In this context, it is proposed to appoint a consultant to, in the first phase, carry out a situation analysis of the Mauritius Island with regard to geothermal potential and the possibility of development of geothermal resources. The consultant would ultimately have to advise the government whether to proceed with a geophysical survey of the potential sites.

3.7 Other Technologies

Under global funds such as the Global Environmental Facility (GEF) and funds from other bilateral and multi-lateral cooperation agencies, the government encourages strategies for technological innovation. Technologies such as hydrogen-based electricity, gasification and fuel cells could be explored on a pilot basis subject to availability of funding from donor agencies.

On the other hand, a land-based oceanic industry is one of the innovative projects, which will be developed with the participation of private sector operators for the exploitation of deep sea water for air-conditioning of green data centres.

3.8 Targets for Renewable Energy Over the Period 2010–25

On the basis of the government's overall energy policy and strategy, the targets for renewable energy in terms of percentage of total electricity generation over the period of 2010–25 are given in Table 7.3. Note that the targeted energy mix has been arrived at based on the assumption that all the forecasted projects get implemented.

Table 7.3: Renewable Energy Targets Over the Period 2010–25

Fuel Source		*Percentage of Total Electricity Generation (per cent)*			
		2010	*2015*	*2020*	*2025*
Renewable	Bagasse	16	13	14	17
	Hydro	4	3	3	2
	Waste to energy	0	5	4	4
	Wind	0	2	6	8
	Solar PV	0	1	1	2
	Geothermal	0	0	0	2
	Sub-total	20	24	28	35
Non-renewable	Fuel Oil	37	31	28	25
	Coal	43	45	44	40
	Sub-total	80	76	72	65
	TOTAL	100	100	100	100

4. Maurice Ile Durable

There are numerous challenges awaiting the country when it strives to reduce its dependency on imported energy sources. In order to support the efforts to promote more efficient use of energy and increase the use of renewable energy, the Maurice Ile Durable (MID) Fund was created in July 2008.

The objectives of the MID Fund are to finance mainly:

1. Schemes for the preservation of local natural resources with a view to achieving sustainable development and adapting to climate change.
2. Projects to explore and harness all potential for local sources of renewable energy and to reduce dependency on imported fossil fuels.
3. Programmes to reduce consumption of fossil fuels and achieve greater efficiency in the use of energy in enterprises, offices, homes, public buildings, transportation sector and hotels.
4. Schemes to encourage innovation by households as well as by businesses to produce energy on their own to meet their requirements and sell surplus energy, if any, at a premium.

In addition, funds are also made available for providing grants for solar water heaters; promoting the use of compact fluorescent lamps by providing the lamps at half the cost price; implementing a bus modernization programme and recycling waste programme; conducting R&D pertaining to the development of renewable sources of energy and consumption trends; organizing awareness campaigns on energy saving and promoting the use of renewable energy sources.

Thus, the main vision of the MID concept is to make Mauritius less dependent on fossil fuels through increased utilization of renewable energy and more efficient use of energy.

5. Energy Efficiency

5.1 Energy Efficiency Bill

The Energy Efficiency Bill has been passed in the National Assembly on 29 March 2011. The bill forms part of the national energy strategy, which aims to reduce the energy demand by 10 per cent by 2015 and improve the country's energy security. The bill will help sensitize the public to become more energy conscious, reduce energy use and costs, protect the environment, improve productivity and contribute to alleviating the effects of climate change. In order to police the implementation of the bill, an energy efficiency management office will be set up. Besides, a new Building Control Bill is being prepared to include in the Building Regulations and Codes the energy efficiency concept and, ultimately, to enforce these new measures in all economic sectors, namely, industrial, commercial, residential, health and education. The rationale behind this bill will be to improve building designs, incorporating the use of energy-efficient equipment. This will also promote lowering the energy demand of the industrial sector, where energy-intensive industries will be required to develop energy management plans and smaller industries will be required to carry out regular energy audits.

The tourism industry, which contributes significantly to the economic growth of Mauritius, will also be addressed by the Energy Efficiency Bill and the Building Control Bill. The strategy to increase the arrival of tourists to two million is likely to have a negative impact on the energy sector; hence new measures have been developed to revamp the energy strategy for the tourism sector, namely, to encourage hotels to install the latest energy-efficient technologies and appliances and adopt (mandatory) new building designs and eco-friendly airport transfer policies, and thus to develop an eco-friendly tourism sector.

5.2 Energy Auditing

The new energy efficiency legislation will make energy auditing mandatory for designated consumers/sectors and regulate the standards of energy auditing.

In order to pursue its energy efficiency and conservation strategy, the Mauritian government will also create a pool of 50 qualified and certified energy auditors in the country. To ensure that the auditors are of the required standard, the government will also develop an appropriate energy auditor certification scheme. Each energy audit will produce an energy efficiency certificate and a recommendation certificate. The Energy Efficiency Management Office will be the regulating authority of energy auditing.

6. Conclusions

The rising price of fossil fuels in recent years has driven the Government of Mauritius to re-engineer its energy strategy towards renewable energy and implementing an energy efficiency programme. By adopting a long-term strategy, Mauritius aims to increase its renewable energy potential so as to raise the contribution of renewable energy in the energy mix to 35 per cent by 2025.

The target is that over the next 50 years Mauritius should be able to achieve 70 per cent self-sufficiency in terms of energy supply through progressive increase in the use of renewable energy. At the end of that period, Mauritius would be able to reduce its greenhouse gas emission by some 70 per cent of its current level. Although the challenges are enormous, the future generations are bound to take innovative and daring decisions to convert these proposals into reality. The opportunity to fully develop the exclusive economic zone of Mauritius is still a long way ahead, but very promising, as energy development from the sea is still in its infancy.

References from Websites

Annual Sugar Industry Energy Survey from the Central Statistics Office
http://www.gov.mu/portal/goc/cso/report/natacc/energy05/sect3.pdf

Energy and Water Statistic 2009 from the Central Statistics Office
http://www.gov.mu/portal/goc/cso/ei833/toc.htm

General information from the Central Electricity Board website
http://ceb.intnet.mu/

Long-term Energy Strategy from the Ministry of Energy and Public Utilities
http://www.gov.mu/portal/goc/mpu/file/finalLTES.pdf

Maurice Ile Durable Fund
http://www.gov.mu/portal/goc/mpu/file/ile.pdf

Outline of the Energy Policy 2007–2025 from the Ministry of Energy and Public Utilities
http://www.gov.mu/portal/goc/mpu/file/Outline%20energy%20policy.pdf

Appendix 1: Energy Conversion Factors

The following energy conversion factors have been used to express the energy content of the different fuels in terms of a common accounting unit, tonnes of oil equivalent (toe).

	Tonne	*toe*
Gasoline	1	1.08
Diesel Oil	1	1.01
Dual Purpose Kerosene (DPK)	1	1.04
Fuel oil	1	0.96
Liquefied Petroleum Gas (LPG)	1	1.08
Coal	1	0.62
Bagasse	1	0.16
Fuel Wood	1	0.38
Charcoal	1	0.74
GWh	toe	
Hydro/Wind	1	86
Electricity	1	86

1 toe = 41.84 gigajoule (net calorific value).

Chapter 8

Energy in Nepal

Suresh Kumar Dhungel

Nepal Academy of Science and Technology
P.B. Box – 3323, Khumaltar, Lalitpur, Nepal
E-mail: skdhungel@hotmail.com

ABSTRACT

Nepal is a landlocked South Asian country located in the lap of Himalayas and bordered to the north by People's Republic of China, and to the south, east, and west by the Republic of India. Nepal's Traditional energy resource comprises mainly of biomass. Commercial energy resources include coal, grid electricity and petroleum products whereas biogas, solar power, wind and micro level hydropower fall into the third category of alternative energy resources. Electricity is mainly generated from hydropower whereas petroleum products and natural gases are imported from foreign countries. The total energy consumption in Nepal was about 4.01×10^{17} J in the year 2008/09. Nepal has been suffering from acute shortage of electricity in recent years, which has resulted in power cuts for as high as fourteen hours per day.

The residential area constantly remains the major area of energy consumption throughout the year in Nepal. Nepalese people consume primary energy far below the world's average per capita primary energy consumption. The total energy consumption per capita of Nepal, as calculated from national data and also from the report of world bank, is ~ 15 GJ at present whereas that of world average is ~ 68 GJ.

Nepal has a huge hydro-power potential. Solar, Wind and Biogas energy are the alternative sources of energy for the Nepalese people, especially in rural areas that are not linked with national grid of electricity. The annual average Global Horizontal Solar Irradiance in Nepal is 4.7 kWh/m^2/day and the annual average wind energy potential measured in some areas was found to be 3.387 MWh/m^2. There is a potential of domestic Biogas plant installation in 1.1 million households in Nepal out of which ~ 0.22 million households have already installed the plants.

Keywords: *Energy, Nepal, Renewable energy, Consumption, Resource, Generation.*

1. Introduction

Nepal is a landlocked South Asian country located in the lap of Himalayas and bordered to the north by People's Republic of China, and to the south, east, and west by the Republic of India. It stretches roughly in rectangular shape covering an area of 147,181 sq. km. with an average length of 885 km from east to west and a width from North to South varying between 145 and 241 km. It has a population of approximately 30 million and it is the world's 93rd largest country by land mass and the 41st most populous country. Kathmandu is the nation's capital and the country's largest metropolis. Nepal is rich in geographical variation with its elevation ranging from 70 m to 8848 m (Mount Everest). Nepal is divided into three parallel belts consisting of the snow covered mountains (Himal) to the North, the green mountains and hills (Pahad) in between, and the plain land (Terai) to the south.

Energy is referred to as capacity of doing work. It exists in different forms. The energy resources can be broadly categorized as renewable and nonrenewable. Energy resources that are naturally regenerated over a short time scale and either derived directly or indirectly from solar energy, or from other natural energy flows such as geothermal, tidal, wave, etc are commonly known as renewable energy resources whereas the energy resources formed and accumulated over a very long period of time in the past, such as oil, coal and uranium, whose rates of formation are many orders of magnitude slower than the rate of their use, so that they will be depleted in a finite time period at the current rate of consumption are called nonrenewable energy resources [S. Bennett, 2007]. Any energy system other than the traditional fossil, nuclear, and hydropower energy sources that have been the basis of the growth of industrial society over the past two centuries; *e.g.*, solar, wind, or hydrogen energy is called alternative energy resource.

Nepalese society have relied for generations on a fairly short list of energy sources such as wood and solar radiation for heating the body, space, agricultural products, utensils, clothes, etc. as well as for cooking.

The direct energy from Sun has remained simple but major source to support life on the entire planet. However, the human instinct does not allow us to be confined to a simple life. With the expansion of community, needs of new technologies were felt to meet the growing demands of increased population and make its lives more luxurious, as a result of which the communities soon began growing at a pace that surpassed natural resources. In this race of developing technologies by utilizing available material resources and human intelligence, some parts of the world ran out of resources faster than other regions, but they maintained their strong, growing economies by importing materials and skills from resource-rich areas. All technologies require energy for their operations and hence create potential threat to environment if the employed energy is not clean in nature. The world has now arrived at a juncture of its developmental history where a clear balance between energy, environment, and economy must be established to ensure sustaining growth of the advancing societies to which Nepal can't be an exception. Nepal has been struggling to meet its people's demand of energy at present and provide energy security for future too, without further degrading the global climate.

Per capita consumption of energy has become an indicator of development of a country. Total energy demand of the world has grown tremendously with the global population explosion due to which the world is facing a state of net deficit of energy supply, which is commonly known as 'Energy Crisis'. Also the excessive consumption of fossil fuels to meet the ever growing energy demand has caused enhanced emission of greenhouse gases (GHGs), which has led the world into an alarming scenario of global warming. The mass consumption of fossil fuels has caused the rapid depletion of non-renewable energy reserves in the world due to which a global conflict has already been triggered in the form of new edition of cold war. At the time of energy crisis, poor people become the first victims as they will either have no access to the energy or have no capacity to afford for the expensive energy available to them. As one of the economically poorest nations in the world, Nepalese people fall in the category of the energy deprived people on the Earth at present with ~54 per cent of its people without electricity through national grids and rest of the ~46 per cent of its population connected to grids but facing power cut for as high as fourteen hours a day.

2. Trend of Energy Consumption

The available energy resources of Nepal are basically categorized into different types, *viz.* traditional, commercial and alternative. Biomass sources such as fuel wood, agricultural residues and animal dung in dry form fall in the category of traditional energy resources whereas the energy resources such as coal, grid electricity and petroleum products fall in the category of commercial energy resources. Biogas, solar and wind power and micro level hydropower are categorized as alternative energy resources, which mainly come as supplement to conventional energy resources.

Table 8.1: The Trend of the Energy Consumption from Different Sources in Nepal in Recent Years

Year	*Types of Energy Consumed (TJ)*			*Total (TJ)*
	Traditional	*Commercial*	*Renewable*	
1995/96	263634.0	27758.5	434.9	291827.4
2000/01	290859.6	43343.9	1217.6	335421.1
2005/06	328093.3	46597.5	2095.2	376786.0
2008/09	348869.5	48902.1	2734.7	400506.3

Recent data of the year 2008/09 **[WECS Report 2010]** showed that the total energy consumption in Nepal was about 4.01×10^{17} J out of which 87 per cent were derived from traditional resources, 12 per cent from commercial sources and less than 1 per cent from the alternative sources. The Table 8.1 shows the breakdown of the total energy consumption from different resources in different representative years from 1995/96 to 2008/09.

Figures 8.1(a) and (b) show the trends of consumption of energy from commercial and alternative resources, respectively.

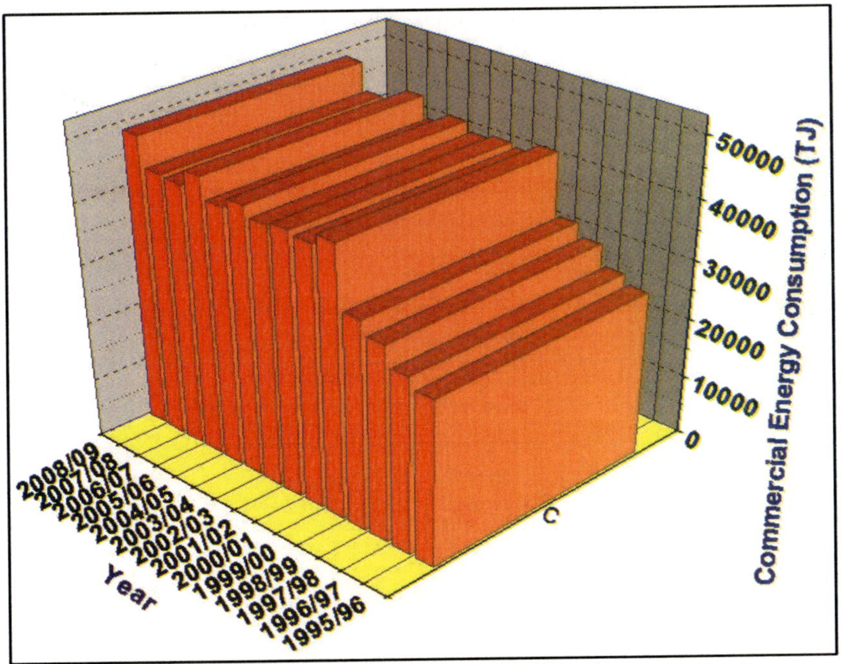

Figure 8.1(a): Trend of Commercial Energy Consumption in Nepal over the Last Fourteen Years

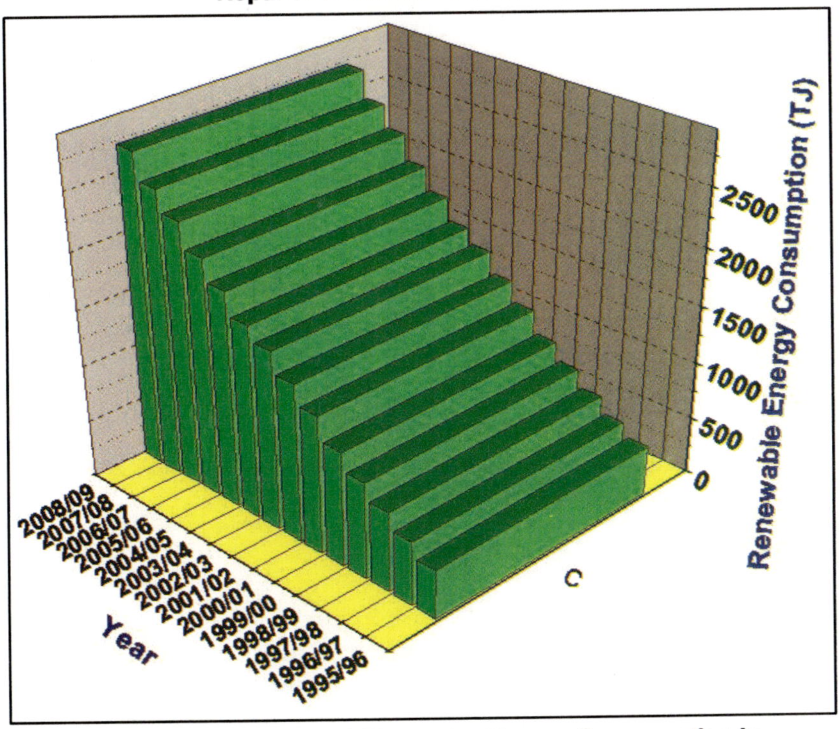

Figure 8.1(b): Trend of Alternative Energy Consumption in Nepal over the Last Fourteen Years

A clear progressive trend of consumption of alternative energy in the recent years can be seen in Figure 8.1(b) whereas the trend of commercial energy consumption, as seen in Figure 8.1(a) seems to be increasing without a fixed trend due to uncertainty in demand-supply dynamics.

Table 8.2 shows the trend of energy consumption in different sectors of Nepal during the past fourteen years. It is clear from the table that the residential area has constantly remained the major area of energy consumption throughout the years. It clearly reveals the fact that Nepalese society is yet to enter the age of industrialization.

Table 8.2: The Trend of Sectoral Distribution of Energy Consumption in Nepal in Recent Years

Year	*Energy Consumed in Different Sectors (TJ)*						*Total*
	Residential	*Industrial*	*Commerical*	*Trnasport*	*Agriculture*	*Other*	
1995/96	267542.3	11771.3	2840.2	8721.0	690.4	262.2	291827.4
2000/01	301143.1	12998.3	4127.7	13591.5	3152	408.5	335421.1
2005/06	337627.5	16839.8	5336.5	13469.5	2888.6	624.1	376786.0
2008/09	256752.2	13369.7	5122.2	20875.9	3646.4	739.9	400506.3

The per capita energy cosumption in a region shows the level of development in that region. Table 8.3 shows the comparison of per capita total primary energy consumption in different regions of the world in recent five years along with that of the world total and Nepal [EIA, DOE 2011].

Table 8.3: Comparison of Per Capita Total Primary Energy Consumption of Nepal with Different Regions of the World Along with World Total in Recent Five Years

Region	*Per Capita Energy Consumption (MBtu) in*				
	2004	*2005*	*2006*	*2007*	*2008*
North America	280.84	279.86	275.97	277.53	270.04
Europe	144.62	144.65	144.96	143.61	142.78
Eurasia	154.49	156.59	153.93	159.73	161.60
Middle East	111.91	119.70	122.58	119.56	124.67
Africa	15.80	16.08	15.79	16.00	16.63
Asia and Oceania	39.48	41.22	42.88	44.44	46.33
World	70.18	71.33	71.90	72.77	73.51
Nepal	2.36	2.58	2.58	2.65	2.70

MBtu: Million British Thermal Units = 1.0551×10^{-3} TJ.

The comparison of the figures in Table 8.3 clearly reveals that Nepalese people consume primary energy far below the world's average per capita primary energy consumption. It is even much lower than that of Africa, which clearly shows that Nepal has to go a long way in terms of primary energy access and its security for its people.

The total energy consumption per capita of Nepal, as calculated from national data and also from the report of world bank is ~ 15 GJ whereas that of the world is 68 GJ.

Among all the forms of energy required for livelihood, electricity plays a crucial role in terms of deciding the living standard of the people. Though electricity occupies only ~2 per cent share in the total energy consumption in Nepal, it plays a vital role in modernization, industrialization and enhancing the income generating activities. Therefore, electricity is taken as the basis of analysis regarding the power demand and supply dynamics in this article. Electricity is mainly generated by hydropower plants in Nepal. Thermal power plants and stand alone solar photovoltaic systems are the next two sources for the generation of electricity in Nepal whereas wind turbines are still in the phase of pilot projects. Nepal Electricity Authority is the sole agency responsible for generation, transmission and distribution of electricity in Nepal, mainly from hydropower and thermal plants whereas alternative energy promotion center (AEPC) has been mandated to promote the alternative energy sources such as solar, wind and biogas.

The fiscal year 2009/10 witnessed new records of demand, generation and import of electricity [NEA Reports 2010]. Annual Peak Demand was recorded 85.28 MW with 8.96 per cent growth over 812.5 MW figure of previous year. Similarly, Annual Energy Demand was recorded 4367.13 GWh out of which 3076.69 GWh was contributed by domestic generation, 612.58 GWh was imported and rest 677.860 GWh was managed by power cuts, which is commonly termed as load shedding in Nepal. Domestic generation comprised of 3064.05 GWh from hydropower plants and 13.12 GWh from thermal plants.

A total of maximum power 9.14 MW has been generated from the solar photovoltaic systems installed in different parts of the country till the end of 2010 [Solar PV Report 2010, AEPC] whereas electricity generated from wind turbines is still not accounted for comparison in consumption.

The consumption of petroleum products in the fiscal year 2006/07 was 947,784 kilo liters while that of liquified petroleum gas (LPG) was 93,562 metric ton [S. Upadhyay, 2008]. It is estimated that there is annual growth in consumption of petroleum products and LPG by ~30 per cent. Since there is no production of natural oil and gas in the country, the entire supply of these products have to be based on import. The sky rocketing price of the crude oil in international market in recent years has made a severe impact on Nepalese economy as the country has been forced to sell the petroleum products to its people at subsidized prices to avoid public protest.

3. Potential for Energy Generation

About 5.6 million hectares (29 per cent of country's area) is covered by forest, which is the prime source of fuel wood that supplies ~75 per cent of the country's total fuel requirement. It is expected that Nepal still will have to depend on fuel wood for many years to come to meet the major energy requirement of the Nepalese people and therefore it poses a continued threat of deforestation and desertification of the fertile land of the country.

Due to the availability of many high current rivers, Nepal has been recognized as a country rich in water resources for hydropower generation with a potential of 83,000 MW, out of which 42,000 MW is considered to be economically feasible in the present condition. The history of Hydropower generation in Nepal dates back to 1911 with the establishment of Pharping Hydropower plant of 500 kW. After a long interval of 25 and 29 years, two more hydropower plants were established with capacities of 900 kW and 2400 kW at Sundarijal and Panauti, respectively. On the basis of the power generating capacity, hydroelectric plants generating powers of < 100 kW, 100 kW- 10 MW, > 10 MW – 300 MW and >300 MW are called Mini-micro, Small, Medium, and Big Hydropower plants, respectively.

The major policy objective of Government of Nepal in recent years is to exploit the nation's vast hydro-power resource potential to meet the energy demand of its people and to generate export revenue for which private companies have been encouraged to invest for the generation of hydroelectricity. The electricity generated by such schemes by promoting public, private, community and cooperative investments will be purchased by NEA as per the Power Purchase Agreement (PPA) done prior to the commencement of the project and distributed to Nepalese households along with the rapid expansion of national grid. This step aims to ensure the reduction in power cuts in Nepal, which in the long run will provide access to electricity for common people and support for poverty alleviation through sustainable industrial growth.

In this connection, NEA has already signed 69 PPAs of total 392 MW capacity till date, out of which 27 projects of total 137.22 MW capacity were signed only during 2009/10. Out of 69 PPA signed, 22 projects with total capacity of 164.8 MW are in operation. Three projects having total capacity of 6.491 MW were commissioned during 2009/10. One hundred twenty PPA applications of total 1600 MW capacity are still under process [NEA Reports 2010].

Also, the local communities have been encouraged to install micro-hydro power plants, which have potential to generate a total of 100 MW of electricity in Nepal, out of which only 15 MW have been generated so far to meet the demand of electricity in 0.13 million households.

Solar, Wind and Biogas energy have come up as the alternative sources of energy for the Nepalese people, especially in rural areas that are not linked with national grid of electricity. Many villages of Nepal are dependent upon the solar energy for cooking and lighting. However, wind energy has not yet been used commercially. Biogas has become a dependable alternative source of energy in rural areas. Biogas development is promoted by government and NGO sectors.

The annual average Global Horizontal Solar Irradiance in Nepal is 4.7 kWh/ m^2/day and the annual average wind energy potential measured in some areas was found to be 3.387 MWh/m^2 [SWERA, 2006]. Nepal has ~ 300 sunny days per annum and thus it is very rich in solar power potential. Similarly, there lies a huge potential of harvesting wind energy in many hilly and mountainous areas of Nepal. However, the energy density varies spatially due to the effect of the local obstacles and the terrain surrounding the point of measurement as well as point of interest. This shows the necessity of measuring the wind parameters through a wind-meteorological tower to calculate actual wind potential of any area in Nepal before installing the wind turbine to harvest the available energy. There is a potential of domestic Biogas plant installation in 1.1 million households in Nepal out of which ~ 0.22 million households have already installed the plants.

Despite the greater initial cost of installation, stand-alone solar photovoltaic systems, solar water heaters, solar dryers are becoming popular day by day in rural as well as urban areas. Similarly, there is good trend of using improved cooking stoves (ICS) and water mills in rural areas of Nepal.

In the context that Nepal has to rely 100 per cent on the imported fossil fuels, research is underway to develop appropriate technique of using biofuel mainly derived from Jatropha Carcus to run its automobiles. There is a potential to grow as high as 1.1 million tons of Jatropha Carcus seeds per annum. A poor country like Nepal must be reluctant in choosing the option to use food grains to produce biofuel, as it is more important to feed a man than to feed an automobile.

4. Future Prospects

The total electricity generated in the country in recent years is 714 MW with approximate power deficit of~ 400 MW [Eco. Survey, 2010].

The Table IV shows the projected demand of electricity for this decade [LSMC Report, 2007]. It is natural that the figures increase as the year progresses due to population explosion, rapid urbanization, industrial growth and the expansion in transmission and distribution of electricity.

Table 8.4: Energy Demand Projection of Nepal with Peak Load

Fiscal Year	*Energy (GWh)*	*Peak Load (MW)*
2010/11	4430.7	967.1
2011/12	4851.3	1056.9
2012/13	5349.6	1163.2
2013/14	5859.9	1271.7
2014/15	6403.8	1387.2
2015/16	6984.1	1510.0
2016/17	7603.7	1640.8
2017/18	8281.8	1770.2
2018/19	8870.2	1906.7
2019/20	9562.9	2052.0

Present state of power crisis and growing demand of electricity in future can be addressed only through augmentation of generation capacity. In the same connection, NEA is set to commission hydropower projects such as Chameliya (30 MW), Kulekhani -3 (14 MW), Upper Trishuli- 3A (60 MW), Upper Trishuli-3B (37 MW) and Rahughat hydropower (32 MW) projects whereas Budhigandaki (600 MW), Upper Seti (127

MW) and Nalsyaugad (400 MW) storage projects are expected to be launched during that period. NEA has already initiated Upper Tamakoshi hydropower project (456 MW) that is expected to be completed in next five years. In the mean time, private power producers are expected to induct at least ~ 200 MW in central grid[N EA Reports 2010].

Alongside the reinforcement in the generation of electrical power, there will be intensification for the development of internal transmission system with its backbone at 400 kV. River basin corridor concept is expected to be adopted while developing transmission network. Separate export and cross border transmission system is planned to be developed at 400 kV to attract investment in export oriented projects. Despite the deficit of supply sources, Government of Nepal aims to continue electrification in the househols of the remaining almost half of the population deprived of electricity.

Several energy policies and plans in the past to tackle the issue of energy crisis were unsuccessful due to lack of political stability in the country as a result of which Nepalese people have been suffering from prolonged period of power cuts per day in recent years. The Government of Nepal has recently declared this state of power deficit as the Energy Crisis in the country and formulated a policy to rescue the country from this state within next five years. The policy has been appreciated as investment friendly in the power sector, especially in the hydropower because the policy encourages the real investor in this sector and discourages the brokers who have owned the licenses for installing hydropower plants in many rivers but have not initiated the works at all in this direction. Hence, it is clear that even if everything goes well as planned by the Government, the people of Nepal still have to suffer from power cuts for about half a decade to come. These years of energy crisis in Nepal may be utilized as an opportunity for promoting alternative energy resources like Solar, Wind, Biogas, Biofuel, etc., if implemeted new ways to make them available to common people of Nepal at affordable cost.

5. Conclusion

Sufficiency of energy resources is a precondition to materialize the attempts to progress human civilization through the development of physical infrastructures and human resources. Nepal is suffering from actute shortage of energy. Unique geographical location, avaialability of natural resources and socio-economic structure of Nepal demand its specific plans and programs to ensure energy security of its people. Nepal has no petroleum products of its own. It has hydropower potential of 83,000 MW, out of which 42,000 MW is considered to be economically feasible in the present condition. The total electricity generated in the country in recent years is 714 MW with approximate power deficit of 400 MW, which has resulted in power cuts for as high as fourteen hours per day. The total energy consumption in Nepal was about 4.01×10^{17} J in the year 2008/09 out of which 87 per cent were derived from traditional resources, 12 per cent from commercial sources and less than 1 per cent from the alternative sources. Nepal will have to depend on fuel wood for many years to come to meet the major energy requirement. The total energy consumption per capita of Nepal is ~ 15 GJ whereas that of the world is 68 GJ. Solar, Wind and Biogas energy have come up as the alternative sources of energy for the Nepalese people, especially in rural areas that are not linked with national grid of electricity. The people of Nepal still have to suffer from power cuts at least for about half a decade to come, which could be an opportunity for promoting alternative energy resources like Solar, Wind, Biogas, Biofuel, etc., if ushered new ways to make them available at affordable cost.

References

Annual Report of Nepal Electricity Authority, 2010.

Economic Survey, 2010, Ministry of Finance, Government of Nepal.

Energy Sector Synopsis Report Nepal, 2010, Water and Energy Commission Secretariat.

Energy Information Administration, online publication 2011, Department of Energy of United States of America.

Final Report of Solar and Wind Energy Resource Assessment in Nepal, 2006, UNEP/ GEF.

Load Shedding Managing Committee Report, 2007, Ministry of water resources, Government of Nepal.

S. Upadhaya, 2008, Energy Crisis and Nepal's Potentiality, The Initiation.

Scott Bennett, 2007, Encyclopedia of Energy.

Status of Solar Photovoltaic Sector in Nepal, 2010, Alternative Energy Promotion Center.

Chapter 9

Improving Energy Efficiency in Nigeria

Badmos Soliu Adebare*, Bamikole Amigun and Bamidele Solomon

National Biotechnology Development Agency, NABDA, Umar Ya'dua way, Lugbe Abuja, Nigeria
****E-mail: badmossoliuadebare@yahoo.com***

ABSTRACT

Energy efficiency and renewable energy are generally acclaimed to be the twin pillars of sustainable energy policy. There are various motivations to improve energy efficiency. There is national security benefits associated with energy efficiency. This is due to the fact that energy efficiency can be used to reduce the level of energy imports from foreign countries thereby saving foreign currency and may slow down the rate at which domestic energy resources are depleted. According to the International Energy Agency, improved energy efficiency in buildings, industrial processes and transportation could reduce the world's energy needs in 2050 by one third, and help control global emissions of greenhouse gases. This paper explains about different approaches suitable to increase energy efficiency in Nigeria. Specifically, the paper also highlights the use of renewable energy, recycling of materials, which eventually lead to reduction in energy usage and air pollution, and energy conservation tactics through behavioral changes. The outcome of this study will be of immense benefit to governmental and non-governmental organizations at national, regional and local levels, energy planners, energy regulators and other relevant stakeholders in the broad range of energy industry.

Keywords: *Energy efficiency, Renewable energy, Sustainable energy, Greenhouse gas, Energy usage, Nigeria.*

1. Introduction

Reducing the impacts of the use of energy has been described as one of the key technical, political and moral challenges facing the world today. While the world works towards the use of cleaner energy, the priority should be to use the energy we generate more efficiently. Energy efficiency measures are cheaper, cleaner and faster to install than any other energy options. Energy efficiency measures have the potential to promote economic development and can lead to job creation and saving of personal income. By reducing energy bills, it frees up money that can be spent elsewhere in the economy. Since a large part of the greenhouse gases emitted into the atmosphere come from energy generation, energy efficiency can also play a pivotal role in the mitigation of climate change. This assertion is contained in the Fourth Assessment Report (AR4) of the Intergovernmental Panel on Climate Change (IPCC), which demonstrated that improved energy efficiency could play a key role in our mitigation of climate change (IPCC, 2007).

In Nigeria, experts have asserted that Nigeria can save up to half of the energy currently consumed in the country if energy is efficiently utilized. The major challenge has been that the energy policy in Nigeria has undermined the importance and gains of energy efficiency to the environment and economic growth. In the midst of the prevailing energy crisis in Nigeria, energy efficiency will play a pivotal role in ensuring greater access to energy.

The concept of energy efficiency seems to be poorly developed in Nigeria. This is due to lack of appropriate and proactive policy to drive this initiative. Also, the baseline information/data are required to guide and strengthen regulatory measures to use energy efficiently in Nigeria and also to guide the development of energy efficiency policy, which will ultimately strengthen regulatory measures to use energy efficiently in Nigeria. This paper focuses on the management of electricity; though energy efficiency is applicable to other forms of energy. Another objective of this study is to identify commercially and behaviorally low-cost ways of reducing energy consumption in the residential including public and private sectors in Nigeria. The information from this study could help to develop policy document for efficient use of energy in Nigeria. The study reported in this article will be of great help to identify renewable energy potential in different regions of Nigeria and serve as a training manual for forthcoming conferences and workshops related to energy.

2. Energy Efficiency

What is Energy Efficiency?

Energy plays a critical role in the development process, first as a domestic necessity and also as a factor of production whose cost directly affects price of other goods and services. It affects all aspects of development such as social, economic, and environmental including livelihoods, access to water, agricultural productivity, health, population levels, education, and gender-related issues. Access to energy has been described as a key factor in industrial development and in providing vital services that improve the quality of life, the engine of economic progress (Amigun et al., 2008). The Millennium Development Goals (MDGs) especially MDG 1, reducing by half the percentage of people living in poverty by 2015, cannot be met without major improvement in the quality and magnitude of energy services in developing countries (Amigun et al., 2008).

Energy efficiency entails the use of energy in a manner that will minimize the amount of energy needed to provide services. This is possible if we improve in practices and products that we use. If we use energy efficient appliances, it will help to reduce the energy necessary to provide services like lighting, cooling, heating, manufacturing, cooking, transport, entertainment etc. Hence, energy efficiency products essentially help to do more work with less energy. For instance, to light a room with an incandescent light bulb of 60 W for one hour requires electrical energy of 60 W/h (that is 60 watts per hour). A compact fluorescent lamp (CFL) would provide the same or better light at 11 W and only use 11 W/h of electrical energy. This means that 49 W/h (82 per cent of total energy) is saved for each hour the light is turned on by replacing the incandescent lamp by a CFL. This saving can be instrumental in provide increased energy access. End-use efficiency is very crucial to achieving energy efficiency. This refers to technologies, appliances and/or practices that improve the efficient use of energy at end users' level. It can be justified by taking a case of the appliances we use in our houses and offices. Though this term is not limited to electrical appliances, it can also be used for other areas of efficiency such as measures to improve the ability of houses to absorb and retain heat in winter and keep out heat in the summer. On the side of utility companies, providing electricity, they can also device ways and technologies to promote the efficient use of energy. This is referred to demand-side efficiency or management (DSM). DSM can be policies implemented by utilities and energy planners that encourage consumers to use energy more efficiently. An example of this is load shifting, which includes encouraging consumers to move their energy use away from peak period.

There are two important approaches to achieving the efficient use of energy. The first one is the technological approach while the second is the behavioural approach. Technological approach involves the need to change the type of technology we use to a more efficient one. A good example is the one about replacing incandescent bulbs with energy efficiency bulbs such as CFLs. The behavioral approach entails changing the ways we do things. An example is switching off appliances when not in use. This will be discussed in subsequent sections.

2.1 Importance of Energy Efficiency

Energy efficiency has become the key driver of sustainable development in many economies in the world. If we use energy efficiently, it will lead to the saving of personal income; families will not have to spend so much money paying for energy. It will help to reduce the building of more power stations, thus the money for building power stations will then be spent on other sectors of the economy. Moreover, more people will have access to energy by saving energy in one part of the country making it available in another part. In Nigeria, where the utility companies do not have enough energy to meet the everyday needs in all sectors at the same time, energy supply is alternated. With good energy management at the residential, public and private sectors, there will be no need to alternate electricity supply.

Most of the energy generated in Nigeria comes from the burning of fossil fuel such as oil and gas. For every kilowatt-hour of electricity we consume, there is an equivalent emission of greenhouse gases (GHGs). Energy efficiency can help to reduce the emission of GHGs and reduce the reliance on petroleum to drive our economy. The negative environmental impacts associated with the generation of energy will also be reduced if energy is used efficiently. Many people can be employed during intervention programmes to change the behavior of people to use energy efficiently. For companies manufacturing electrical appliances, there will then be competition among them more manufacturing efficient appliances to capture the patronage of consumers.

3. Energy Generation in Nigeria

The report of Energy Commission of Nigeria (ECN) states that there are nine electricity generating stations in Nigeria (ECN, 2008). Three of these stations are hydro based while six are thermal based and they are all owned by the Government under the Power Holding Company of Nigeria (PHCN). All of them have an installed capacity of 6000MW. However, for many reasons ranging from shortage of gas supply to lack of maintenance, these stations are performing far below the installed capacity. Recently published figures show that Nigeria is generating 2000MW of electricity (Nigeria Punch News paper). Part of the electricity generated is exported to neighboring Niger Republic. Electricity demand in Nigeria is very high as about 60 per cent of Nigerians do not have access to electricity. Most of these people live in rural areas. Although many gas-powered stations have been commissioned to increase generation capacity by 4000MW, this will still not be enough. Due to the fact that the energy generated in Nigeria is grossly inadequate, there is, therefore, the need to promote energy efficiency culture.

4. Justification for the Study

Energy policies in many developing countries including Nigeria have not really put into consideration the importance and gains of energy efficiency to the social, environment and economic development. This could be that the concept is poorly developed in these countries. In many developing countries, there is inadequate data that will guide the development of policy, which is required to strengthen regulatory measures to use energy efficiently.

The objective of this study therefore is to:

- ☆ To elicit information that will serve as a guide to draft policy that will strengthen regulatory measures to use energy more efficiently in Nigeria.
- ☆ To identify commercially and behaviorally low-cost ways of reducing energy consumption in the residential, public and private sectors in Nigeria
- ☆ To identify renewable energy potentials in the different regions of Nigeria, as illustrated in Figure 9.1.

5. Energy Intensive Behaviours in Nigeria

As mentioned in previous section of this paper that one of the ways to tackle the inefficient use of energy is to change our behaviors. A lot of energy is wasted in

Figure 9.1: Map of Nigeria Showing Different Regions of the Country

Nigeria because households, public and private offices and industries use more energy than is actually necessary to fulfill their needs. One of the reasons is that they use old (obsolete) and inefficient equipment and production processes. Other reason observed is the unwholesome practices that lead to energy wastage.

Some recommendations to achieving energy efficiency in Nigeria are as follows:

5.1 Adaptation to the Use of Incandescent Light Bulbs

The common name for incandescent bulb in Nigeria is "yellow bulb" because of the yellowish color of the light rays from the bulbs. The use of incandescent bulbs for lighting is energy intensive. Only about 5 per cent of total energy used by an incandescent bulb is converted to light energy, the remaining 95 per cent is converted to heat energy (Lebot, 2009). The energy rating of the incandescent bulbs found in the Nigerian market range from 40 W to 200 W. High rating bulbs are used in places where low voltage is experienced to get a brighter effect. High rating incandescent bulbs are used for outdoor lighting because they appear brighter.

Energy consumed in Nigeria can be drastically reduced if Nigerians replace their incandescent bulbs with energy efficiency bulbs. The energy saving bulbs found in the market were of power rating 20W, 26W, and 36W. If a particular household using 20 incandescent bulbs of 60W decides to replace them with energy saving bulbs of 20W, instead of spending 1200W/h (20 x 60W) for lighting, they will be spending 400 watts per hour (20 x 20W). Thus this saves approximately 67 per cent of energy for lighting alone. This is a huge saving. On a larger scale, if Nigeria as a country replaces one million incandescent bulbs by energy saving bulbs, the country will be saving about 40MW of electricity. This is enough to provide electricity to many communities in Nigeria. If each of the 36 states and the Federal Capital Territory (FCT) replaces one million incandescent bulbs each, we can save up to 1480 MW of electricity.

5.1.1 Policy Action

Policy option for Nigeria will include phasing out the incandescent bulbs from the Nigerian system and putting a ban on the import and production of incandescent bulbs. Policy to encourage the import and production of energy efficient light bulbs will enhance the efficient use of energy. Government should put in place strategies to reduce the cost of energy saving bulbs. Awareness creation is also needed to change the attitude of Nigerians on the need to save energy by using the right technology. This can be achieved through media campaign.

5.2 Putting on Light to Advertise Goods

Many people who sell certain goods such snacks and electrical materials switch on light during the day to draw the attention of people to buy their goods. Operators of fast food centers also have similar practices for which they use incandescent bulbs to heat their food and at the same time draw the attention of people to their products. This practice is energy intensive and should be discouraged.

5.2.1 Policy Action

Policy option is that the government should impose tax on energy consumption for industries and privately owned firms. It should be made mandatory for these private institutions to carry out energy audit and make them public in order to facilitate the designated agency to impose reasonable tax on them. The energy audit should be done by government designated agencies or firm for transparency. Designs for houses should be properly screened by the designated government agency to ensure that they comply with energy efficiency standards of buildings.

5.3 Switching Off Outdoor Lighting during the Day and Keeping Electrical Appliances on Standby Mode

Many Nigerians do not switch off their outdoor lighting during the day. This is particularly very common in commercial and residential areas in many major cities in Nigeria. This is also common even in public institutions such as Universities and Government agencies.

Putting an electrical appliance on standby mode is not the same thing as switching it off. Electrical equipment consumes energy when on standby mode.

Although the energy they consume is not the same as when they are switched on, but putting them off when not in use can save significant amount of energy.

5.3.1 Policy Action

Policy should be made to create awareness through radio campaign and television advertisements. By introducing energy efficiency culture into the school curriculum and involving both the religious leaders and the traditional gate-keepers for effective information dissemination the task can be accomplished.

5.4 Proliferation of Private Water Boreholes

In the major cities in Nigeria, significant number of people has boreholes in their houses. This arises because of the inability of government to provide water in many parts of the country. The use of privately owned boreholes is on the increase. The machine used for pumping water from the aquifer is an energy intensive machine and is generally has power rating up to 2000 W. Since water and energy are inextricably linked, these machines exert a lot of stress on Nigerian Electricity Regulator –Power Holding Company of Nigeria (PHCN) facilities.

5.4.1 Policy Action

Access to water is the right of the people and it is the responsibility of government to consistently provide water for her citizens. This is the best way to discourage the use of private boreholes. A lot of energy will be saved if government and accredited private companies provide water from a central system.

5.5 Industrial Activities in Residential Areas

Many cities in Nigeria are not properly planned. The practice of establishing industries in residential areas is unhealthy as it creates hurdles for power supply in residential buildings. With this kind of practice, the agencies responsible to supply electricity are not able to plan on how to allocate energy to the various sectors.

5.5.1 Policy Action

Policy should be made to encourage the proper planning of cities, so that residential and industrial areas are separated. This will help the government to plan how they can effectively provide electricity for the two sectors.

5.6 Multiple Use of Inefficient Heating Equipment

The use of heating equipment for cooking and heating water should be discouraged in the residential and private buildings. Government should encourage the use of renewable source of cooking and heating for households. Solar heaters are one of the examples of renewable energy system and similar are the clean fuel such as ethanol gel fuel, and biogas technology. Most of these renewable energy appliances and technology also reduce the build-up of CO_2 in the atmosphere. Heating equipment consume about 60 per cent of the energy used in houses. For example, in places like hotels where several water heating equipment are installed in several rooms sometime numbering up to 100 rooms or more, the use of solar heaters in these buildings will help to save a lot of energy.

5.6.1 Policy Action

Government should make policy that will encourage the use of renewable sources of energy. Incentives should be given for being energy efficient to encourage the widespread use of renewable energy technologies.

5.7 Purchase of Second-Hand (Used) Appliances

The Nigerian market is flooded with all kinds of second-hand appliances. Over 90 per cent of Nigerian use one secondhand product or the other. They are cheaper compared to the new ones. Many Nigerians are on the opinion that secondhand products are more durable than the new ones. This assertion could be based on the fact that there are a lot of substandard goods in the market and the secondhand goods tend to last longer than them. Many of the secondhand products come from European and North American countries and they may have been manufactured long time ago. The efficiency of these products is quite doubtful and the possibility exists that they may have been rejected by the former users to purchase more recent and efficient appliances.

5.7.1 Policy Action

Policy to standardize the secondhand product imported into the country is necessary. There is also need to make policy that will encourage Nigerians to purchase new and modern appliances.

6. Barriers to Energy Efficiency Development in Nigeria

It was identified that the following are barriers to the development of energy efficiency in Nigeria. (Edjekumhene and Brew-Hammond, 2001).

6.1 Lack of Policy and Legislation

Lack of policy and legislation to address the inefficient use of energy is a key barrier to the development of energy efficiency. Policy and legislation will help to change behaviour towards an energy efficient economy. Private and public institutions should also be encouraged to make their own policy to promote the efficient use of energy. The government can make it mandatory for public, large and small scale private organizations to establish an Energy Management Department or Unit.

6.2 Lack of Trained Personnel and Energy Efficiency Professionals

Inadequately trained personnel and professional is another factor inhibiting the development of energy efficiency. Nigeria as a country lacks adequate number of experts on energy efficiency who could drive the development of the concept and policy to promote energy efficiency.

6.3 Energy (Electricity Access)

Access to electricity is a problem in Nigeria. Over 75 per cent of the total population does not get electricity supply for up to 24 hours. The general notion is that there is no energy to save. They are of the opinion that when the energy is made available, then the issue of energy efficiency can be discussed. Awareness creation and enlightenment campaign are needed to erase this notion from the minds of Nigerians. People should be made to understand that if they save energy, there will be enough energy to go round everybody. This can help to solve the disruptive supply of electricity.

7. Best Practices in Energy Efficiency

This section focuses on best practices in energy efficiency in other parts of the world and looks at the possibility of domesticating some of these practices in Nigeria. The practices are in no way exhaustive (EIC, 2002).

7.1 Standard and Label (S&L)

In many countries of the world, especially the Industrialized Nations, the use of standards and Labels (S&L) are increasingly becoming common. An energy label is attached to electrical appliance to display the accurate energy consumption information on the product, such information will help the buyer to take decision whether to buy the product or not. In many of the countries in Organization for the Economic Cooperation and Development (OECD), energy labeling is now fully operational and the appliances that are commonly labeled include refrigerators, freezers, and air conditioners and a range of other appliances such as rice cookers, boilers, lighting products, and washing machine (Harrington and Damnics, 2004).

There are two types of labels - *Endorsement Labels* and *Comparative Labels.* Endorsement labels point out to consumers that products belong to the "most energy efficient" class of products or meet a predetermined standard or eligibility criteria (Harrington and Damnics, 2004). This type of label merely informs the consumer that the products meet certain required standard. Endorsement labeling can be done specifically to provide information on energy efficiency or for other purposes.

7.2 Minimum Enegy Performance Standards (MEPS)

Minimum Energy Performance Standards (MEPS) is also referred to as "standards" or "efficiency standards" in some countries. MEPS are specified minimum energy efficiency levels products must meet before they can be legally sold in any country (Harrington and Damnics, 2004). Here, specific energy standards are set before products are allowed into a country and sold. For example, a country may decide to set a standard that refrigerators consuming more than 400 kwh will not be allowed into the country.

7.3 Retrofitting Homes and Public Buildings

The practice of retrofitting homes and public buildings is now practiced in many parts of the world to reduce energy consumption. Owing to the fact that many homes and public building have been built long time ago and are equipped with all kinds of inefficient appliances, it is now a common thing for owners of home and government to replace this old (obsolete/outdated) equipment with newer and more efficient ones such as replacing incandescent bulb by energy efficient bulb such as Compact Fluorescent Lamps (CFL) and replacing modern and energy efficient refrigerators with old and inefficient refrigerators. Different refrigerators are designed for different climate. Using a refrigerator designed for temperate region in a tropical climate will lead to inefficient use of energy. A proper enforcement mechanism should be put in place by the Government in this regard.

7.4 Landscaping and Energy Efficient Building

There are natural ways by which we can keep our homes comfortable and reduce energy bill. A well placed tree, shrub or vine in our homes can provide shade and act as windbreak. This can help to reduce the energy we spend on cooling because the shade from these trees can keep our home cool. Also sustainable architectural designs can be put in place to reduce the additional lighting required in buildings.

8. Renewable Energy Potential in Nigeria and Energy Efficiency

Renewable energies include wind, ocean wave and tides, solar, biomass, rivers, geothermal (heat of the earth), etc. They are called 'renewable' because they are regularly replenished by natural processes. Their operations also reduce the carbon dioxide emissions into the atmosphere, thereby leading to decrease in the level of greenhouse gases in atmosphere. Technologies that have been developed to harness these energies are called renewable energy technologies (RETs) or sometime also called "clean technologies" or "green energy" (Ekouevi, 2001). Because renewable energies are constantly being replenished from natural sources, they have security of supply, unlike fossil fuels, which are negotiated on the international market and subject to international competition, and geopolitical uncertainties sometimes may even result in wars and shortages.

8.1 Why Should Nigeria Promote Renewable Energy?

- ☆ Their rate of use does not affect their availability in future, thus they are inexhaustible.
- ☆ The resources are generally well distributed all over the world, even though wide Spatial and temporal variations occur. Thus all regions of the world have reasonable access to one or more forms of renewable energy supply unlike fossil fuel which is unevenly distributed.
- ☆ They are clean and pollution-free, and therefore are sustainable natural form of energy.
- ☆ They can be cheaply and continuously harvested and therefore regarded as sustainable source of energy.

Renewable energy can be set up in small units (decentralized unit) and is therefore suitable for community management and ownership. In this way, value from renewable energy projects can be kept in the community-enhancing rural development. In Nigeria, this has particular relevance since the electricity grid does not extend to many rural areas and in some remote areas extension of grid line of electricity is alarmingly expensive due to transmission and distribution losses. This presents a unique opportunity to construct power plants such as biogas technology closer to the places where they are actually needed. In this way, much needed income, skill transfer and manufacturing opportunities for small businesses would be injected into rural communities.

RETs have the potential to produce more jobs than fossil fuel or nuclear industries. When RETs are properly integrated into National development plans and implemented, they can substantially reduce greenhouse gas emission and simultaneously increase employment and also serve as a source for increasing foreign currency reserve of the government.

Replacing some of the household, public, commercial and industrial energy applications with renewable energy could help in achieving energy efficiency in Nigeria.

9. Conclusion and Recommendation

Policy should be made to ban the import, manufacture and use of incandescent bulbs in Nigeria. Such policy should encourage the gradual phase out of incandescent bulbs from the system and encourage the adoption of energy saving bulbs. Agencies responsible for standardizing goods imported into the country should be adequately equipped to combat the influx of substandard and energy inefficient goods into the Nigerian market. Example of such agency is the Standard Organization of Nigeria (SON), with the mandate for preparing standards for products and processes and ensuring compliance with Federal Government policies on Standards Methodology and Quality Assurance of both locally manufactured and imported products and services in Nigeria. The influx of secondhand (used) products into the Nigerian market is a big threat to the efficient use of energy. In many instances, the secondhand products are preferred over new ones by many Nigerians mainly because of the price. Some of them were also found to claim that the secondhand products are more durable than the new ones. This notion is based on the presence of substandard new goods which are not durable. Many of the secondhand products are imported from the temperate region, thus they may not be designed for use in the tropical region. This can contribute significantly to the inefficient use of energy in homes and offices. Policy should be directed to gradually stop the import of secondhand (used) goods. This could be done by placing high tariff on secondhand goods to discourage their import and use.

Considering the relevance of energy efficiency for National development, it will be necessary for government to set up and equip an agency with the mandate for promoting energy efficiency. The agency will ensure that energy efficiency policy and programmes are implemented. They will also ensure that information on energy efficiency are well disseminated, and also ensure that the training and re-training of staff in the different establishments are periodically done.

For medium to large scale industries, it should be made mandatory for them to establish an Energy Management Unit (EMU). The Unit should be responsible for ensuring that energy is properly managed within the organization. This policy should also be applicable in public offices such as the universities and government ministries. EMU should be trained to carry out energy audit of their various institutions. Legislation should be made to make it mandatory for private companies and government owned institutions and ministries to publish the report of their energy audit. Government should introduce energy tax that will be proportional to the total energy consumed by institutions. Apart from helping in taxation, the energy audit will also help the utilities to plan on how to put in place energy efficiency mechanisms. Revenue from such tax can be channeled to promote the efficient use of energy in other areas.

Since water and energy are inextricably linked, the proliferation of water borehole in many town and cities in Nigeria is energy intensive. This is because the Nigerian government has failed to provide water in many parts of the country. The energy spent daily to pump water from the aquifer by private individuals can be drastically reduced if government spends extra money to provide water for her citizens. Access to water is the right of every citizen in Nigeria. Policy should be directed toward providing water and other infrastructures that will lead to efficient use of energy in Nigeria. Lastly, the use of renewable energy should be promoted in the household, industries and other sectors to ensure effective energy use and management.

References

Amigun, B., Sigamoney, R., and von Blottnitz, H. (2008). Commercialization of Biofuel in Africa: A review". Renewable and sustainable Energy Review. 12, pp 690–711

ECN, (2008). Assessment of Energy Options and Strategies for Nigeria: Energy Demand, Supply and Environmental Analysis for Sustainable Energy Development pp (2000-2030). Report No. ECN/EPA/2008/01.

Edjekumhene, I. and Brew-Hammond, A. (2001), "Barriers to the Use of Renewable Energy Technologies for Sustainable Development in Ghana", Proceedings of the African High-Level Regional Meeting on Energy and Sustainable Development for the Ninth Session on the Commission on Sustainable Development, Denmark: UNEP. Energy Commission of Nigeria

EIC (2002), Best Practice Guide: Economic and Financial Evaluation of Energy Efficiency Projects and Programs, Colorado, Ecoenergy International Corporation (EIC).

Ekouevi (2001), "An Overview of Biomass Energy Issues in sub-Saharan Africa", Proceedings of the African High-Level Regional Meeting on Energy and Sustainable Development for the Ninth Session on the Commission on Sustainable Development, Denmark: UNEP Collaborating Centre on Energy and Development.

Harrington L. and Damnics M. (2004). Energy Labeling and Standards Programme Throughout the World. A publication of the National Appliance and Equipment Energy Efficiency Committee, Australia. NAEEEC Report 2004/04

IPCC (2007). Climate Change 2007: The Physical Science Basis. Contribution of Working Group I to the Fourth Assessment Report of the Intergovernmental Panel on Climate Change. Cambridge: Cambridge University Press.

Lebot, B. (2009). Energy Efficiency and Market Transformation: A Short Overview of Best Practices. A paper presented during the Inception Workshop of the UNDP-GEF Project to Promote Energy Efficiency in Residential and Public Building in Nigeria, 14th July 2009.

Smith, K. R. (1994), "Health, Energy, and Greenhouse-Gas in Household Stoves", Energy for Sustainable Development, Vol. 1, No. 4, Bangalore, International Energy Initiative, pp. 23-29.

Chapter 10

Evolution of Energy Efficiency and Conservation in Nigeria

Ismail Ibraheem Idris

Raw Materials Research and Development Council,
PMB 232 Garki, Abuja, Nigeria
E-mail: ismaili1629@gmail.com

ABSTRACT

Nigeria is the most populous country in Sub-Saharan Africa, with nearly one quarter of Sub-Saharan Africa's population and is one of Africa's leading exporter of crude oil, however, Nigeria has been in energy crisis for over two decades. International Energy Agency (IEA) reported in 2007 that the total energy consumed in Nigeria was 4 Quadrillion Btu (107,000 kilotons of oil equivalent), of which combustible renewable and waste accounted for 80.2 percent of total energy consumption. This high percent share represents the use of biomass to meet off-grid heating and cooking needs, mainly in rural areas. IEA data for 2008 indicate that electrification in Nigeria covers only 47 per cent for the country as a whole. In urban areas, 69 per cent of the population had access to electricity compared to rural areas where coverage of electrification was only 26 per cent. Approximately 81 million people do not have access to electricity in Nigeria at present and the nominal electricity generating capacity in Nigeria is less than 6000 MW. The actual generated power is about half of the installed capacity of the power plants.Due to the high percentage waste in energy use, it is widely believed that Nigeria can save up to half of the energy currently consumed in the country if energy is efficiently utilized. This paper discusses on the energy policy and resources of Nigeria, areas of energy wastage, challenges in implementing the policy and the way forward.

Keywords: *Nigeria, Energy efficiency and Conservation.*

1. Introduction

Nigeria is Africa's most populous country and the seventh most populous country in the world with over 150 million people of which the majority are black (one out of every four black persons is a Nigerian). It is listed among the "Next Eleven" economies, and is a member of the Commonwealth of Nations. The economy of Nigeria is one of the fastest growing in the world, with a growth rate of 9 per cent in 2008 and 8.3 per cent in 2009

Nigeria is one of Africa's leading exporters of crude oil, but despite this it has been in an energy crisis for over two decades. International Energy Agency (IEA) reported in 2007 that the total energy consumed in Nigeria was 4 Quadrillion Btu (107,000 kilotons equivalent of oil) of which combustible-renewables and waste accounted for 80.2 per cent. This high percentage share represents the use of biomass to meet off-grid heating and cooking needs, mainly in rural areas. Due to the high percentage waste in energy use, it is widely believed that Nigeria can save up to half of the energy currently consumed in the country if energy is efficiently utilized.

This paper aims to discuss the energy resources and policy of Nigeria, areas of energy waste, challenges in implementing the policy and the way forward.

2. Energy Resources of Nigeria

Nigeria is blessed with abundant energy resources, the major ones are: coal, petroleum, natural gas and solar energy.

2.1 Coal

Coal was the first fossil energy resource discovered in Nigeria. Coal mining in Nigeria began in 1916 with a production out-put of 24,500 tons per annum. This rose to a peak of 905,000 tons in 1958/59 with a contribution of over 70 per cent to commercial energy consumption in the country. Available data show that coal of sub-bituminous grade occurs in about 22 coal fields spread over 13 States of the Federation. The proven coal reserves so far in the country are about 639 million tons while the inferred reserves are about 2.75 billion tons. Following the discovery of crude oil in commercial quantities and the subsequent conversion of railway engines to diesel from coal this led to a fall in the production of coal from the beginning of the sixties to only 0.009 million tons in 2008.

2.2 Petroleum

Petroleum is the main stay of the Nigerian economy and its exploration has witnessed steady growth over the past few years. The nation had a proven reserve of 25 billion barrels of predominantly low-sulphur light crude oil in 1999. This substantially increased to 34 billion barrels in 2004 and currently is about 36.5 billion barrels. It is projected that proven reserves will reach up to 68 billion barrels by year 2030. Oil production in the country also increased steadily over the years; however, the rate of increase is dependent on economies and geopolitics, both production as well as consumption in the country. Nigeria's current crude oil production is limited to about 2.4 million barrels per day only, which is partly due to the uprising in the Niger Delta and to the restriction imposed by OPEC (Organisation of Petroleum Exporting Countries). Figure 10.1 presents Nigeria's oil production and consumption trend from 2000 to 2009.

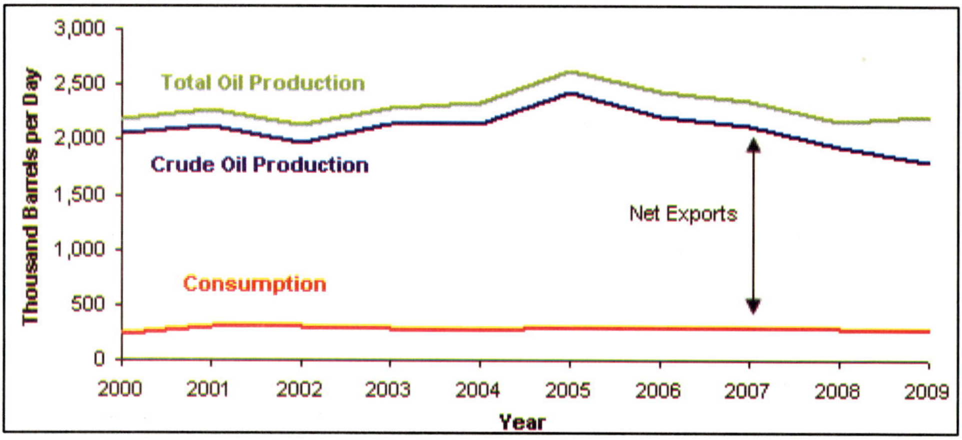

Figure 10.1: Nigeria's Oil Production and Consumption Trend from 2000 to 2009 (*Source*: US Department of Energy)

2.3 Natural Gas

Nigeria had reserves of about 187.44 trillion standard cubic feet of high quality sweet gas in 2005 (Kukpolokun, 2006). Natural gas reserves are known to be substantially larger than oil resources in energy terms. Gas discoveries in Nigeria are incidental to oil exploration and production activities. Consequently, as high as 75 per cent of the gas produced was being flared in the past. However, gas flaring was reduced to about 36 per cent as a result of efforts by the government to monetized natural gas. Domestic utilization of Natural gas is mainly for power generation, which accounts for over 80 per cent, while the rest are used in the industrial sector and very neg-ligible for household use. Figure 10.2 shows Nigeria's natural gas production from 2004 to date.

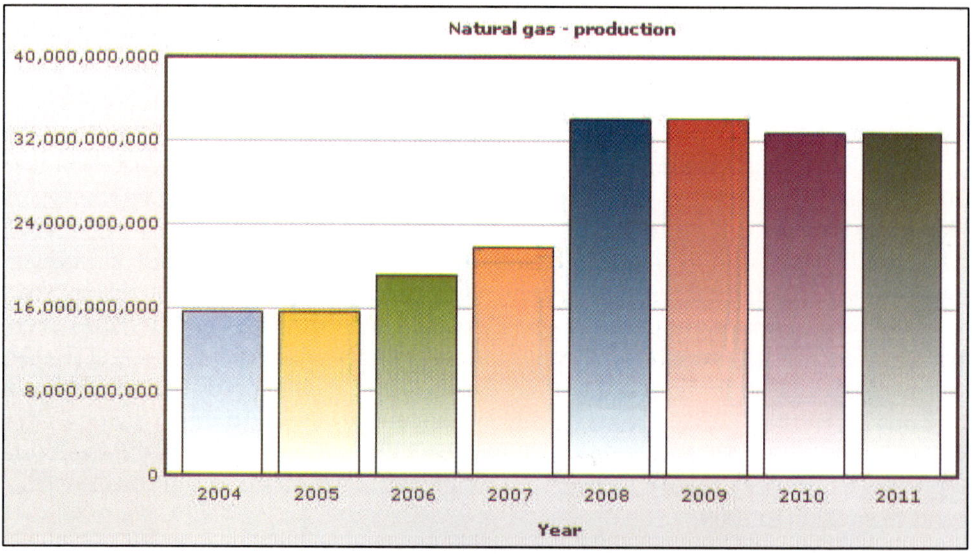

Figure 10.2: Natural Gas Production in Nigeria from 2004 to Date (*Source*: Index Mundi)

2.4 Renewable Energy

Nigeria is blessed with a large amount of renewable energy resources such as solar energy, biomass, wind and hydroelectricity. Table 10.1 presents the estimated renewable energy resources of Nigeria.

Table 10.1: Nigeria's Renewable Energy Resources

Energy Source	*Capacity*
Hydropower, Large Scale	10,000MW
Hydropower, small scale	734 MW
Fuel wood	13,071,464 hectares (forest land 1981)
Animal waste	61 million tones/yr
Crop residue	83 million tones/yr
Solar Radiation	3.5-7.0 kWh/m^2-day
Wind	2.4 m/s (annual average)

Source: ECN, Renewable Energy Master Plan, November 2005.

Except for large scale hydropower plants, which serve as a major source of electricity in Nigeria, the current state of exploitation and utilization of the renewable energy resources in the country is very low and limited largely to pilot and demonstration projects.

3. Electricity in Nigeria

The installed electricity generating capacity in 2005 was about 6,861MW. Electricity in Nigeria is generated from several sources as shown in Figure 10.3 but there is a wide gap between installed capacity of the power plants and the actual power generation from such plants. As reported in THISDAY newspaper of September 2009, electrical power generation was only 2450 MW. Figure 10.4 shows the installed capacity and actual generation of electricity over the years.

This provides the reason for only 47 per cent electrification in Nigeria as a whole, as reported in 2008 by the International Energy Agency (IEA). In urban areas, 69 percent of the population had access to electricity compared to rural areas where electrification was only 26 percent. Approximately 81 million people do not have access to electricity in Nigeria at present. Per capita electricity consumption in Nigeria was 140 Kwh in 2004, which is extremely low compared to 1337 Kwh in Egypt and 4560 Kwh in South Africa (Akin, 2008).

4. Inefficient Energy Generation and Utilisation

Despite the enormous domestic endowments of non-renewable and primary renewable energy resources discussed in this article, there are persistently inadequate quantity, poor quality and poor access to energy in Nigeria. These are chiefly attributed to inefficiency in generation and utilization.

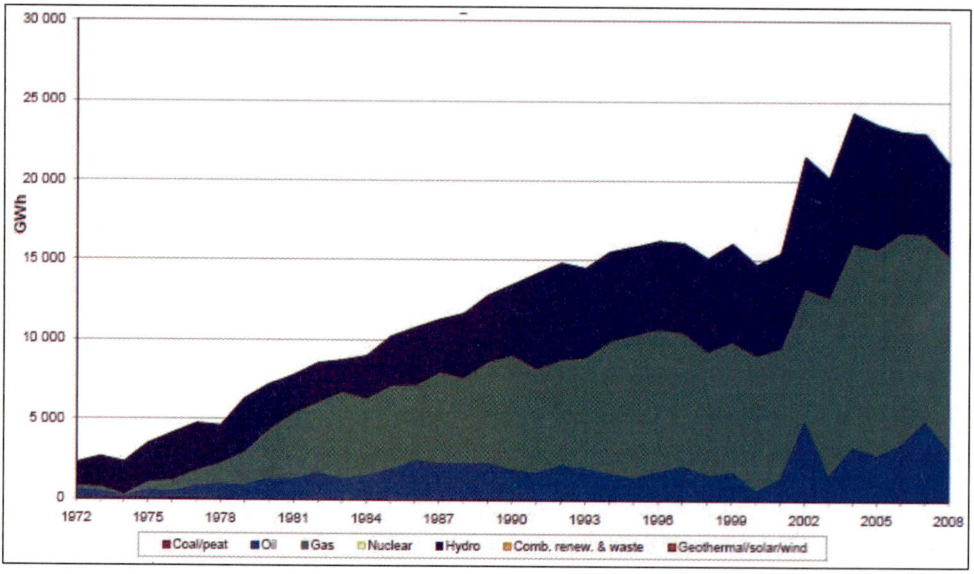

Figure 10.3: Comparison of Electricity Generation in Nigeria from Different Fuel Resources (*Source*: IEA)

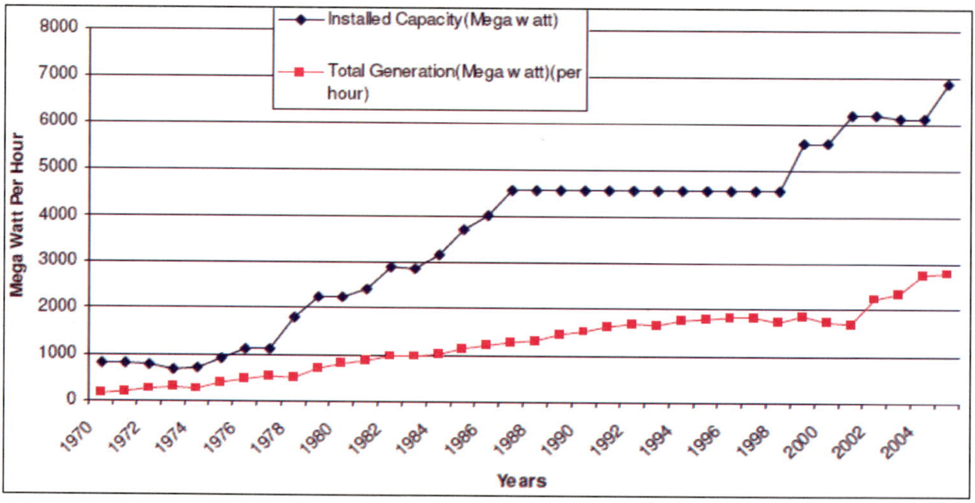

Figure 10.4: Electricity Generations during 1970-2004 (*Source*: African Econometric Society)

4.1 Inefficiency in Generation

In Nigeria, electricity is generated from a central location and distributed through long distances to other parts of the country. Energy is lost when transmitted through long distances. The transmission losses on the Nigerian grid are 35 per cent. So if 100 MW power is generated only 65 MW gets to the consumers. Figure 10.5 compares

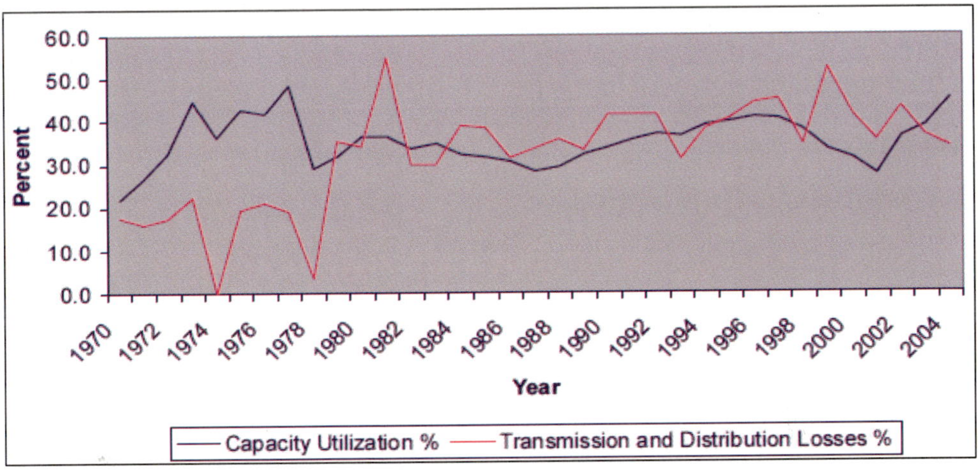

Figure 10.5: Capacity Utilization, Transmission and Distribution Losses from1970-2004
(*Source*: Akin Iwayemi, 2008 International Association of Energy Economics (IAEE) Istanbul Conference Proceedings, June 2008)

electricity capacity utilization and losses in transmission and distribution over the years.

In addition, oil extraction in Nigeria is characterized with waste. It was reported by Nigerian National Oil Spill Detection and Response Agency (NOSDRA) that approximately 2,400 oil spills have been recorded since 2006. Also, Nigeria ranked

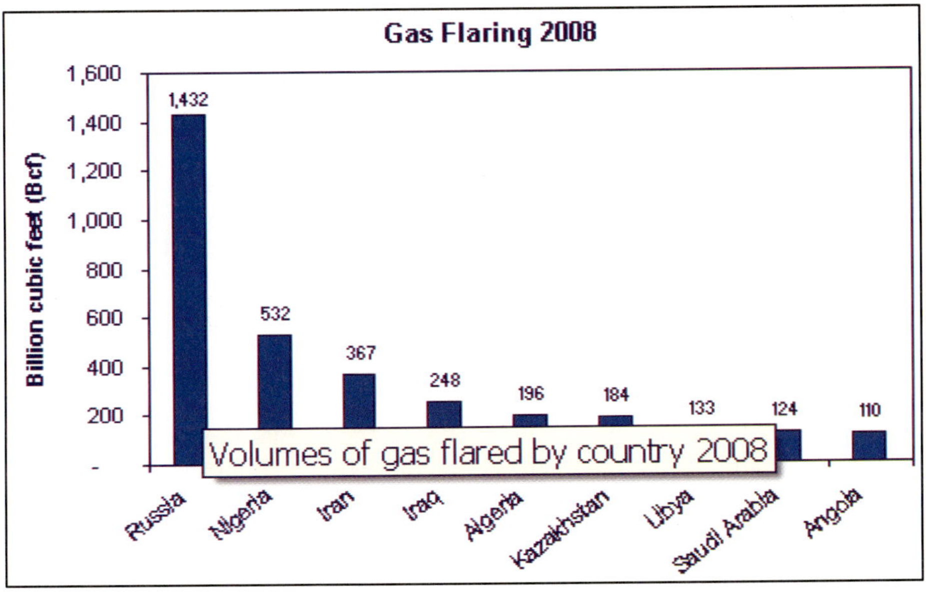

Figure 10.6: Comparison of Gas Flaring in Nigeria with Other Countries in the World in 2008
(*Source*: : National Oceanic and Atmospheric Administration)

second in gas flaring during petroleum production in 2008 as indicated by Figure 10.4. As most of the oil fields lack the infrastructure to produce and market associated natural gas, it is often flared. Nigeria flared 532 Billion Cubic Feet (Bcf) of natural gas in 2008, down from 593 Bcf in 2007. Nigerian National Petroleum Corporation (NNPC) claimed that flaring costs Nigeria US$1.46 billion in the form of lost revenue.

4.2 Inefficiency in Energy Use

Most of the energy generated in Nigeria is wasted through inefficient use in households, public and private offices and industries. More energy is used than is actually necessary to fulfill their needs. The prime reasons for this are the use of old and inefficient equipment and obsolete production processes. In the following sub-sections a closer look at some of these areas are presented.

4.2.1 In-efficient Energy Use in Households

According to a survey conducted in 2009 by Community Research Development Centre (CREDC), over 65 per cent of households claim to use incandescent bulbs. Incandescent bulbs are not efficient means of lighting, as only 5 per cent of the energy used is converted to light and the rest 95 per cent is wasted as heat. The reasons why most households use incandescent bulb are that, it is cheaper than energy saving bulbs and it gives light even at low voltage as most houses experience low voltage due to overcrowding on transformers. Lighting constitutes almost 18 per cent of the total power usage as compared to other countries with only 8-10 per cent.

Also, most households in Nigeria use second hand refrigerators and air conditioners, which were discarded from Europe and America due to their inefficiency and emission of green house gases.

In addition, offices and residential houses leave their outdoor lights switched on during the day. This is due to regular power outage during the dark that may linger into the day, thus, causing most people to forget to put out their lights, while some people switch the lights on permanently to know when power is restored.

Furthermore, in the household sector, there is considerable energy loss due to inefficient traditional three-stone stoves(wood/charcoal fuel fired), used for cooking mainly in the rural areas. These stoves have thermal efficiencies of less than 10 per cent.

4.2.2 Transportation

Nigeria lacks an organized and efficient transport system. The public means of transportation are irregular and uncomfortable. This explains why every middle income earner strives to own a car so that he/she can move about his/her business activities freely and comfortably. However, most cars on Nigerian roads are 15-20 year old imported from Europe and America. Statistics provided that in 2009 alone 13,619 new cars and 187,364 used cars were imported which means that for every 14 vehicles on the road, 13 were used ones. This accounted for high inefficiency in energy use for transportation.

4.2.3 Intensive Energy Use in Process Industries

Energy use in process industries in Nigeria is characterized by wastage as contained in the "National Energy Policy". Energy audit studies have shown that as much as twenty five percent of industrial energy can be saved through simple housekeeping measures.

A study conducted by Aderemi et al in 2009 on the assessment of electrical energy use and efficiency in the food industries showed that 39.1 per cent of the electrical equipment used in the selected food industry of the study area were well above 15 years in age. The equipment became less efficient due to wear in some of their parts. As a result, the quantity of product that was fed into them was reduced by 30 to 40 per cent before the machine could run. In some cases, the processes have to be re-run severally to achieve product specifications. This, no doubt, consumed more energy than necessary.

In addition, other contributing factors to in-efficiency in energy use are; worn out or slack/misaligned belts that need timely replacement or the tensioning and power factor of electrical equipment among others. Table 10.2 shows areas of energy waste in food industries.

Table 10.2: Sources of Energy Wastage in Food Processing Industries

Sl.No	*Ways by Which Electrical Energy is Wasted in Food Industry*	*No. of Firms*	*Per cent*
A	Slack or worn our belts.	72	41.4
B	Generated heat on (or from) electrical machine in use.	102	58.6
C	Undersized main supply cable.	60	37.0
D	Air leakage from ovens, refrigerators and any other drying and cooling equipment.	54	33.3
E	Poor control of sunlight towards having negative effect on company's architecture.	54	31.0
F	Lack of usage of sunlight as an alternative to purcahsed electrical energy.	12	8.3
G	Lack of usage of the heat generated from a cooling system.	54	31.0
H	Worn out pulleys.	48	29.6
I	Wear on gear teeth resulting in excessive backlash.	30	17.2
J	Wear on drive sprockets/slack chain.	60	35.7
K	Failure of couplings/misalignment.	66	39.3
L	Lubrication failure in gearboxes resulting in failed bearing or gear teetch.	66	40.7

Source. Aderemi *et al.*, African Journal of Food Science.

5. Economic and Environmental Benefit of Energy Efficiency

Nigeria would not have been in an energy crisis if appropriate efficient energy generation and utilization measures were put in place. Some of the benefits that would accrue from more efficient energy utilization are:

- ☆ Reliable and wider access to power supply,
- ☆ Competitiveness of goods and services; locally and internationally,
- ☆ Free up capital for use in other sectors of the economy,
- ☆ Reduction of impact on the environment from energy production and utilization, and
- ☆ Reduction of poverty due to increase in industrial productivity.

6. Energy Efficiency Measures in Nigeria

It was in realization of these benefits that the government undertook some measures by formulating The Energy policy, which contained specific action plans to promote energy efficiency such as establishment of the Energy Efficiency and Conservation Centre. Similarly, Energy Commission of Nigeria, in conjunction with UNDP, conducted energy audit in the commercial buildings and textile industries and Pilot replacement of one million incandescent lamps with CFL in collaboration with Cuban government is on-going. Some of these measures are discussed here.

6.1 National Energy Policy of the Federal Republic of Nigeria

6.1.1 History

The levels of energy utilization in an economy, coupled with the efficiency of conversion of energy resources to useful energy, are directly indicative of the level of development of the economy. In order to ensure optimal, adequate, reliable and secure supply of energy and its efficient utilization in the country, it is essential to put in place a co-ordinated, coherent and comprehensive energy policy. The policy will serve as a blue print for the sustainable development, supply and utilization of energy resources within the economy, and for the use of such resources in international trade and co-operation.

It was in pursuance of the above vision that in 1984, the Federal Ministry of Science and Technology produced the first Draft of the *Energy Policy Guidelines*. The contents were however limited in scope and depth. The Energy Commission of Nigeria, in furtherance of its mandate, produced a draft of the National Energy Policy in 1993. This was later reviewed in 1996 by an Inter-ministerial Committee, under the Chairmanship of the Ministry of Science and Technology. The document was yet to be approved by the Federal Executive Council. In view of significant changes in the orientation of the economy, especially as regards increased private sector participation, it became necessary to review the document of 1996, prior to its approval. This led to a review in 2003.

6.1.2 Energy Efficiency and Conservation Policy

Though energy efficiency is not a resource per se, the national energy policy gave it a place of pride as it recognized that energy utilization in Nigeria is far from being efficient and thus, it provided that it is necessary to promote energy efficiency and conservation in all sectors of the economy as follows:

6.1.2.1 Policies

1. Energy conservation shall be promoted at all levels of exploitation of nation's energy resources.
2. The nation shall promote the development and adoption of energy efficient methods in energy utilization.

6.1.2.2 Objectives

1. To ensure the prudent exploitation of the nation's non-renewable energy resources
2. To enhance energy security and self-reliance
3. To reduce the cost of production of energy-dependent goods and services
4. To reduce adverse impacts of energy utilization on the environment
5. To increase the proportion of hydrocarbon resources available for special applications such as industrial feedstock and for export
6. To eliminate avoidable investments in energy supply infrastructure

6.2 Establishment of the National Centre for Energy Efficiency and Conservation

To achieve the set objectives and address the energy problems in Nigeria the National Centre for Energy Efficiency and Conservation (NCEEC) was established in 2007. The objectives of the centre include the creation of the policy framework that will ensure the efficient use of the Nation's energy resources. The centre is also a source of authoritative information and leadership on sustainable energy systems and in particular, seeks to:

- ☆ Undertake research into energy usage habits of industrial, institutional and household concerns with the view of finding optimal energy balance.
- ☆ Determine the optimal infrastructure expansion plan for energy networks.
- ☆ Generate reliable data on both traditional and new energy sources that will ascertain their real values in our energy mix. This includes data survey, experimentation and testing, analysis of reliability and cost performance of the existing systems.
- ☆ Create and operate energy efficiency laboratories for the testing and calibration of transport, production and general energy related equipment.
- ☆ Research on linkages between energy and other themes, including economy and social development and impact on environment and climate change.
- ☆ Educate and train researchers through postgraduate degrees and short course programs on energy efficiency.

7. Challenges in Implementing Energy Efficiency and Conservation Measures

Despite the efforts of the government and non-governmental organizations the road to having an efficient mechanism that would cater for energy generation and utilization for sustainable development in Nigeria is still fraught with many challenges such as:

- Low level of awareness
- Lack of economic incentive(s)
- Absence of code or regulation
- No enforcement or energy utilization law
- Lack of energy auditing/assessment programmes
- No comprehensive database of energy use in different sectors of the economy
- Lack of funds to implement energy efficient programmes
- Low human capacity to implement and enforce energy efficiency programmes and auditing
- Highly subsidized Energy tariffs, which encourage the energy users to waste and discourage investment in energy efficiency programmes.

8. Ways Forward

Even though implementing energy efficiency measures in Nigeria is faced with many challenges, with concerted efforts from relevant stakeholders enabling environment could be created by adopting all or some of the following measures.

8.1 Compulsory Annual Energy Audit of Industries, Commercial and Government Buildings

Energy auditing should be made mandatory for industries, commercial and government buildings as it is practiced in developed economies. If the established energy limit is exceeded, the organization should be sanctioned appropriately.

8.2 Establishing Energy Standard and Codes

Currently, there are no energy standards and codes in Nigeria. Standard Organization of Nigeria (SON), Energy Efficiency and Conservation Centre and other relevant agencies should collaborate to establish energy standards and codes for buildings and all industrial processes and products.

8.3 Product Labeling

All energy consuming appliances should certify for energy efficiency and product labeling should be made compulsory.

8.4 Establishing an Enforcing Agent

Energy Efficiency and Conservation Centre should be given appropriate authority to enforce and sanction erring individuals and organizations.

8.5 Provision of Economic Incentives

All tiers of government should set aside a portion of their annual budget for soft loans provision at very low interest for funding Energy Efficiency and Conservation (EE &C) projects. Subsidies of up to 30 per cent of initial cost of a certain quantity of energy efficient equipment and appliances should be given to end-users, funds should be deployed to designated organizations to purchase energy efficient equipment and appliances in bulk and facilitate to distribute through retail to end-users, Initial purchase taxes such as VAT should be waived for EE&C equipment users and income taxes and levies on EE&C equipment should be made subject to rebates.

8.6 Creating Awareness on Energy Conservation and Efficiency

Promoting awareness and educating the public on the benefit of energy conservation and efficiency through seminars, workshops, radio jingles and newspaper advertisements could be effective means to achieve the set objectives. Training and re-training of professionals should also be encouraged.

8.7 Appropriate Energy Pricing

Energy tariffs should be left to market forces to discourage waste in energy usage.

9. Conclusion

It is evident that energy efficiency and conservation measures are gradual evolving in Nigeria, especially with its inclusion in the National Energy Policy and the establishment of the Centre for Energy Efficiency and Conservation. The recommendations made in this article should be carefully looked into in order to accelerate the emergence of a strong culture for energy efficiency and conservation. People should be made to realize that energy is a basic necessity to everyone and everywhere, whether it is the remotest village of developing countries or the mega cities of developed nations. Also, energy is the live-wire of every economy, thus, investments in energy-saving products and practices can lower energy bills, promote overall economic efficiency and create jobs, increase cash flow and operating margins, provide businesses with a critical competitive edge.

References

Abubakar, S. Sambo, Strategic Developments in Renewable Energy in Nigeria, www.ecn.gov.ng

Abubakar, S. Sambo, 2008. Matching Electricity Supply with Demand in Nigeria, www.ecn.gov.ng

Abubakar S. Sambo, 2007. Creating Enabling Environment for Energy Efficiency and Conservation (EE &C) Programmes in Nigeria, A Paper Presented at the WEC-Africa Forum on Energy Efficiency, Abuja, January 8- 10, www.ecn.gov.ng

Akin Iwayemi, 2008. Nigeria's Dual Energy Problems: Policy Issues and Challenges, "Bridging Energy Supply and Demand: Logistics, Competition and Environment" 31st IAEE International Conference, Istanbul, Turkey.

www.iaee.org/en/publications/newsletterdl.aspx?id=53 (accessed April 10, 2011)

A. O. Aderemi *et al.*, 2009. Assessment of electrical energy use efficiency in Nigeria food industry, African Journal of Food Science, Vol. 3(8) pp. 206-216. http://www.academicjournals.org/ajfs (accessed April 10, 2011)

Ed. Etiosa Uyigue, 2009. Energy Efficiency Survey in Nigeria: A Guide for Developing Policy and Legislation, Community Research and Development Centre, www.credcentre.org (accessed April 10, 2011)

Ed. Etiosa *et al.*, 2007. Promoting Renewable Energy and Energy Efficiency in Nigeria, *The Report of a one-day Conference which held at the University of Calabar Hotel and Conference Centre 21st November www.credcentre.org* (accessed April 10, 2011)

Energy Commission of Nigeria, National Energy Policy of the Federal Republic of Nigeria, 2003, www.ecn.gov.ng

F. M. Kupolokun, 2006. Nigeria and the Future of Global Gas Market, the Baker Institute, Energy Forum Houston USA, May 2. http://www.rice.edu/energy/publications/docs/NIGERIA_FutureGlobalGas_Speech.pdf (accessed April 16, 2011)

http://allafrica.com/stories/200909170131.html (accessed April 16, 2011)

http://www.nceec.org (accessed April 16, 2011)

http//www.iea.org/stats/pdf-graohs/NGPES01.pdf) (accessed April 10, 2011)

http://www.indexmundi.com/nigeria/oil_production.html (accessed April 16, 2011)

M. Adetunji Babatunde and M. Isa Shuaibu, 2009. The Demand for Residential Electricity in Nigeria: a Bound Testing Approach, African Econometric Society, 14th Annual Conference On Econometric Modelling For Africa 8 - 10 July 2009 Sheraton Hotel, Abuja, Nigeria www.africametrics.org/documents/./papers/Babatunde_Shuaibi.pdf (accessed April 16, 2011).

Chapter 11

Study of Potential Improvements of Tobacco Curing Process in View of Energy Aspects

K.T. Jayasinghe

Energy and Environmental Management Centre,
National Engineering Research and Development Centre of Sri Lanka,
Sri Lanka

E-mail: jayasinghe69@yahoo.com

ABSTRACT

Tobacco curing is the process undertaken in the curing barns to remove the moisture in fresh picking leaves before final processing. Required thermal energy to the process is obtained by combusting paddy husk in a furnace attached to the curing barn. Temperature inside the barn has to be maintained in different levels for the different time intervals in order to achieve the quality of the cured leaves. According to the present set up of curing barns and firing chambers, it requires around seven days to complete the process.

The paper covers the study of the present performance of tobacco curing barns and investigates the potential improvements in order to modify the existing tobacco barns in view of energy aspects. The study was conducted in tobacco barns, which are located in Matele district area of Sri Lanka. Temperature variations inside the barns were monitored throughout the process in order to find out the heat transfer patterns. While concerning the energy terms, the temperature variations inside the barn and furnace and the paddy husk consumption are the most important factors, and hence those factors were monitored continuously for a few batches in different barns. The heat distribution and ducting system were studied to find out the heat transfer efficiency from the furnace to the barn. The study outcomes and the improvements based on the outcomes are discussed in this paper. It is expected to reduce the curing period up to three days, half of the existing curing period, in order to achieve efficient curing system.

Keywords: *Tobacco, Curing, Barn, Furnace, Ducting, Heat transfer, Paddy husk, Automation.*

1. Introduction

Curing of tobacco leaves is done inside an oven called "Tobacco Barn". Most tobacco curing barns in Sri Lanka were built several decades ago and almost all of the barns were built by the owners and fueled by wood logs and barks. Those home made barns are used for bulk curing and the method of heat transfer is an indirect. Furnace attached to the barn is also home made and of ancient type. In 1997, Tobacco Company developed a grate type paddy husk furnace and the furnace was introduced to the tobacco barns in the country by replacing traditional system of fire wood combustion. Now a days almost all of the tobacco barns in the country are operated with paddy husk. It is estimated that the total annual paddy husk consumption for tobacco curing is in the range of 18,000 – 20,000 tons and about 1,100 barns are in operation.

Since there is no positive attention forwarded for the research and development activities related to the improvement of furnace or the barns efficiency, the farmers who are involved in this industry have faced several problems such as uneven heating, scarcity of paddy husk, removing high quantity of ash, longer curing period, and periodic replacement of ducts.

2. Present Curing System

After picking, the tobacco leaves have to be dried before final processing. The leaves are then sorted and strung together in bunches and hung over poles in drying barns.

2.1 Arrangement of Tobacco Barn

There is not any special material or technique used while constructing the barns and normally it looks like a single room building. The walls of the barn are constructed out of engineering bricks or cement blocks and roof is made out of Galvanized-corrugated sheets. The floor area inside the barn neither cemented nor perfectly made. In an average size barn, there are 18 poles (six layers and three poles in each layer) are laid at equal distances inside the barn in order to hang the tobacco bunches. The arrangement of tobacco bunches hanging poles are given in the Figure 11.1.

While the main charging door is placed at the front side of the barn, the paddy husk furnace is located at the opposite side of the barn. The other two side walls (lengthy sides) have four rectangular openings each of dimensions 4′ x 1′ where each wall has two openings close to ground level. The sliding doors are available in each opening to control the opening area in order to maintain the heat flow in the barn. In addition to these openings, a 6′ x 4′ opening is also available on the roof top (called REGIN) with an adjustable door to maintain the inside moisture content.

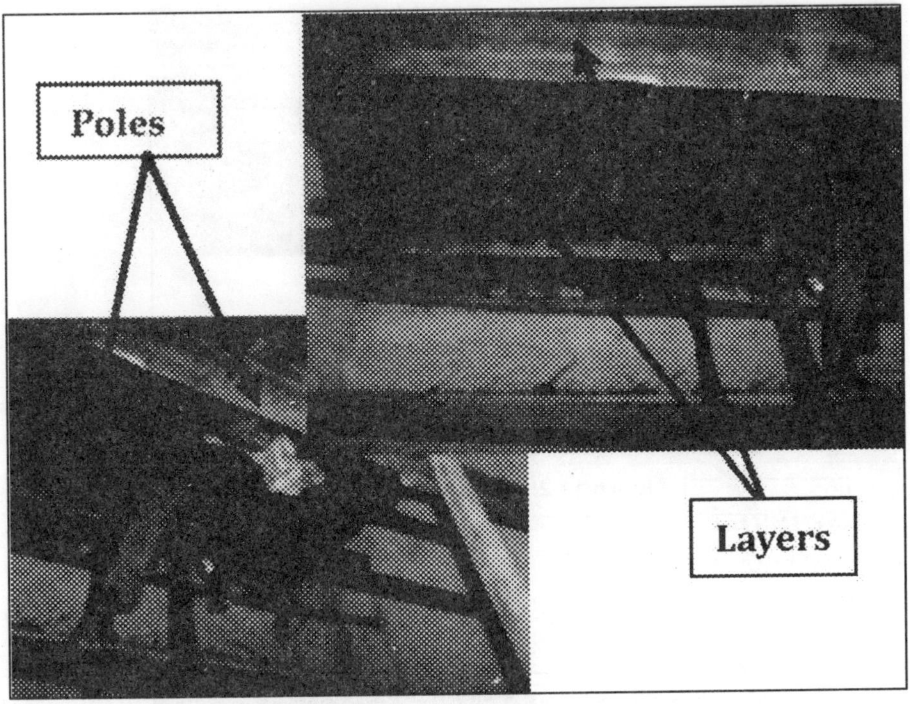

Figure 11.1: Arrangement of Tobacco Bunches–Hanging Poles

2.2 Furnace

The paddy husk burning furnace is attached to the outer wall of the barn, which is the rear side wall of the furnace. The grater consist of 12 fire clay plates, which are placed as a step ladder arrangement and the shape of this grate provides the ventilation for combustion and easy paddy husk flow to the bottom. The top of the grater is used to place the paddy husk charging container. Three adjustable plates are placed in between top of the grater and the bottom of the paddy husk container and these can be individually adjusted to feed the paddy husk for the combustion. The unburnt paddy husk and ash particles get collected to a tray placed at the bottom of the furnace and it is located somewhat below the ground level. Figure 11.2 shows arrangement of the furnace.

2.3 Heat Inlet to the Barn

The heat generated by combusting paddy husk is transferred to the barn via caste iron pipe of diameter 12 inches, which is connected from the furnace and the inner side of the barn. The arrangement of this cast iron pipe is shown in the Figure 11.3.

2.4 GI Ducting System (Heat Distributing System)

The end of the cast iron pipe of 12" diameter is connected to the galvanized iron ducting system to distribute the heat throughout the barn. Outlet of this ducting system is vertically extended as a chimney and carries away the unused heat from

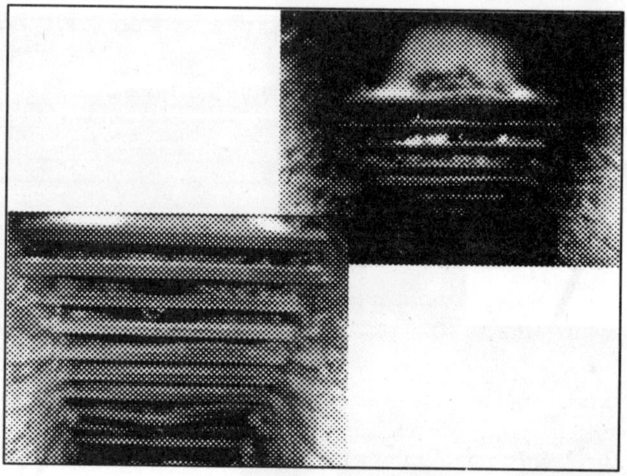

Figure 11.2: Arrangement of Furnace

Figure 11.3: Heat Inlet Ducting System

the barn. The heat carried by the ducting system is emitted to the barn as a mode of radiation and then this heat is distributed throughout the barn as a mode of natural convection.

This ducting system consists of several segments that can be disassembled easily to remove the ash collected in the ducts. The arrangement of the part of the ducting system is shown in Figure 11.4.

3. Data Analysis

Temperature variations at eight locations inside the barn were monitored throughout the process at five minutes interval. Also the furnace inlet, outlet, and the stack temperature were monitored in order to find out the furnace performance. The paddy husk charging time, quantity, and ash removing time were recorded in order to analyze the combustion performance.

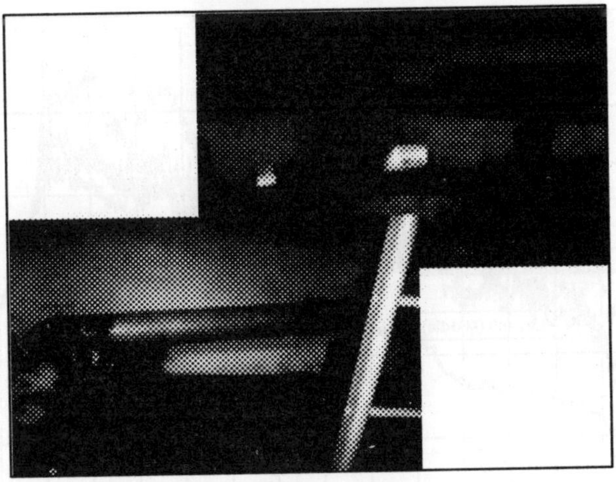

Figure 11.4: Furnace Inside Heat Transfer Ducting System

3.1 Dry Bulb Temperature Variations in the Barn

The arrangement of temperature measuring locations inside the barn is given below.

- ☆ First Layer (Bottom): Three Locations
- ☆ Third Layer: Single Location
- ☆ Fourth Layer: Two Locations
- ☆ Sixth Layer (Top): Two Locations

The analysis is based on the average temperatures in each layer and the variations are shown in Figure 11.5.

X axis of this graph shows the number time intervals each of five minutes during the curing process. According to the graph, this particular batch takes 1500 x 5 minutese (~ 5 days) for curing process.

Figure 11.5 shows that the heat transferring in each layer is very slow from bottom to top layers. For an example, while bottom layer taken one day to reach 50 °C temperature, third, fourth and top (6th) layers have taken 2.1, 2.3 and 3.5 days respectively to reach the same temperature level. This is mainly due to the tight packing of tobacco leaves in each layer and there is no effective heat flow path.

The graph also shows that initially (before adding heat) the temperature variations of all layers are uniform. This is mainly due to heat generated by barn itself with an effect of solar radiations. Moisture formation inside the barn has increased and flew upwards after adding heat into the barn as a result of which the temperature of the top layer dropped gradually at the end of the first day.

The graph also indicates that the temperature of top layers never reach the maximum temperature of adjacent bottom layer even at the end of the process. As a result the cured leaves are not uniform.

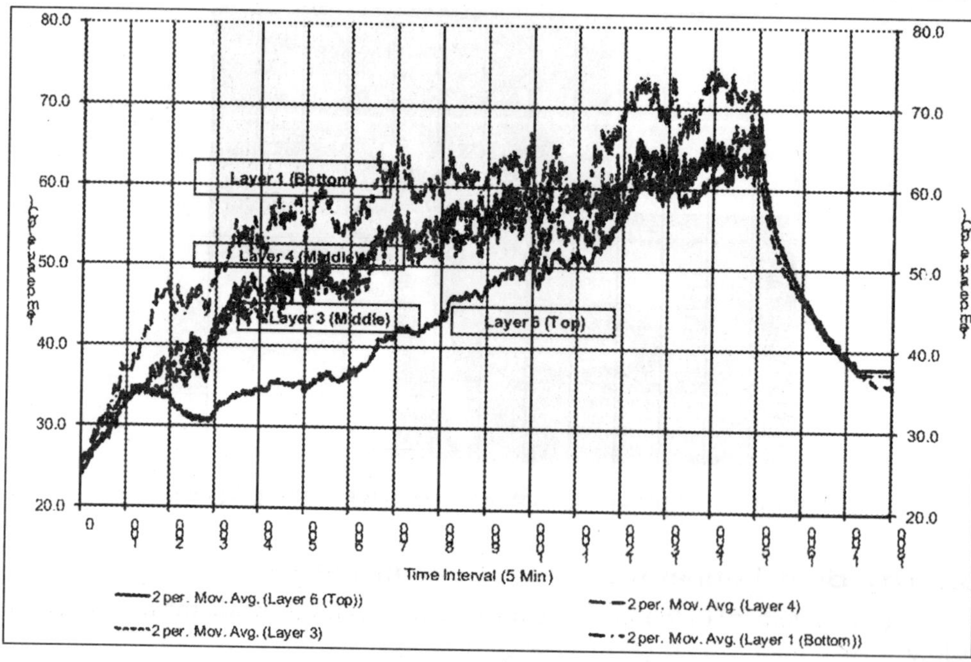

Figure 11.5: Average Temperature Variations in the Barn in Four Layers

The temperature of the layers suddenly varied within a few degrees and could not be maintained. This mainly depends on the paddy husk feeding rate to the furnace.

3.2 Heat Transfer to the Barn

Temperature variation in the furnace (Hearth) and the stack were monitored in the same time intervals as discussed in 3.1. The tabulated results are graphed and shown in Figure 11.6.

According to this graph, the average stack temperature was maintained around 200 °C - 250°C during the curing process and the inner temperature of the furnace gradually increased up to ~ 900 °C. This shows that the heat transfer efficiency from the furnace to the barn is around 75 per cent. {~ (900 °C – 200 °C)/(900 °C)} and therefore the heat loss through the flue gases is around 25 per cent. In general, the heat loss through flue gases of biomass combustion system with this type of furnace is around 20 – 30 per cent whereas there is no considerable amount of heat loss through the stack in the tested curing barns.

3.3 Paddy Husk Consumption

The paddy husk consumption rate is changed according to the process temperature maintained in the barn. However, the total paddy husk consumption to complete a curing process is around 3750 kg. The amount of ash formation is quantified periodically and the estimated total ash formation is around 1000 kg per batch. That is closely around 25 per cent of the total paddy husk consumption.

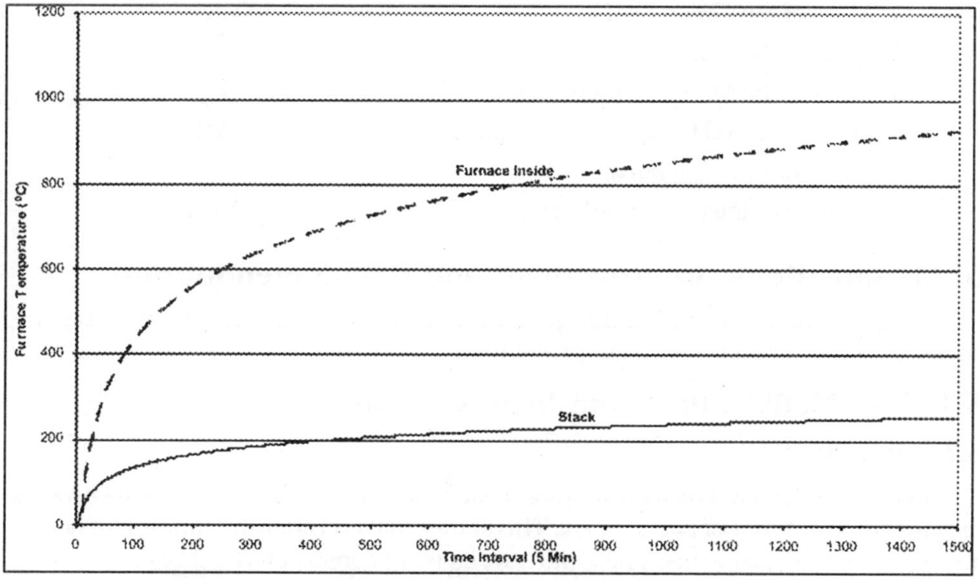

Figure 11.6: Average Temperature Variations in the Stack and Inner Side of the Furnace

4. Furnace Efficiency

In practice, the percentage of theoretical ash formation by combusting paddy husk with 10 per cent moisture content is around 20. The quantity of ash formation in this particular furnace under test is around 25 per cent. Therefore, by comparing the above figures, it is seen that there is not much waste of heat during the combustion of paddy husk and hence the combustion efficiency of the barn is at acceptable level.

- ☆ Calorific Value of Paddy Husk = 15.2 MJ/kg
- ☆ Moisture Content of Paddy Husk = 10 per cent
- ☆ Total Consumption of Paddy Husk = 3987 kg
- ☆ Total Heat Content = 60602 MJ
- ☆ Total Unburnt Husk and Ash Generated = 997 kg
- ☆ Theoretical Ash Content = 20 per cent
- ☆ Total Unburnt Paddy Husk = 199 kg
- ☆ Waste Heat (With the Ash) = 3030 MJ
- ☆ Energy Taken to the Barn = 57572 MJ
- ☆ Furnace Efficiency = 95 per cent

5. Overall Efficiency of the Barn

The overall efficiency of the barn is calculated based on the heat taken by the moisture to cured leaf. The values estimated by using the particular tested batch data are given below.

- ☆ Mass of the Green Leaf = 3,500 kg
- ☆ Mass of the Cured Leaf = 525 kg
- ☆ Mass of the Moisture Removed = 2,975 kg
- ☆ Heat Required to Remove Moisture = 7,810 MJ
- ☆ Heat Input to the Barn = 49,239 MJ
- ☆ Overall efficiency of the barn = 16 per cent

6. Modifications, Improvement and Recommendations

Since all the items and techniques that have been used in this industry are ancient, the identified potential improvements can be made.

6.1 Barn Modifications and Improvements

6.1.1 Barn Walls

Even though there is no considerable heat losses through the stack, curing process required high amount of paddy husk. This shows that considerable amount of heat is absorbed by the barn walls. These barn walls were constructed out of engineering bricks or cement blocks and those materials have high capability of heat absorption. Also propagated thermal cracks on the walls leak considerable amount of heat. This is mainly due to incomplete walls of the barns that are still to be given the finishing touch. Therefore, the heat loss through walls can be reduced by applying an insulating material layer inside the wall surfaces.

6.1.2 Barn Floor

There was not any barn with inner floor modifications in order to reflect the heat radiation which emits through the heat transfer ducting system. The irregular shape of the floor and the soft soil layer help to absorb more heat than the naturally made heat reflecting floor. Therefore, the heat loss due to absorption by floor can be reduced by applying a layer of heat reflecting material over the floor prior to which the floor should be properly leveled and cemented.

6.1.3 Air Ventilation Controlling

The barn has several openings (air vents) on walls and roof top in order to control the humidity level. Wider the vent opening more is the wastage of thermal energy. Therefore, it is necessary to control the vent opening according to the temperature inside the barn. Proper vent controlling system is required to control the heat flow. This system should have to measure the inner temperature of the barn.

6.1.4 Door Sealing

Doors of the tested barn were not properly sealed due to which the leakages of heat had taken place. Also, these doors were made up of GI sheets and were not insulated. It is necessary to make an air tight door and apply insulated material layer on the inner surface of the door.

6.1.5 Barn Loading System

As discussed under the sub titles 2.1 and 3.1, the barn is tightly packed while loading and there is not any space or path to flow hot air and to remove moisture. Due to these disturbances, curing product is uneven and curing process is slow as indicated by Figures 11.1 and 11.6. This can be easily overcome by maintaining spaces between tobacco leaves hanging poles while loading. This method can not be practically done in the present system and a simple modification has to be done to the leaves hanging cross bars as described below.

The wooden web pieces each of size 6" in length and 2" in height are placed on the top surface of cross bars at intervals of 2′ length. This web piece has to be fixed in "Zig Zag" ("Z") pattern each layer. Then the tobacco hanging poles can not be pulled outwards; while loading, due to these wooden pieces. Figure 11.7 shows the wooden web fixing details.

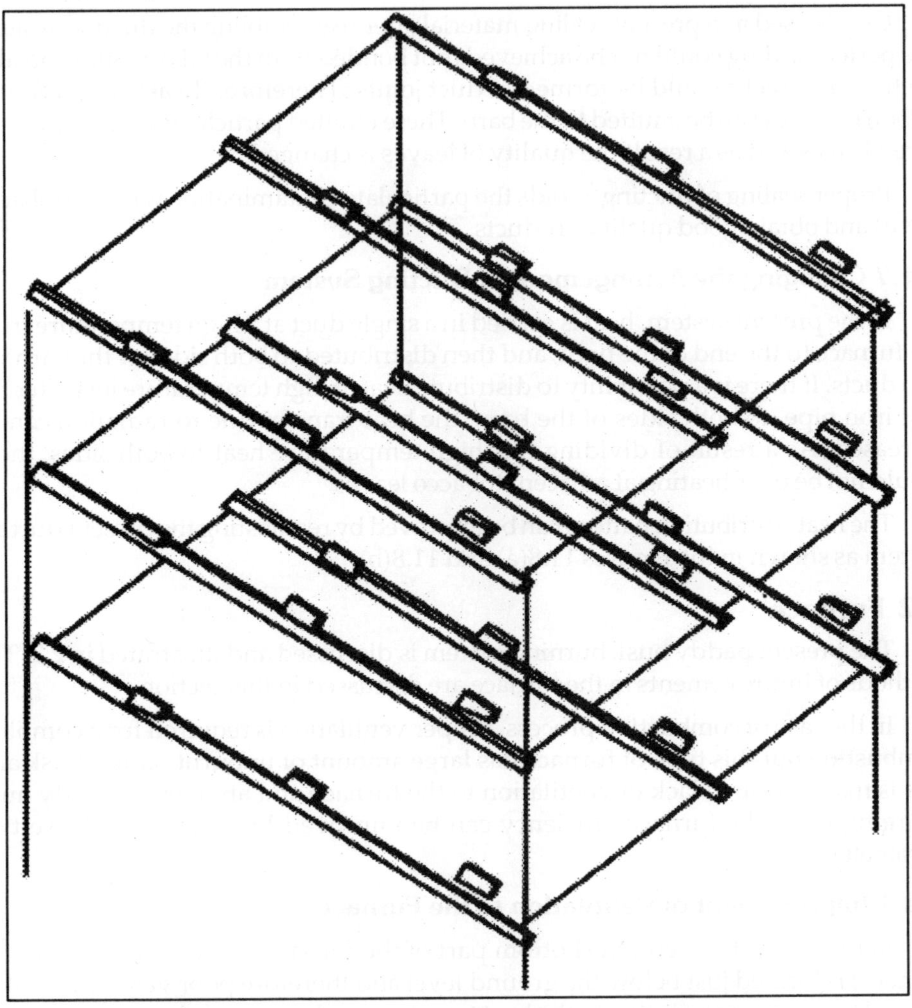

Figure 11.7: Wooden Web Fixing Details to Cross Bars

6.1.6 Heat Transfer Ducting System

Presently available ducting system is discussed in 4.1. Replacement of the ducting system in every two seasons requires an additional cost to the curing process. In the system, the ducting system has to be disassembled and reassembled after each curing process. The main purpose of this is to remove fly ash collected in the ducts. Therefore due to this repetition the ducting system would be damaged, mainly because the circular shape becomes irregular and difficult to reassemble the adjacent parts. If there is any method to remove fly ash collected in the duct, the ducting system can be permanently fixed.

The fly ash collected can be removed without dissembling the ducting system by introducing cleaning ports of 2" diameter at the bottom side of the ducting system. An additional air blower is required to apply pressure to raise air after each curing process. Permanent fixing of the ducting system can reduce the ducting cost.

Clay is used as a present sealing material after reassembling the ducting system. The perfect sealing could not be achieved (not bonded with the GI ducting) and also the thermal cracks could be formed at duct joints. Therefore, fly ash and unburnt carbon particles can be emitted to the barn. These emitted particles will react with the cured leaves and as a result the quality of leaves is changed.

Proper sealing of ducting avoids the particulate contamination with the tobacco leaves and obtain good quality products.

6.1.7 Changing the Arrangement of Ducting System

In the present system, heat is carried in a single duct at a high temperature from the furnace to the end of the barn, and then distributed to both sides of the barn via two ducts. If there is a possibility to distribute heat at high temperature just after the cast iron pipe, to both sides of the barn, the heat transfer due to radiation can be increased. As a result of dividing this high temperature heat to both sides, there would not be over heating at adjacent tobacco leaves.

The heat distribution pattern can be improved by readjusting the present ducting system as shown in the Figures 11.8(a) and 11.8(b).

6.2 Furnace

The present paddy husk burning system is discussed and illustrated in 2.2. The methods of improvements in the furnace are discussed in this section.

In the case of combustion process, proper ventilation is required for a complete combustion but this type of furnace has large amount of unburnt paddy husk and this is mainly due to lack of ventilation to the furnace and an uneven paddy husk charging rate. The furnace efficiency can be improved by controlling these two parameters.

6.2.1 Improvement of Ventilation to the Furnace

In the present system, the bottom part of the furnace (*i.e.* almost 1/3rd of the furnace) is located just below the ground level and therefore poor ventilation takes place. The main reason is due to the heat transferring duct is laid close to the ground

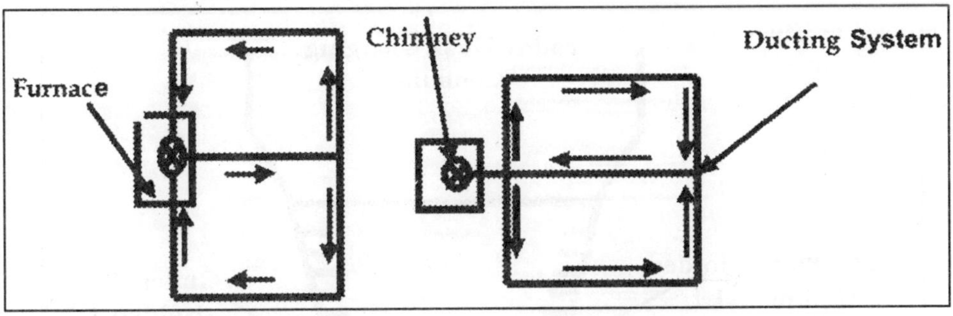

Figure 11.8a: Sketch of Present Heat Flow Arrangement

Figure 11.8b: Sketch of Proposed Heat Flow Arrangement

level and it has tapped 1/3rd height from the furnace bottom. Figures 11.9(a) and 11.9(b) illustrate the sketches of present and proposed furnace layouts.

This can be avoided by placing the cast iron pipe at a distance some what higher than the present level and by reconstructing the furnace not beyond the ground level.

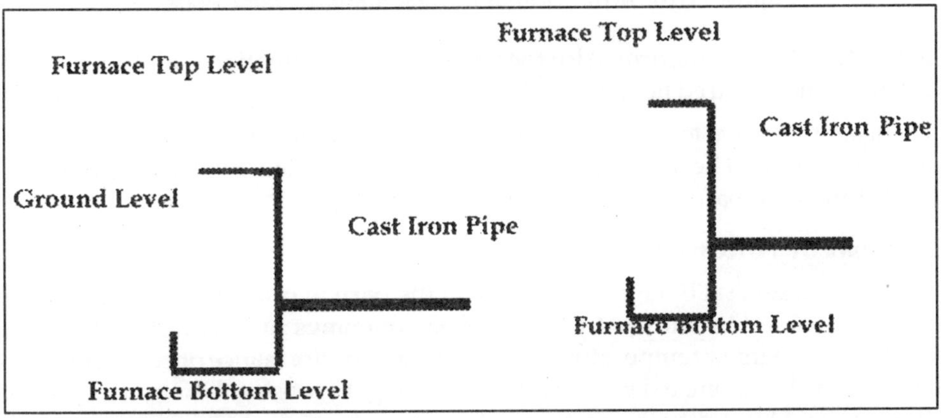

Figure 11.9a: Sketch of Present Furnace Arrangement

Figure 11.9b: Sketch of Proposed Furnace Arrangement

6.2.2 Re-adjusting the Grater Plates

In the present grater system, 12 to 14 grater plates are used. The vertical space between two plates is about 2" and those plates are horizontally offset about 1.5". The space is provided to supply required air for combustion but the spaces between the plates may not be the optimized one. Therefore, it is necessary to do several trial tests by adjusting the grater plates in both directions to find out the optimum distance. Figure 11.10 shows the arrangement of readjusting grater plates which can be used easily.

6.2.3 Paddy Husk Charging System

At present, paddy husk charging to the furnace is done manually. Therefore, the flame in the hearth can not be maintained uniform as a result of which the pattern of

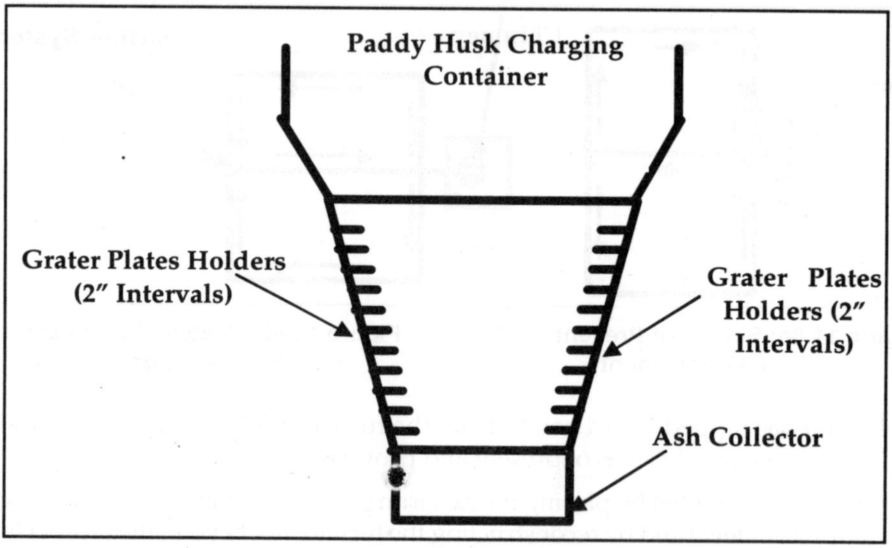

Figure 11.10: Arrangement of Readjusting Grater Plates

heat produced is not uniform. Also the barn operator's attention is always required to maintain the required heating level.

The uniform heat level can be maintained by introducing continues paddy husk charging system. The feeding system can be controlled by sensing the inner temperature of the barn.

6.3 System Automation

There are several openings available in the barn in order to remove moisture generated inside the barn. At present, those openings are controlled manually according to the inner temperature of barn and the performance of curing leaves. If the system can be automated to control those openings by sensing the inner temperature of the barn and humidity the escaping of useful energy via the openings would be minimized. However, such system should be easily understandable by even a common man because most of the barns are operated by uneducated persons.

6.4 Hot Water System

The hot water distribution system can be introduced instead of the hot air ducting system in order to obtain required thermal energy.

This system would consist of water heating container, hot water feed pump, radiators and blowers and necessary pipes for hot water distribution. Similar system is used in rice mills for paddy drying process.

The above mentioned items increases the capital cost. Even though the paddy husk can be used as a fuel to boil water; considerable electrical energy is required to operate the other components. Therefore the running cost can also be increased. However, the quality of the cured leaves can be improved with this system.

7. Conclusions

1. The uniform temperature variations inside the barn can be achieved after simple modifications to the barn and furnace such as internal wall insulating, ducts improving, leakage avoiding, etc. These improvements can be done by the barn owners without a high capital investment. The curing time can be reduced up to 3 to 4 days and this reduces paddy husk combustion.
2. The furnace modifications such as grater plates adjustment, hot air ducting rearrangement, etc. will help to achieve the optimal combustion conditions and initially those modifications have to be applied to the depot centers curing barns.
3. The methods such as system automation, hot water system, etc. need to be initiated by the large scale manufactures.
4. Any methods discussed in this paper will help to reduce the heat loss and therefore will cause to reduce curing time and paddy husk consumption as a result of which the curing cost will be reduced.

Acknowledgements

The author highly acknowledges Eng. D D Ananda Namal, Deputy General Manager, National Engineering Research and Development Centre for his contribution to collect the required data and guidance provided to evaluate the collected data. The author also appreciates Mr. Intage Kareem, former area manager in Galewela tobacco depot centre, for his full cooperation for the successful completion of this study. He also acknowledges the support staff in Galewela leaf collecting depots and other united tobacco processing plant officers for sharing their valuable experiences with me to succeed in this work.

References

Energy Audit Report in Energy and Environmental Management Centre, 2006. Study on Tobacco Barns at Ceylon Tobacco Depot, Galewela-E&EMC/MIS-208-718/ 2006.

Jaluria Yogesh, 1980. Natural Convection Heat and Mass Transfer, Pergamon, Oxford.

Osborn Peter D, 1985. Handbook of Energy Data and Calculations, Butterworth, London.

Chapter 12
The Energy Sector of Togo

Abdoulaye Robil Nassoma

Direction Générale de l'Energie,
BP: 4105 Lomé Togo
E-mail: naspaz@hotmail.com

ABSTRACT

The final energy consumption per capita of Togo in 2008 is 0.29 toe (ton oil equivalent). This value is very low compared to the African average which is 0.5 toe/per capita. Biomass energy represents 71 per cent of the total final consumption. Electricity and petroleum products account for 3 per cent and 26 per cent of the total final consumption. Thirty four percent of the total population lives in urban areas and consume 94 per cent of electricity while 66 per cent of the rural population consumes only 6 per cent of total electricity consumed. The total final consumption has increased by more than 27 per cent between 2000 and 2008 whereas the national population rose nearly by 21 per cent and the economic growth was recorded to be 34 per cent over the same period. The total consumption of biomass increased and petroleum products increased by 20 per cent and 45 per cent, respectively between 2000 and 2008. Similarly, the Electricity consumption has grown by 36 per cent during the same period. This shows the growth in overall consumption in Energy in Togo from the year 2000 to 2008.

Keywords: Togo, Biomass, Energy consumption, Energy policy, Energy system information.

1. Introduction to Republic of Togo

Located at the southern edge of West Africa, the Republic of Togo covers an area of 56,600 km^2. With a shape of stripe, Togo is limited at the west by Ghana, at the east by Benin, Burkina Faso at the north, and at the south by the Atlantic Ocean. It stretches nearly 400 miles north, 55 miles coastline on the Gulf of Guinea and 75 miles of maximum width from east to west. Figure 12.1 shows map of the Togo and its Flag.

Figure 12.1: Map of Togo and its Flag

According to estimates by the Department of Statistics, the country's total population reached 5,596,000 in 2008 and estimates showed that the population of Togo reached to 5,700,000 in 2010 where the annual population growth rate is of 1.9 per cent. Overall, the data show that the population is heavily rural with 66 per cent of the total population whereas the rest 34 per cent is urban population. French is the official language of Togo and its Gross Domestic Product (GDP) is US $ 900. Cotton, Cocoa, Coffee generate 40 per cent of income by export and Togo is the fourth largest producer of Phosphate in the world. In the year 2008 alone 645 GWh of electricity was consumed in Togo with a per capita consumption of 115 KWh. The total installed capacity for the generation of electrical power in Togo is of 200 MW out of which 65 MW comes from hydropower plants and 135 MW is generated by thermal power plants.

2. Energy Policy in Togo

Togo went through an energy crisis from 2006 to 2009. More than 70 per cent of the electricity needed was imported during that period. The imported electricity was mainly of hydropower origin. Due to climate change, rains became irregular, leading to the draining of rivers and a severe energy crisis.

The days of energy crisis seem to have been forgotten after ContourGlobal has come into existence and has been producing 100 MW of power. However, building new power plants is not the solution, diversifying energy source with an emphasis on renewable energy, and energy efficiency should be the new agenda for energy in Togo. Energy audit is the first strategy toward energy efficiency since it would reveal where energy is wasted.

Along this line the country initiated projects of energy efficiency such as:

- ☆ The control of public administration buildings in the first step of the process, which will later include every building of a certain size,
- ☆ The promotion of Compact Fluorescent Lamps (CFLs) in substitution of incandescent lamps with a program to distribute 400 000 CFLs, and
- ☆ Investments in the renovation of the grid lines to reduce transportation losses.

There is not any written document as energy policy of Togo but the energy efficiency program has launched some projects. It is expected that the officially documented energy policy of Togo will be in place very soon. In order to plan for the development of energy sector, a thorough knowledge of past, present and a good anticipation of the future are essential. Such an approach requires capacity building in particular to collect, validate, manage, and analyze a large set of data essential for decision making, which is in fact called the Energy Information System. Efforts have been made to publish such data every year since 2004.

3. Energy Sector in Togo

The energy sector in Togo relies on two main types of energy:

- ☆ Modern energy (electricity)
- ☆ Biomass energy (firewood, charcoal, vegetal waste, etc.).

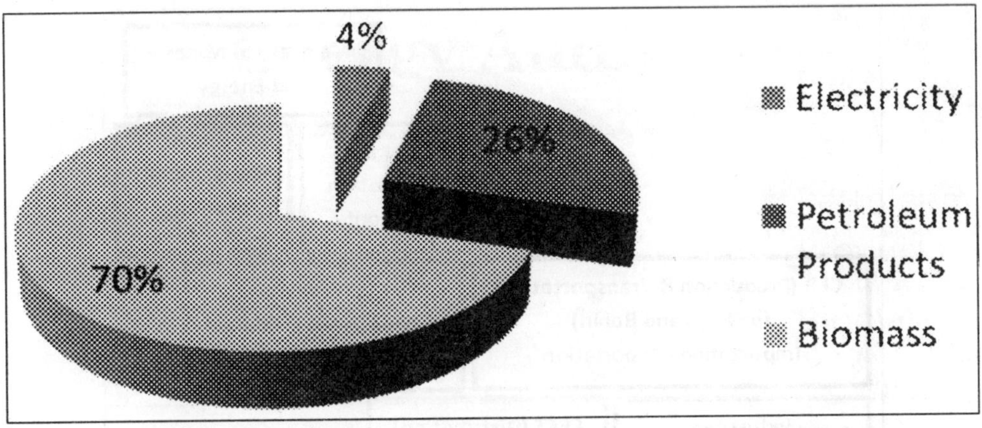

Figure 12.2: Breakdown of Total Energy Consumed in Togo in 2009

Figure 12.2 shows that the Biomass energy alone contributes 70 per cent of the final energy consumption against 26 per cent petroleum products and only 4 per cent electricity in 2009.

Only 22 per cent of households in the entire country and 4 per cent in rural areas of Togo have access to electricity. It used to import over 70 per cent of the electricity consumed from its neighboring countries Ghana, Ivory Coast and Nigeria. But since the arrival of a new independent producer ContourGlobal the import of electricity has dropped dramatically. ContourGlobal has installed capacity to generate 100 MW of power and has been generating since October 2010. Biomass energy, mainly obtained from firewood and vegetal charcoal, is the major energy source used to meet basic needs such as cooking, processing of agricultural products, traditional catering and preparation of local drinks, peanut oil, bakery products, pottery, etc.

4. Organizational Structure

The sector is ruled by the ministry of mines and energy, which is divided into three main departments:

1. The department of mines and geology,
2. The department of hydrocarbons and
3. The department of energy.

The department of energy is the execution office of the ministry in charge of energy matters. Its role is to:

- ☆ Elaborate the sector's policies,
- ☆ Define and implement investment programs for the development of the sector and
- ☆ Elaborate and propose regulation texts related to the sector.

The department is assisted in its works by the Authority of Regulation of the Energy Sector (ARSE), the distribution company (CEET), and the production and transports company (CEB) as shown in Figure 12.3.

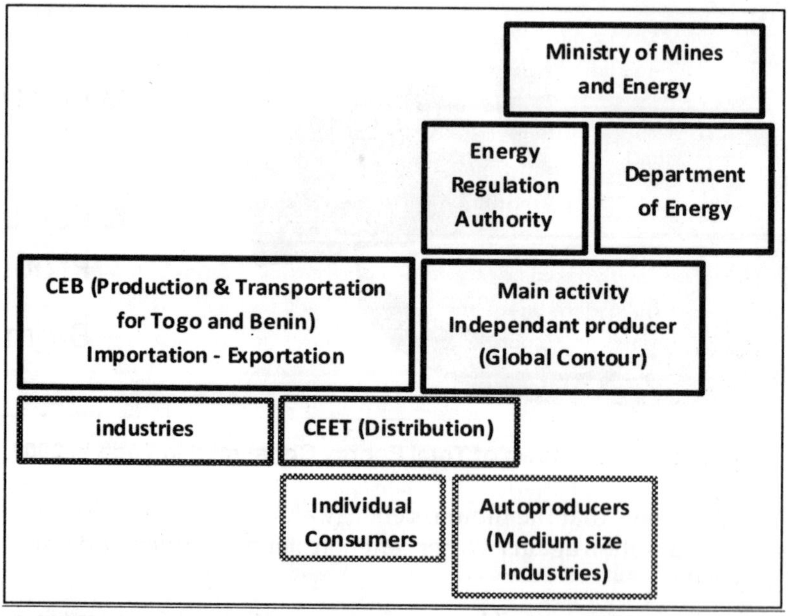

Figure 12.3: Organizational Structure of Energy Sector in Togo

5. Potential for Power Generation from Different Resources

5.1 Solar Power

The Solar Energy Laboratory of the University of Lomé and the Directorate of National Meteorology at different latitudes of the country estimated the average global solar energy radiated on a horizontal plane to be 4, 4 kwh/m^2/day for Atakpame and 4.5 kwh/m^2/day for Mango. These powers can exceed 700 Watt/m^2, especially in the dry season when the sky is clear with lower humidity of the air.

5.2 Hydroelectric Power

In Togo, several potential hydropower sites have been studied. The latest survey conducted identified 39 sites of which 23 are of individual potential greater than 2 MW. Most of this potential lies on Mono and Oti rivers. The potential power of all of these sites is 224 MW.

5.3 Wind Power

Togo has a very low potential to generate power from wind as the wind varies from 2 to 6m/s. However, a private company named DeltaWind has been conducting feasibility studies and planning to produce electricity.

5.4 Other Sources of Power

Togo used to import 70 per cent of the electricity consumed in the country from neighboring countries, Nigeria, Ghana and Ivory Coast. The import has dropped dramatically since Contour Global has started its production.

6. Power Production Scenario

The total power capacity installed in Togo is 200 MW out of which 65 MW from hydroelectricity and 135 MW from thermal plants. The production of biomass energy in 2008 was estimated to be 2130 ktoe out of which 2109 ktoe from fuel wood and 21 ktoe from agricultural residues. Similarly, the production of energy from charcoal was estimated to be 400 ktoe in 2008. The power produced locally in 2009 was 229 GWh in which 42 per cent comes from hydropower and 58 per cent from thermal plants.

The total production of hydropower in Togo was estimated to be 154 GWh in 2010. This production comes from hydro and thermal power plants of the Electricity Community of Benin (CEB, CompagnieEnergieElectrique du Togo (CEET), and self-producers. The rest of electricity supply comes from imports of the Volta River Authority (VRA) of Ghana and the Ivory Electricity Company (CIE) of Côte d'Ivoire. These imports are estimated to be 666 GWh and a total supply of 692 GWh in 2007. The Figure 12.4 shows the contribution made by different sectors to supply electricity in Togo.

ContourGlobal is the biggest producer of electricity in Togo and it has 100 MW capacity installed and is expected to produce up to 850 GWh per year. However, the exact figure is not available it has been in operation for less than one year. Others Independent producers are large industries such as SNPT (Société Nouvelle des Phosphates Togo), NIOTO (New Oilseed Industry of Togo), and some hotels. Despite of being connected to the main grid such large industries have their own power plant for power backup in case power shortage or problem with the main grid. Their production in 2008 was estimated to be 6 GWh.

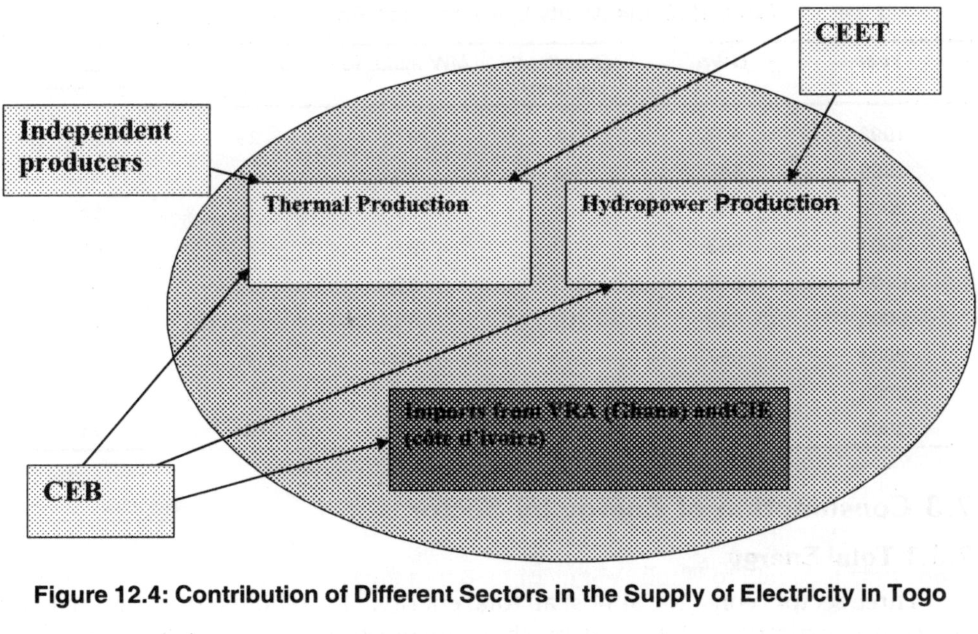

Figure 12.4: Contribution of Different Sectors in the Supply of Electricity in Togo

7. Energy Consumption Pattern Over the Years

7.1 Gas

Table 12.1 presents the domestic gas consumption pattern in Togo from the year 2000 to 2008. The trend shows that the gas consumption goes on increasing year after year.

Table 12.1: Domestic Gas Consumption in Togo

Year	*Consumption of Domestic Gas (t)*	*Equivalence of Charwood (t)*
2000	1130	3814
2001	1130	3814
2002	1130	3814
2003	1170	3949
2004	2260	7628
2005	2260	7628
2006	2900	9788
2007	2931	9877
2008	3628	12226
Total	**18539**	**52750**

7.2 Electricity

Table 12.2 presents in details the pattern of consumption of electricity in Togo from the year 1998 to 2006.

Table 12.2: Electricity Consumption Pattern in Togo

Year	*GWh*	*Growth in per cent*	*MW Installed*	*Growth in per cent*	*Load in per cent*
1998	433	-9	97	29	51
1999	545	26	90	-7	69
2000	542	-1	95	6	65
2001	553	2	97	2	65
2002	558	1	99	2	64
2003	623	12	98	1	73
2004	667	7	102	4	75
2005	684	3	106	4	74
2006	**688**	**1**	**110**	**4**	**71**

7.3 Consumption of Energy by Sector

7.3.1 Total Energy

Three sectors consume almost all total energy. Households come first with 67 per cent consumption followed by the transportation sector with 22 per cent

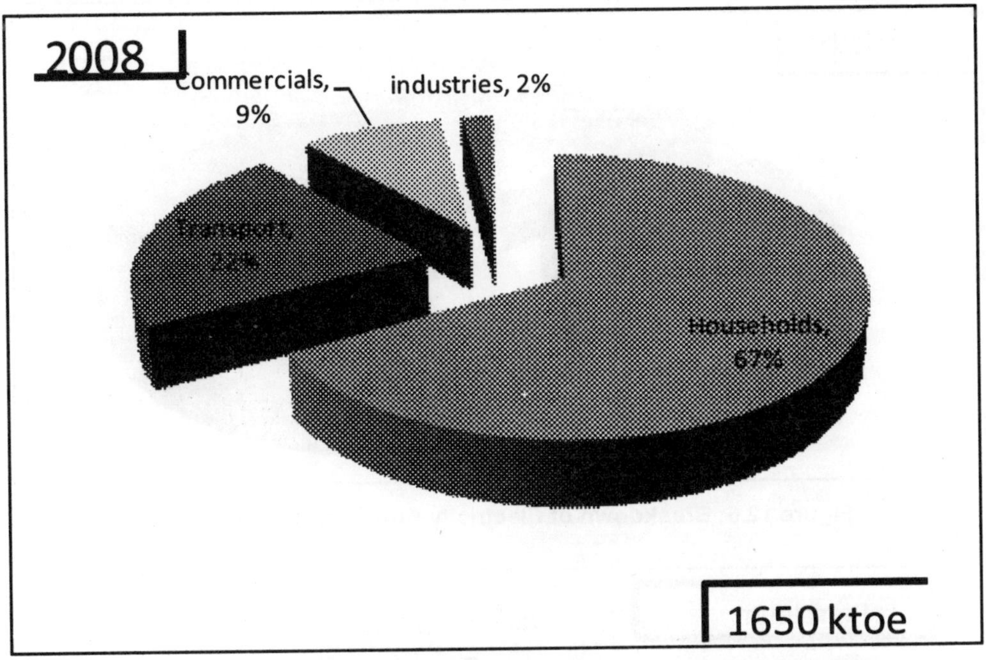

Figure 12.5: Distribution of Final Energy Consumption by Sector (*Sources*: DGE, CEET, CEB, STSL)

consumption, and finally, public and commercial services with 9 per cent consumption. The industrial sector consumes less than 2 per cent of the total consumption of energy in Togo as shown in Figure 12.5.

7.3.2 Electricity

The total electricity consumed in 2008 was 825 GWh. Households consumed 54 per cent of the electricity, followed by industry with 31 per cent and commercials services and administrations with 15 per cent as shown in Figure 12.6.

7.3.3 Petroleum Products

The consumption in transportation sector accounts for 83 per cent of final consumption of petroleum products, which is followed by 11 per cent consumption in household sector and 5 per cent in industrial sector. Non-energy uses such as lubricants and bitumen account for only 1 per cent, as shown in Figure 12.7.

7.4 Distribution of Total Energy Consumption in Different Sectors

7.4.1 Households

The energy consumption of households is characterized by a high prevalence of biomass (firewood, charcoal and vegetable waste), which represents almost 93 per cent of consumption. Consumption of other energy sources account for 7 per cent out of which 3.6 per cent comes from kerosene and 3 per cent from electricity. The

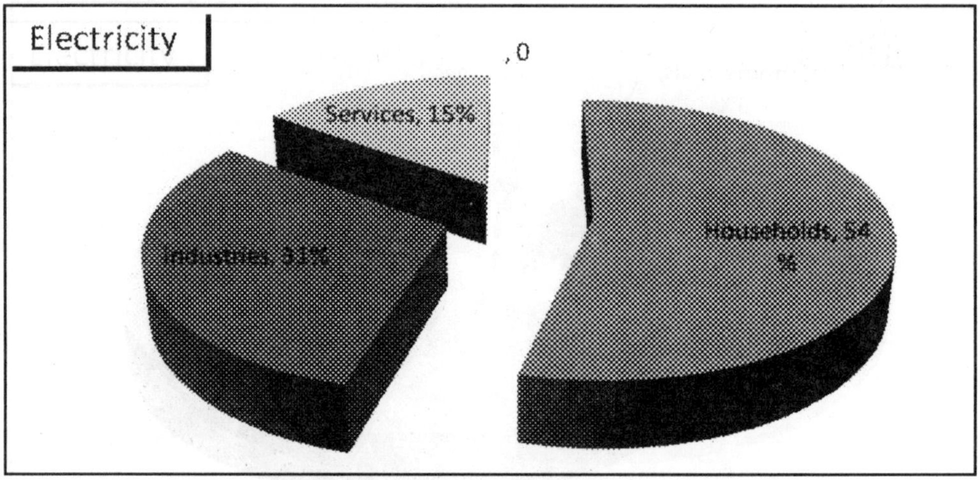

Figure 12.6: Breakdown of Electricity Consumption by Sector

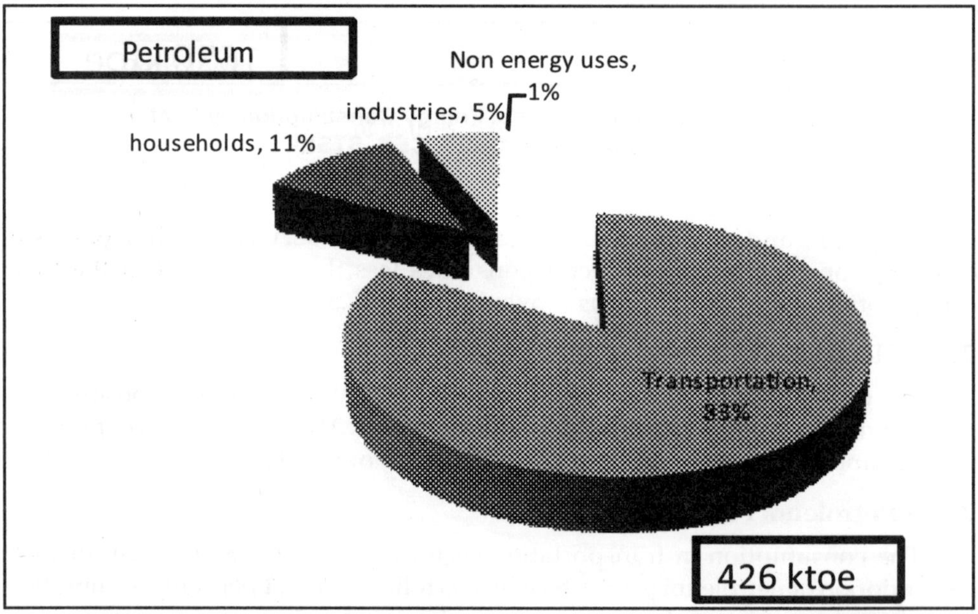

Figure 12.7: Distribution of Consumption of Petroleum Products by Sector

consumption of LPG (Liquefied Petroleum Gas) is only 0.4 per cent of household energy consumption as shown in Figure 12.8.

7.4.2 Industrial Sector

The energy consumption of the industry sector is divided between consumption of fuel (54 per cent) and electricity (40 per cent). This sector also consumes a bit of diesel (6 per cent of its consumption) as shown in Figure 12.9.

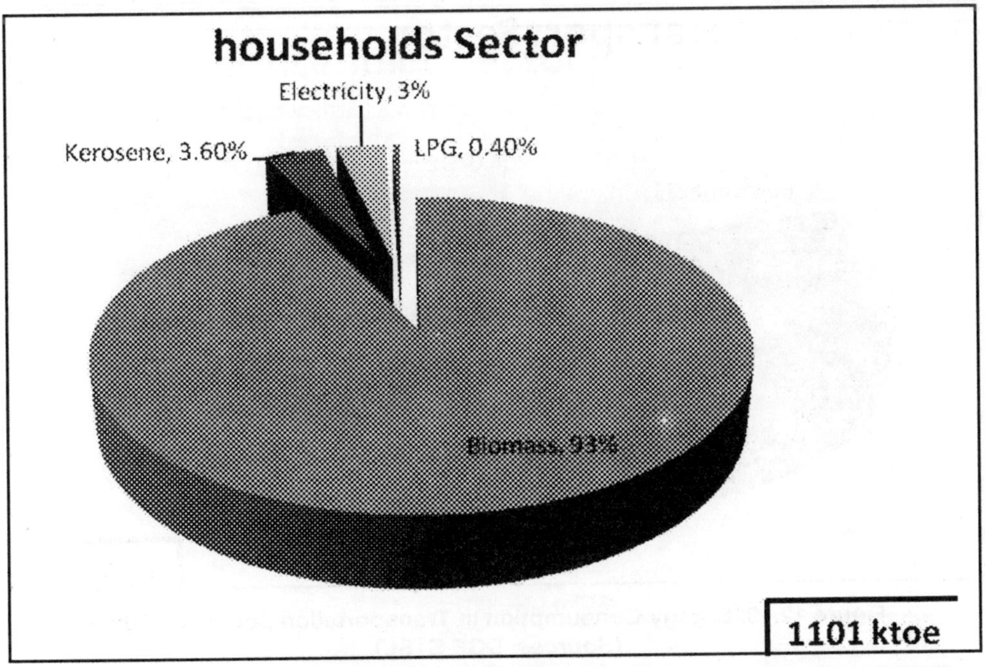

Figure 12.8: Distribution of Total Energy Consumption in Households in 2008 (*Sources*: DGE, CEET, CEB, STSL)

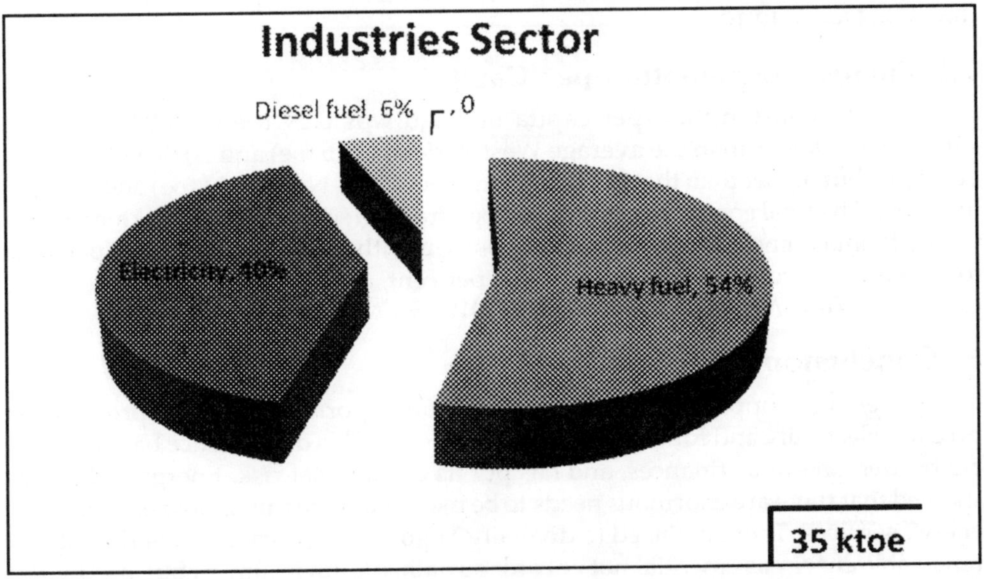

Figure 12.9: Energy Consumption in Industrial Sector in 2008 (*Sources*: DGE, TE)

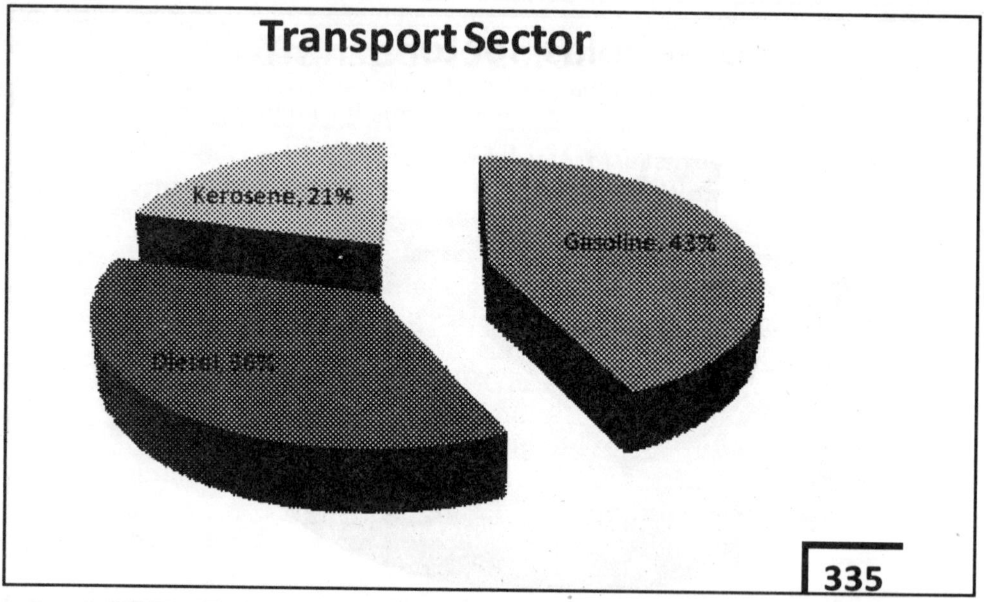

Figure 12.10: Energy Consumption in Transportation Sector in 2008 (*Sources*: DGE STSL)

7.4.3 Transport Sector

For the year, 2008 in transport sector, consumption of Gasoline, Diesel fuel, and Kerosene were 43 per cent and 36.21 per cent of total consumption, respectively, as shown in Figure 12.10.

7.5 Energy Consumption per Capita

Energy consumption per capita of Togo was 0.29 toe in 2008, which is substantially lower than the average West African (0.45 toe) and African (0.50 toe) per capita but higher than that of other countries such as Niger (0.14 toe) and Senegal (0.24 toe). The total energy consumed in Togo from all sources was 1650 ktoe in 2008 where Biomass energy is in dominant position with a contribution of 71 per cent followed by petroleum products with 26 per cent, and electricity with 3 per cent. *(Source: SIE Togo, Niger EIS, EIS Senegal, ECOWAS, ENERDATA).*

8. Conclusion

The energy supply in Togo is dependent on imported petroleum products to produce electricity and for transportation purposes. This dependence has created a big burden on public finances, and has put its economy at risk. Energy indicators showed that there are enormous needs to be met relating to public access to modern energy services. There is a need to diversify Togo's energy resources and establish renewable energy as essential not only for sustainable environment but also for the accessibility of it. Changes are required in the way we use energy. Taking into account these needs today, it requires efficient management of the energy that must be integrated into a comprehensive program of planning and development sector. Efforts are being made to supply the necessary energy needed for consumption, but energy still remains expensive. Fortunately, low cost strategies can be implemented for improving energy efficiency. Energy audits are part of these strategies but it needs necessary expertise to make the right choices.

Reference

Department of Energy, Energy Report of the Energy Information System, 2010.

Chapter 13

Energy Saving Potential in Public Buildings: A Case of Mulago Hospital at Kampala

Davis Bariho Bagamuhunda

Energy Systems Engineer,
Uganda Industrial Research Institute, Technology Development Centre,
P.O. Box 7086 Kampala, Uganda
E-mail: dbariho@uiri.org

ABSTRACT

In an era of increasing power supply deficit, high prices of petroleum products, concerns about CO_2 emissions, pollution and the uncertainty about the security of supply, adoption of energy conservation technologies and practices play significant roles by providing sustainable energy supply solutions for businesses and enterprises. Energy auditing presents one of the valuable methods for energy cost optimisation, pollution control and safety aspects and suggests the methods to improve the operating and maintenance practices. Beyond simply identifying the sources of energy use, energy auditing prioritises the energy uses according to the greatest to least cost effective opportunities for energy savings. In this paper a detailed energy audit for Mulago hospital is presented. A comprehensive study of the electrical system, lighting system, steam system and all other major energy consuming equipment was conducted. The audit involved carrying out various measurements and analyses of all major energy consuming sectors to realistically assess losses and potential for energy savings. The analysis included simple payback calculations where investments are required to be made to implement recommendations and to establish their economic viability. To evaluate the energy saving potential, prevailing tariff and recent year's energy consumption were considered. Many energy saving proposals are made. The savings that can be achieved with small investment are sizable. The calculated total payback period is 3.92 years and the overall identified annual energy saving potential is 2.4 million kWh of electricity. An electrical load reduction of 550 kW from hospital is anticipated, after implementation of energy conservation measures.

Keywords: *Energy auditing, Energy conservation, Energy consumption, Energy saving potential, Payback period, Electrical load reduction.*

1. Introduction

Uganda is one of the countries, facing major challenges of securing its energy supplies, while mitigating the effects of climate change, preserving the environment, and maintaining a competitive economy. Energy is a vital factor in Uganda's continued economic development, but today the country faces many energy-related challenges that threaten to undermine its development.

For a number of years, there has been significant public investment, primarily in an effort to expand the electricity supply. Nevertheless, the problems facing the energy sector still include an inadequate supply, a situation which is exacerbated by consumers' inefficient use of the energy that is available.

Mulago Hospital is the National referral Government hospital in Uganda. It provides specialist services in Surgery, Internal medicine, Pediatrics, Obstetrics and Gynecology, Oncology, Radiology with computerized tomography (CT scan), Intensive care,Renal dialysis, Dentistry, Oral surgery, Orthopedics including limb fitting, Ear,Nose and Throat (ENT), Dermatology, Genital/Urinary (urology) medicine, Neurosurgery, Cardiology and Cardiothoracic surgery, accident and emergency services among others. The hospital complex is divided into two parts; Lower Mulago and Upper Mulago and currently has a 2000 bed capacity for in-patients.

New equipment have been acquired and super training in intensive care, Open Heart surgery, Brain surgery, Urology, Infectious diseases to mention but a few, has been undertaken. Currently, the medical equipment and lighting systems consume a lot of energy from the power sources in the hospital. The ever increasing consumption of energy in the hospital is partly attributed to the electric boiler for steam generation and other electric appliances used in the hospital together with the poorly rated lighting system. This further is attributed to the absence of measures meant to identify the potential of recovering wasted energy from the flue gases.

The major objective of this study was to quantify the current energy being utilized at the hospital and to generate energy saving measures that can enable efficient energy utilization.

1.1 Energy Sources for Mulago Hospital

The major sources of energy are Electricity and High Speed Diesel (HSD). High Speed Diesel is used as fuel for the Incinerator and Diesel Generator (DG) sets. Electricity is supplied through two feeders; for which an 11KV high tension line from Wandegeya substation is purchased from UMEME. High speed diesel fired generator sets are used to supply the hospital's essential loads during power blackout. The Incinerator installed for burning medical wastes is also fired with high speed diesel.

1.2 Description of the Electrical System

Mulago hospital's main switch room receives electricity from Wandegeya substation through two 11KV high tension feeders. Until October- 2008, even though single feeder was utilized at a time, the total demand of the hospital was shared on two bills. During the audit period, the power meter installed for the stand-by feeder - 2 was removed by Umeme for maintenance and was replaced in the month of March. On Mulago hill (except lower and upper Mulago hospital premises) there are around 19 Umeme feeders supplying power to various support service facilities with individual power meters installed. There are two staff quarters and one doctor's village which receives power supply through the Umeme power meter. The simplified single line diagram of Mulago hospital electrical distribution network is shown in Figure 13.1.

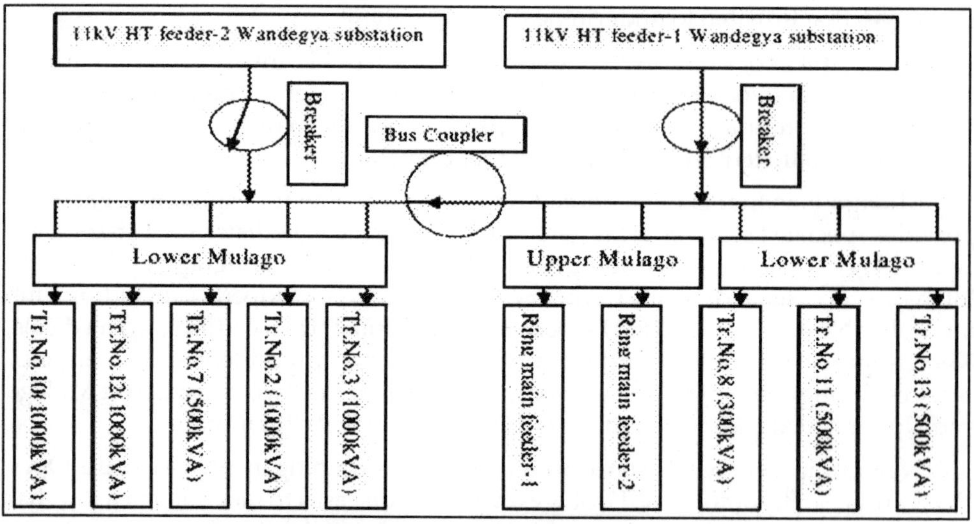

Figure 13.1: Single Line Diagram of Mulago Hospital

Electricity supplied by Umeme is billed under Industrial HV tariff and details of the tariff are shown in Table 13.1

Table 13.1: Tariff Structure for Industrial HV Category

Time of Use	*New Rate*
Peak	UGX 238.7 per kWh
Shoulder	UGX 192.7 per kWh
Off-Peak	UGX 135.3 per kWh
Average lanffper month	UGX 187.2 per kWh
Fixed Monthly Sen/ice Charge	UGX 30,000
Maximum Demand Charge up to 2,000 kVA	UGX 3,300 per kVA/month

Apart from the electricity consumption, on an average, 20 liters of high speed diesel is used per day in the incinerator for burning the medical waste.

1.3 Description of the Steam System

Mulago Hospital has two sets of electrical boilers of rated capacity 1250 kW and 150 kW, with a stand-by facility. The design steam pressure and temperature from the boilers is 150 psi and 180 °C. These boilers are operated between 6:00 am to 6:00 pm every day. Boilers are installed with condensate recovery system from the users. However this was not operational. Higher capacity boiler is operated manually and smaller capacity boiler operates in auto-mode. The auxiliary power consumption of electrical boiler is very small mainly in the fractional power feed pump. Steam driven pump is installed for condensate return collected from different users to boiler house. Specifications of the boilers in detail are shown in Table 13.2.

Table 2 Specifications of Boilers

Parameters	*Unit*	*Main Boiler*	*Sterilize Boiler*
Make	-	Electrode	HVE Thermo duct
Design Pressure	Psi	165	165
Working Pressure	Psi	150	150
Rating power	kW	1250	150
Test Pressure	Psi	250	225
Code	BS	18945500	5500.199
Year of Installation	-	17.09.90	17.09.90

Boiler steam is generated around 8 kg/cm^2(115 psi) and reduced across the pressure reducing valve to around 4 kg/cm^2 (57 psi). At the boiler house, steam distribution header has been installed and outlet steam lines from two boilers (running and Stand-by) are connected to main header. To different end users (Kitchen, laundry section), 150/100 mm size pipes are drawn from main distribution line. Boilers at sterilization section are connected to different end user (central pharmacy, central sterilize suppliers departments). All steam and condensate lines are insulated with glass wool and lagged with aluminium material. Apart from these two boilers at old Mulago, the orthopaedic department's small capacity sterilization boiler is installed and it operates as per requirement. It is currently operating for 3 hours per day.

During the study period two boilers were in operation at part load. Steam generation from main boiler was greater than 1ton per hour; the same quantity was measured from the feed water line to the boiler and loading time. The generated steam pressure was 8.0 kg/cm^2 before cut-off.

The boiler feed pump is switched ON/OFF manually based on gauge level. The boiler is continuously in ON position between 6:00 am and 6:00 pm. The boiler at sterilization section operates in auto-mode, where feed water pump and electrical heaters switched ON/OFF based on user end load. The steam generating pressure is around 6.0 kg/cm^2. The estimated steam generation quantity from feed water end is around 100 kg per hour, which is much lower compared to design value. The return condensate from the process area is drained continuously and connected steam driven pump is not operational. The boiler continuously gets fresh feed water from the treatment plant, a practice that not only leads to high electricity consumption but also increases the chemical requirement of the treatment plant.

The hospital has installed separate pump house near the entrance of hospital main gate. The pump house is maintained by National Water Sewerage Corporation (NWSC). The hospital has also installed intake storage tank and with the help of the pump, water is transferred to hospital overhead tank. The intake to the tanks is from two sources; Mulago as well as Nakasero/Gun hill NWSC city distribution tanks. From the overhead tank, water is supplied to various departments, building blocks and utilities by gravity. For the pump house an independent energy meter is installed. The pump house consists of three pumps of rated capacity 75 kW each. During the normal operation, one pump is operated for 16 hours per day and the over head tank level control is monitored manually.

1.4 Description of the Lighting System

Lower Mulago, Upper Mulago, dental school and hostel, guest house and doctors mess were found to be lit with different lamps and luminaries for different applications. The different lamps used were General Lighting Source (GLS: Incandescent lamps), Fluorescent tube lights (FTL), Compact fluorescent lamps (Energy savers: CFL), High pressure mercury vapor lamps (HPMV), High pressure sodium vapour lamps (HPSV), and Operation lights (50 W halogen lamp). The new Mulago connected lighting load was 145 kW. During the study, operating lighting load was measured to be 113.12 kW. The operating lighting load was 76 per cent of the total connected load and remaining 24 per cent of the lights were in failure condition. The total connected load of old Mulago complex was 106 kW. During the study, the operating/working lighting load was 87.1 kW. The operating lighting load was 79 per cent and remaining 21 per cent of the lights were in failure condition.

The total connected load of the dental school and hostel premises was 13.2 kW. The measured working load was 10.16 kW. The operating lighting load was calculated to be 77 per cent and remaining 23 per cent of the lights were in failure condition. In the guest house, doctors mess, tutors college which were separately metered, 60W incandescent bulbs were used widely. All the fluorescent lamps had conventional copper/aluminium chokes. The control of all the lighting circuits was manual through designated individual/group switches. Energy savers were installed in few sections as an energy conservation measure.

All the fluorescent lamps (18 W, 36 W, 58 W, 40 W, and 65 W) were equipped with low loss copper chokes. Approximately 5 W-7 W power losses take place in each copper choke. The rated power factor of each copper choke was estimated to be 0.5 lag. Majority of the places like ward areas in new Mulago hospital, corridors were equipped with 58 W, 36 W fluorescent lamps. Incandescent lamps of 60, 75 and 100 watts were provided in the causality building, dental hostel, radio-therapy, private outpatient wing, and doctor's mess, which are energy inefficient.

1.5 Other Equipments

Mulago hospital has installed sophisticated medical equipment and supporting equipment at various wards and operation theatre. The break-up of installed equipment inventory is given below in Table 13.3.

Table 13.3: List of Connected Equipment

Location	*Nos.*
Computers	188
Printers	56
Hospital equipments	316
Others (Fridges, laundry equipment, kettle, Xerox M/c)	294

Operation theatres were facilitated with air- conditioning. The details of air conditioning (A/C) units in old and new Mulago hospital are given in Table 13.4.

Table 13.4: List of Connected Air Conditioning Units

Location	*Nos.*	*Cooling Capacity, TR*
New Mulago area	30	1.5
New Mulago area	4	1
Old Mulago area	30	1.5

The operating hours of the A/C was approximately 8-12 hours (on/off). The air -conditioning system at Intensive Care Unit (ICU) was found to be in continuous use. The mortuary was, located in the General ward area, with in-built cold storage facility and temperature of freezer/cold room was maintained between 5-10 °C. The system could accommodate 20-25 bodies. For cold storage purpose at different departments, 50 freezers were installed; these units are in operation as per the set temperature. The power consumption of these freezers was found to be 400- -600 W during ON position. The hospital has canteen facility for patients who are residing in the hospital. Every day over 1500 patients cook from the kitchen.

2. Materials and Methods

The energy audit covered an in-depth study of the electrical, lighting system, steam system, and all other major energy consuming equipment. The audit involved various measurements and analysis of all major energy consuming sections to realistically assess losses and identify potential for energy savings. The analysis included simple payback calculations where investments are required to implement recommendations and to establish their economic viability.

2.1 Instruments Used

Modern specialized measuring instruments were used to support the energy audit investigations and analysis. These included: a power analyzer (Keycard ALM-32&ALM10), Ultrasonic water flow meter, Thermo hunter,Anemometer and Lux Meter.

During the audit, the researcher conducted interviews with hospital engineering team. The detailed energy audit was carried out during March- and May 2010. Measurements and recordings of energy consumption were carried out based on the recorded information. Study visits were made to the hospital on a weekly basis to obtain information regarding the extent of the problem at hand. Energy consumption data for the last 4 years was collected for analysis from the hospital and Umeme.

2.2 Electrical Measurements

Electrical power measurements were carried out on Wandegeya feeder- 1 of the main switch room on the high tension side. Similarly, power measurements were carried out on the high tension side of transformers 2, 10 &12 of lower Mulago and ring main feeders 1 and 2 of upper Mulago. Power measurements were also carried out at the Power/Motor control Cubicle (PCC/MCC) levels of the lower and upper Mulago areas. The different electrical parameters like voltage (V), Current (A), power (kW, kVA, and kVAr), power factor (PF), frequency (Hz) and total harmonic distortion (THD) levels of both voltage and current were recorded at different time intervals.

3. Results and Discussion

3.1 Energy Consumption at Mulago Hospital

The energy consumption patterns at different systems of Mulago Hospital are presented in this section.

3.1.1 Energy Consumption Details of Main Switch Room Feeders

There are totally 21 metering points for which the hospital pays to Umeme. Out of the 21 meters, two meters are for the main switch room feeders and other 19 meters are for support services and staff quarters. The monthly demand and energy consumption profile of feeder-1 and 2 are provided in Figure 13.2.

The monthly bills paid for consumption of electricity according to Umeme tariff structure for the years 2007 and 2008 are calculated and summarised in Table 13.5.

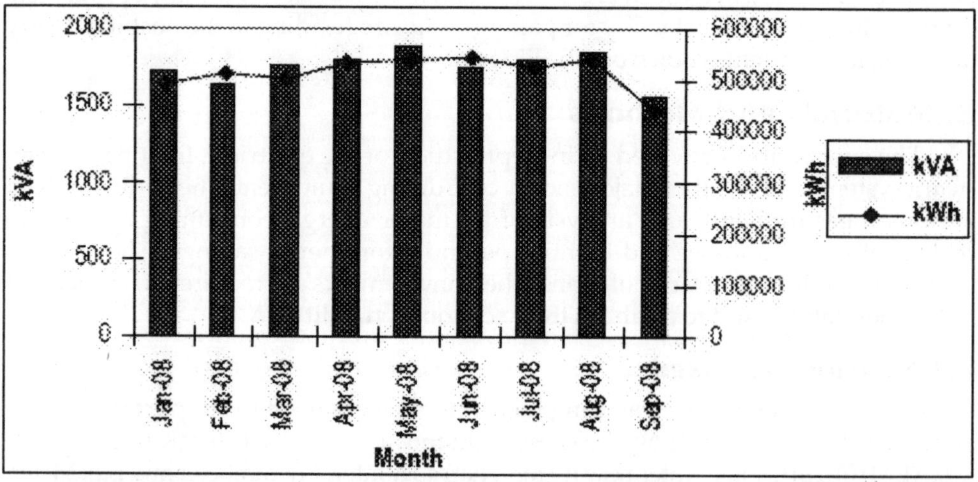

Figure 13.2: Monthly Demand and Electricity Consumption of Feeder 1 and 2

Table 13.5: Cost of Electricity Consumption for the Years 2007 and 2008

Description	*Cost*	*2007 (Jan to Dec)*	*2008 (Jan to Sep)*
Feeder-1 (UMEME Meter No. E245103)	Million UGX	1199.6	928.9
Feeder-2 (UMEME Meter No. E245102)	Million UGX	221.6	165.1
Total	Million UGX	1421.2	1094.0

In total, Mulago hospital (switch room feeders, support services and staff quarters) consume around 6.98 Million kWh per annum. It pays a bill of around 1,823 Million UGX annually. The captured load trend of the main switch room HT feeder-1 is provided in Figure 13.3.

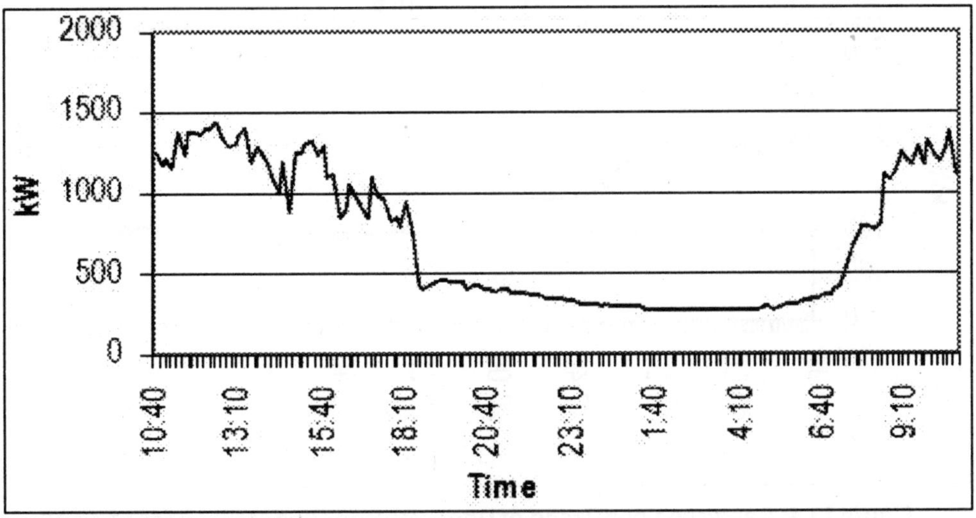

Figure 13.3: Captured Load Trend of Main Switch Room HT Feeder-1

Figure 13.3 shows that the load of the hospital drops below 500 kW after 18.00 hours till 6.00 hours and this is due to no operation of 1250 kW (rated) electrode boiler. During peak tariff time, maximum load of 948 kW was observed.This is due to extended operation of main electrode boiler for 20 to 30 minutes after 18.00 hours. From the measurements and data logging of the main Switch room HT feeder- 1 the total power consumption of the hospital per day was observed to be ~ 16765 kWh and these figures were found to be comparable with the reference of Umeme energy readings.

The 11 kVA transformer operated at maximum efficiency at a percentage loading of around 45 per cent. The transformation losses occurring in the individual transformers 2, 10 and 12 is given in Table 13.6.

The captured load trend of upper Mulago ring main feeder -1 and 2 is shown in Figure 13. 4.

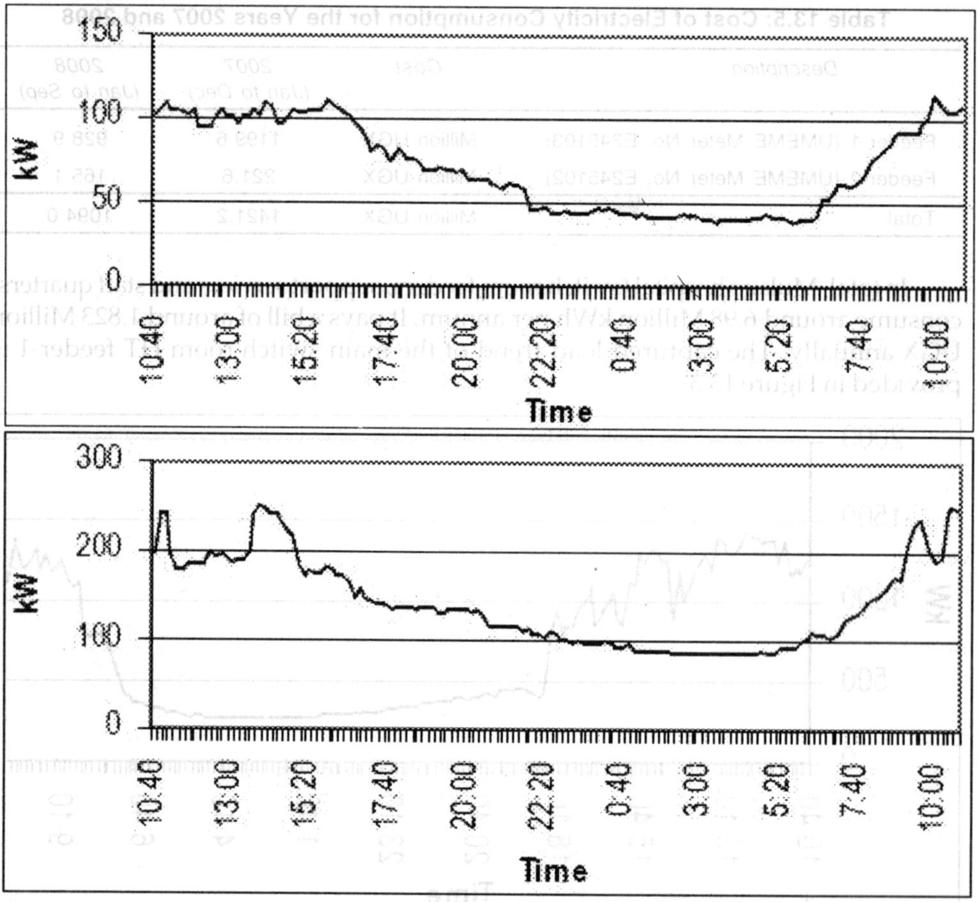

Figure 13.4: Captured Load Trend of Upper Mulago Ring Main Feeder 1 and 2

Table 13.6: Transformer Loading and Losses

Transformer No.	*Rating kVA*	*Measured Average*	*Per cent Loading kVA*	*Annual Losses kWh*
Lower Mulago				
Transformer 2	1000	500	50	27120
Transformer 10	1000	168	16.8	19894
Tmnstoirnei 12	1000	163	16.3	19754

It can be observed from Figure 13.4 that there is a peak load variation of 45 kW from the normal load for around three hours during day time and this is due to the operation of sterilization electrode boiler. The load details of on major section feeders (PCC/MCC level) are given in Table 13.7.

Table 13.7: Section-wise Load Distribution

Day Time Average Load-1055 hW

Load Break-up

Load	kW	Per cent on Total Load
Lower Mulago		
Electrode boiler	500	47.3
Sterilization boiler	90	8.5
Laundry and kitchen	18	1.7
ICU's & mortuary	26	2.4
Lifts	10	0.9
Lighting (new Mulago all areas)	113	10.7
Upper Mulago		
Lighting fold Mulago areas except Baylor college, radiotherapy, Taso, Mjab, cancer ward, dental school and hostel)	40	3.8
Sterilization boiler old Muiago	47	4.4
Baylor college	52	49
Radiotherapy	5	0.5
Taso (NGO)	15	1.4
Mjab (NGO)	9	0.9
Dental schoof	28	2.6
Cancer lab and ward	55	5.2
Other hosptial areas and equipments	50	4.7
Total	**1057**	**100.0**

3.1.2 Energy Consumption Pattern in the Steam System

The daily power consumption of boiler including small auxiliary equipment is given in the Table 13.8.

Table 13.8: Energy Consumption of Boilers

Parameters	Avg. Load, kW
Main Boiler	490
Sterilization Boiler	91
Sterilization Boiler - orthopaedic department	45
Daily Consumption of boilers, kWh	*6200*

The main boiler load is almost constant between 490 to 530 kWh on hourly basis. During the evening hours before switching- off boiler, electrical load is coming down. Daily load curve of main boiler is given in Figure 13.5.

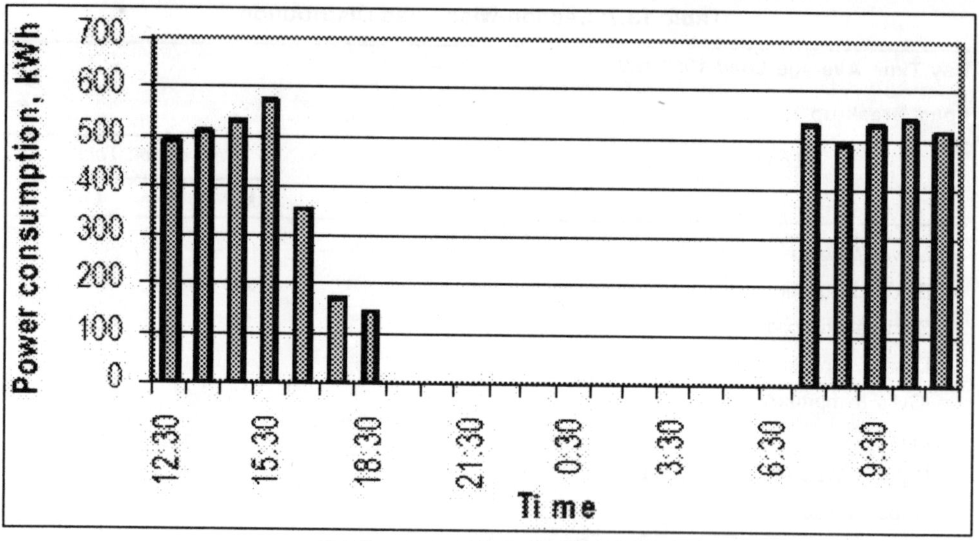

Figure 13.5: Daily Load Curve of Main Boiler

Power consumption of the boiler connected to the sterilization section was calculated to be 91 kW. The operating time of boiler was 60—70 per cent of working time. The estimated daily power consumption was estimated to be 700 kWh. The power consumption of the sterilization boiler at the orthopedic department of Old Mulago was 135 kWh per day for three hours of operation. The daily average power consumption of two running boilers was measured as 6200 kWh. The boiler and steam system consumed about 38 per cent of the total electrical energy (16,500 kWh per day) of the main hospital consumption (Switch room feeder). The observed boiler side parameters (temperatures, pressures etc) are given in Table 13.9.

Table 13.9: Boiler Operating Parameters

Parameters	*Unit*	*Main Boiler*	*Sterilization Boiler*
Steam generating pressure	kg/cm^2	8.0	6,0
Steam temperature	°C	175	154
Estimated Steam quantity	TPH	< 1 -0	0.5
Surface Temp	°C	38	42

Boiler Efficiency

As electrical boiler works like an instant heater, the total electrical energy converts into heat energy to raise the temperature and pressure of feed water during the heating process. During the same period, radiation and convention losses take place to maintain boiler conditions from surface. The boiler surface temperature was 10 °C well above the ambient temperature. Surface heat losses were calculated to be ~ 1 per cent of total input. Apart from this, blow down losses take place in small quantity. Considering these losses, efficiency level of the boiler was calculated to be 98 per cent.

Steam Distribution

Insulation in all steam lines was peeled off and the status of insulation was found to be poor, where bare steam pipe line temperatures were above 110 °C. Continuous drop in steam lines up to user end from generation was observed (150–105 °C). Apart from main boiler steam header at boiler room, remaining steam lines and near user steam lines were bare.

The outside steam lines from sterilization boiler were un-insulated. Condensate return lines were also not insulated. The surface temperatures of insulated lines should be within permissible limits above 5–10 °C of the ambient temperature. Most of the traps were found to have malfunctioned or damaged.

Table 13.10: Quantity of Steam Utilization in Main boiler

Equipment	*Nos.*	*Quantity, kg/h*
Main kitchen		
Sleam Cooker - General	6	200–500
Steam Cooker - General	2 (small)	150–300
Steam Cooker - Private	2	200–500
Laundry		
Pressing m/c	1	100
Rolling Press	1	Not in use
Washing m/c	8	50–75
Drying m/c	7	50–75

The quantity of steam generation at sterilization section boiler was very small and inside boiler room itself major leakages were observed. The utilization of equipment of this low pressure steam operating hours was less.

Pumps: The measured power consumption of pumps is given below in Table 13.11.

Table 13.11: Details of Power Consumption of the Pumps

Pump	*Power Cons. (kW)*
Pump No. 1	69.7
Pump No. 2	69.4

One pump was in continuous operation and switched off to avoid the overflow from overhead tank. For the current hospital consumption rate, one pump operated for 16 hours in a day to meet the water demand. The measured water and energy consumption towards water pumping of hospital was 1,811 m^3 and 1,131 kWh per day, where the pumps operated for 16 out of 24 hours a day. Installed online flow meter and energy meter measurements were in line with audit measurements. The evaluated operating efficiency of major pumps is given below in Table 13.12.

Table 13.12: Efficiency Evaluation of Pumps

Parameters	*Unit*	*Pump No. 1*	*Pump No. 2*
Flow rate	m^3/h	116.5	116.5
Head	m	85	85
Power	kW	69.7	69.4
Pump efficiency	Per cent	42.0	42.2

Considering the present level of motor efficiency as 92 per cent.

It is observed that pumps operating efficiency is less. The expected operating efficiency of the pumps for present operating head and flow range is 70 per cent. This reveals that the present pumps' efficiency drop is >20 per cent.

3.1.3 Energy Consumption Pattern in Lighting System

The operating lighting load (210.4 kW) of the hospital wards/departments/blocks was evaluated to be 79 per cent of the total connected load (~264.2 kW). 21 per cent of the connected lights were faulty and not in working condition. Table 13.13 shows the operating lighting load of the different blocks, ward in old Mulago and New Mulago hospital premises.

Table 13.13: Operating Load of Different Blocks, Departments in the Hospital

Sl.No.	*Department*	*Operation Load (kW)*	*Failure Lamps (kW)*
	New Muiago Hospital		
1.	Casualty building	10.8	6.7
2.	Private out patlent wing	3.3	0.71
3.	Block-A	12.02	2.35
4.	Block-B	29.6	2.7
5.	Block-C	16.0	3.1
6.	Admin block	29.4	6.3
7.	General ward	9.2	9.0
8.	Street lighting	2.8	3.5
	Old Mulago Hospital		
1.	Clinical areas	57.4	15.3
2.	Radiotherapy	2.33	0.58
3.	Baylaw college	27.4	0.79
	Dental school and hostel		
1.	Dental school and hostel	10.16	3.04
	Total Connected Load, kW	**210.4**	**54.07**

It was observed that single phase voltage of hospital incoming panel is varying between 227 V ~ 247 V in lighting circuit and other equipment. The low loss copper chokes were rated as 220–240 V. Most of the fluorescent lamp fittings had no reflectors. Most of the timer controls were faulty and the lights were glowing round the clock. In a few places in old Mulago hospitals, the timer controls were working as per the settings. However, many of the light fittings in corridors, street lighting in parking area were found to be "ON" during the day time due to failure of the timer control.

The light levels at various rooms in wards/blocks were measured using Lux meter. The lux level was found to be very less in areas like HT main panel room and outside the dental college where it is suggested to provide some light.

3.4 Energy Consumption Pattern in other Equipment

After measuring the power consumption in individual equipment by sampling, other major electrical load of equipment was estimated as given in Table 13.14.

Table 13.14: Estimated Power Consumption of Major Equipment

Equipment	Operating Hours (On Position)	Power Consumption (kW)
Computer accessories	8–10	14
A/C split units	8–12	67.5
Fans	8–10	2
Sterilizes/Boilers	4–5	80
Freezers	10–12	25
Mortuary	10–15	15

The major electrical power consumption was measured in cancer institute totaling to 40 kW, which is mainly from freezers and medical equipment. Power consumption by Dental chairs, while in use, was measured to be 1 kW per chair. In the sterilization section small portable compressor of 3.7 kW was installed but operating hours was very less. Near oxygen hospital a small compressor was in use, as per the requirement.

4. Conclusions and Recommendations

Based on the above findings, a number of energy conservation measures were drawn. These together with their economic analyses are summarized in Table 13.15.

Table 13.15: Summary of Overall Potential Savings

Sl.No.	Proposals	Annual Energy Savings Potential, kWh	Annual Cost Savings Million, UGX	Investment Cost Million, UGX	Pay Back Years
	Electrical Measures				
1.	Switching-off the 1000 kVA transformer no. 2 provided for main electrode boiler after the installation of solar steam generator	27120	5.99	Nil	Immediate
2.	Switching-off the primarily charged stand-by transformers-3, 7 and 8	37668	8.32	Nil	Immediate
3.	Demand reduction by installing capacitors of PCC level	888 kVA	3.45	39.31	11.4

Contd...

Table 13.15–*Contd...*

Sl.No.	*Proposals*	*Annual Energy Savings Potential, kWh*	*Annual Cost Savings Million, UGX*	*Investment Cost Million, UGX*	*Pay Back Years*
4.	Solar steam generating system for cooking application	2146200 (7200 kVA)	465	2050	4.4
5.	Replace water supply pumps	146000	63.7	70	1.09
6.	Avoid the operation of water pump during peak hours	-	0.17	Nil	Immediate
7.	Retrofitting of 2 x 58 W-5' fluorescent tube light (TFL) with De-lamping 1 x 5' - 58W fluorescent tube light in old Mulago clinical areas corridor and waiting areas (with reflectors)	9252	2.04	0.92	0.4
8.	Replacement of 58W - 5' fluorescent tube light (TFL) with 4' - 36W fluorescent tube light (with reflectors and low loss copper choke) in the corridors, waiting areas of old and new Mulago hospital premises	29550	6.52	22.3	3.4
9.	Replacement of 60W incandescent light with 20W energy savers (CFL's)	9490	2.09	10.34	4.94
10.	Replacement of 250W mercury vapour lights with 135W sodium vapour for the street lighting and rectification of timer controls	4927	1.09	8.1	7.44
11.	Replacement of 60W incandescent light with 20W energy savers (CFL's) in guest house and doctors meets and tutors college (separately metered)	5740	2.7	3.6	1.3
12.	Replacement of 250W mercury vapour lights with 135W sodium vapour for the security lighting in guest house (separately metered)	2190	1.03	2	1.94
	Grand Total	**2418137 (8088 kVA)**	**562.1**	**2206.57**	**3.92**

The detailed energy audit identified an annual energy saving potential of 2.4 million kWh of electricity. The proposals that fall under the category of 'short term' were quite significant. The identified energy saving potential is summarized in Table 13.16.

Table 13.16: Identified Saving Potential

Particulars	*Electrical Energy, Million kWh*	*Electrical Cost, Million UGX*
Annual consumption	6.98	1823.8
Study findings on saving potential	2.41	562.1
Saving potential in per cent	34.5	30.82

As could be seen from the energy conservation opportunities, the savings that can be achieved with small investment are quite significant. A load reduction of 550 kW can also be achieved after implementation of energy conservation measures.

References

ERA, 2006., Umeme Limited end-user tariffs http://www.era.or.ug/DistributionTariff.php (Accessed 30th March 2010)

Fisher, F.M.,1962. A Study of Econometrics: The Demand of electricity in the United States of America, North Holland Publishing Co., Amsterdam pp. 256-283.

Houthker, H.S.,1973. Some calculations on electricity consumption in Great Britain, Journal of Royal Statistics, 114, pp. 359-321.

Per, L., 2008. Energy Management Handbook. Royal Institute of Technology, Sweden, pp. 65-73.

Personal communication with Mr. Kizito Joseph, Engineering department, Mulago hospital, March 15, 2010.

Sebastián T., 2002. BASIC of Sean Generación, Energía Engineering and Environmental Protection Publications, pp. 56-64.

Shashank,J., 2004, Report on Comprehensive Energy Audit for Mpanga growers tea factory, Ministry of Energy and Mineral Development, Kampala, Uganda.

Abbreviations and Acronyms

APFC : Automatic power factor controller
CFL : Compact Fluorescent lamp
DG : Diesel Generator
DOL : Direct on -line
DSM : Demand Side Management
ECO : Energy Conservation Opportunities
En : Energy Efficiency
GLS : Incandescent Lamp
HPMV : High Pressure Mercury Vapour lamp
HPSV : High Pressure Sodium Vapour lamp
HSD : High Speed Diesel
HT : High Tension/High Voltage
HVAC : Heating Ventilation Air conditioning system
Hz : Frequency
IDA : International Development Association
IEEE : Institution for Electrical and Electronics Engineers
IMS : Industrial Mentholated Sprit
KL : Kilo Litre

KV : Kilo Volt
KVA : Kilo Volt ampere
KVAr : Kilo Volt ampere reactive
kWh : Kilo Watt hour
LT : Low Tension/Low Voltage
MCC : Motor Control Cubicle
MD : Maximum Demand
MEMD : Ministry of Energy and Mineral Development
MT : Metric Tones
MW : Mega Watt
NWSC : National Water and Sewerage Corporation
OLTC : On load tap Changers
PCC : Power Control Cubicle
PF : Power Factor
PHE : Plate heat Exchanger
PV : Photovoltaic
SIDA : Swedish International Development Agency
SS : Substation
TERI : The Energy and Resources Institute
TFL : Twin fluorescent tube light
TFR : Transformer
THD : Total Harmonic distortion
TPH : Tones per Hour
TR : Tonnes of Refrigeration
UGX : Uganda Shillings
V : Voltage
VFD : Variable Frequency drive
VSD : Variable Speed drive

Chapter 14

Utility- and Private Sector-Driven Energy Efficiency in Uganda's Electricity Market

Geofrey Bakkabulindi[1] *and Izael P. Da Silva*[2]

[1]*Head of Energy Efficiency Program, Centre for Research in Energy and Energy Conservation (CREEC), Makerere University, Uganda*

E-mail: gbakkabulindi@tech.mak.ac.ug

[2]*Director, CREEC, Makerere University, Uganda*

P.O. Box 7062, Kampala, Uganda

ABSTRACT

Uganda's energy sector faced a major crisis in the mid 2000's that led to chronic power shortages in most parts of the country. Although this crisis is now slowly abating, it raised awareness of the need for energy efficiency both from the perspective of the utility and private sector companies. Investments in new power plants are costly and can take many years. Energy conservation and efficiency can be viewed as a virtual power source since saved energy will be availed to other consumers without implementing measures like load shedding. This paper presents measures that were undertaken by the government, private sector and local power distribution utility in Uganda to actively encourage companies, especially large consumers, to conserve energy. The penalty and reward scheme introduced in early 2010 has led several companies to audit their energy usage and adopt efficient energy practices like never before in the country. In addition, the Private Sector Foundation of Uganda has played the role of a catalyst for this process by part-funding smaller companies to install energy efficient equipment.

Keywords: *Electricity market, Energy audit, Energy conservation, Energy efficiency, Power factor correction, Power quality, Uganda.*

1. Introduction

Uganda's current national grid electrification rate is around 5 per cent [1]. Most of this remains concentrated in the urban centres where population accounts for only about 15 per cent of the country's total population [2]. The generation capacity as of 2009 was 527 MW with hydropower generation accounting for 59.8 per cent, thermal power 38.0 per cent and from bagasse 2.3 per cent [2]. The fact that about 60 per cent of the country's total electricity capacity comes from hydropower generation contributed to Uganda's energy crisis experienced between 2004 and 2007. The crisis was the worst experienced in the country since the mid 1980's during the civil war. One of the positive consequences of this crisis was the increased awareness of the need to promote energy efficiency across the board to reduce the impact of such crises in the future. An investigation into the role played by the Ugandan government, the local utility company (UMEME), and the private sector in promoting energy efficient practices following the crisis among electricity consumers is presented here. The initiatives have had successes and failures, which will also be highlighted using specific case studies.

2. Ugandas Energy Crisis

Whereas the current share of hydropower generation is about 60 per cent, prior to the energy crisis this value was much higher. The major hydropower plants, Nalubale (180 MW) and Kiira (120 MW), are located on the river Nile just after it flows out of Lake Victoria. Therefore, changes in water levels in this lake affect the hydropower output. Figure 14.1 shows the overall trend of power generation between 2004 and 2008. The figure shows that there was a sharp decline in generation between

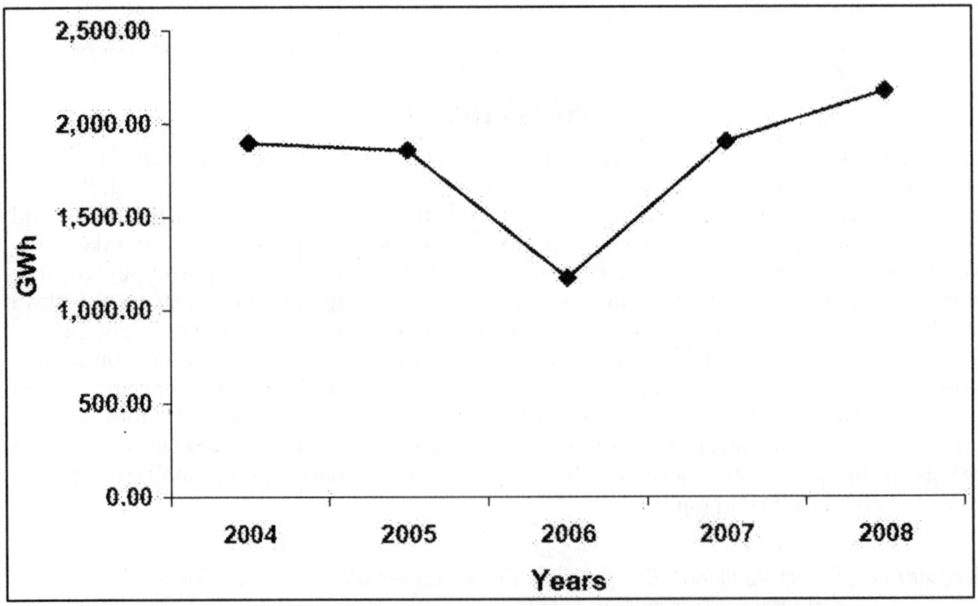

Figure 14.1: Trend of Power Generation from 2004 to 2008

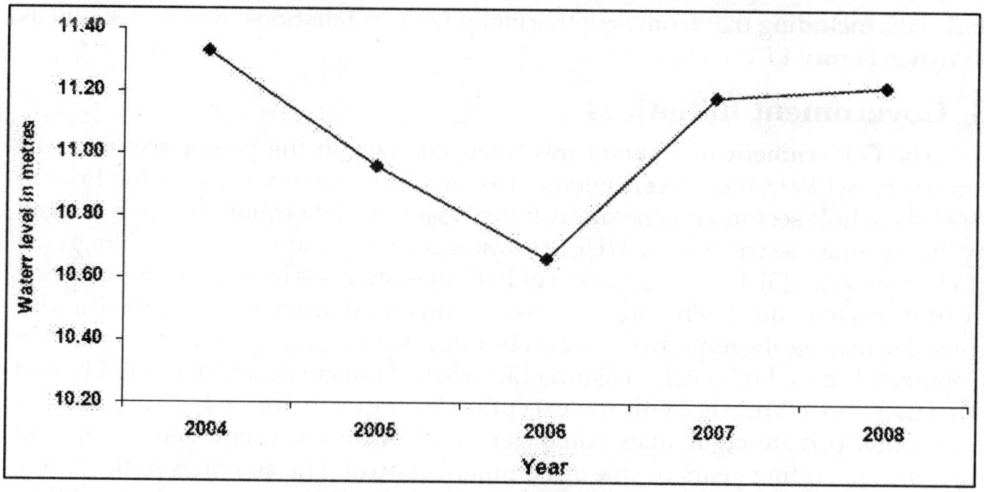

Figure 14.2: Trend of Variation in Water Level at the Dam of L. Victoria between 2004 and 2008

2004 and 2007. This decline was related to the fall in water levels in Lake Victoria during the same time. This relationship is shown in Figure 14.2, which gives the trend of recorded lake levels at the dam during that period.

In addition, there was a steady annual increase in the number of customer connections in the years leading up to the crisis with the highest percentage increase of 11.39 per cent recorded in 2006 [2]. Therefore, the shortage of electricity was also partly due to increased demand during the same period. The ensuing electricity shortage across the country was characterised by widespread load shedding. Several areas would go without electricity in intervals of two days without being followed by one day with power. However, priority areas such as large hospitals and military installations were provided with constant power throughout this period to keep critical activities in operation.

The impact on the economy was immediate. Several small and medium enterprises were forced to buy back-up diesel generators to remain in business. The resulting increase in operation costs subsequently raised the cost of goods and services countrywide. Industrial companies struggled to meet the demand for manufactured goods leading to chronic shortages of goods like sugar and flour. Residential consumers turned to kerosene lanterns for lighting, which increased incidences of smoke-related illnesses indoors and carbon dioxide emissions. Charcoal became the predominant form of fuel for cooking and widespread deforestation ensued to meet this demand.

The Ugandan government was quick to find ways of mitigating the problem. Installations of thermal power plants totalling 200 MW were initiated to beef up the existing hydropower installations. As lake levels rose again between 2007 and 2008, hydropower generation rose from 1,905 kWh in 2007 to 2,176 kWh in 2008 representing a 14.2 per cent increase [2]. The overall increase in power generation between 2007 and 2008, including that from new thermal power installations, was 30 per cent as shown in Figure 14.1.

3. Government Initiatives

The Government of Uganda instituted changes in the power sector in the Electricity Act 1999, which were intended to improve efficiency in the sector. Prior to 1999, the whole sector, *i.e.* generation, transmission and distribution, was managed by the Uganda Electricity Board (UEB) forming a monopoly in a vertically integrated electricity market [3]. Following the Act of 1999, the sector was unbundled into different institutions to control generation, transmission and distribution. The institutions created to manage the respective power sub-sectors were Uganda Electricity Generation Company Limited (UEGCL), Uganda Electricity Transmission Company Limited (UETCL) and UMEME. With the exception of transmission, which remained a monopoly, private companies could get involved in electricity generation and distribution ending years of sole government control. The activities of the newly created institutions were to be regulated by the Electricity Regulatory Authority (ERA). It was hoped that the new policy would improve the sector's financial viability and hence reduce its dependency on government subsidies.

Following the energy crisis above, the government instituted measures through the Ministry of Energy and Mineral Development (MEMD) to mitigate the electricity shortfall on both the demand and supply side. On the supply side, as a medium term measure, grid-connected thermal power plants were installed in Lugogo (50 MW), Namanve (50 MW), Kiira (50 MW) and Mutundwe (50 MW) giving a total output of 200 MW by 2010. The increased use of renewable energy is a major objective of Uganda's energy policy. Therefore, generation using hydro sources was increased through the construction of small hydropower schemes often operated by Independent Power Producers (IPPs). Investors in rural electrification schemes are able to receive facilitation up to 50 per cent of the capital cost through the Rural Electrification Agency (REA). Table 14.1 shows the electricity energy and peak power demand since 2001 as well as the forecasts beyond 2010. The growth in demand ranges between 7 to 9 per cent [3] meaning that generation will have to be increased to meet this demand.

On the demand side, the government has initiated activities aimed at improving the efficient use of energy starting from household level. The share of electricity use among the different consumers is 25.6 per cent in residential, 13.8 per cent in commercial, 60.5 per cent in industrial sector and the rest being used for street lighting [1]. One initiative undertaken was in 2007 whereby the government procurement of 800,000 compact fluorescent tubes for distribution free of charge to commercial and residential consumers in and around the capital, Kampala. In this scheme, each beneficiary received three CFLs free in return for three incandescent bulbs. Since CFLs are up to 80 per cent more efficient than incandescent bulbs, this exercise was intended to reduce the peak demand contribution from lighting. There was dramatic reduction in load shedding throughout the city following this exercise. However, the real impact of the CFLs on this could not be accurately verified since later that year the thermal power plant of 50 MW in Kiira was commissioned. Subsequent studies, however, showed that most of the beneficiary households were paying less in electricity bills than before the exercise.

Table 14.1: Demand Forecasts in Uganda's Electricity Market

Year	*Energy (GWh)*			*Peak Demand (MW)*		
	Low	*Medium*	*High*	*Low*	*Medium*	*High*
2001	1,437	1,437	1,437	270	270	270
2002	1,695	1,506	1,544	274	283	289
2003	1,767	1,767	1,767	308	308	308
2004	1,843	1,843	1,843	317	317	317
2005	1,767	1,684	1,849	279	317	345
2006	1.968	2,025	2,057	380	380	380
2010	2.320	2,674	2,896	442	498	528
2015	2.850	3,785	4,442	535	697	796
2020	3.501	5,359	6,813	647	976	1.200
2025	4,300	7,586	10,449	783	1,367	1.809
2002-25	4.28%	7.20%	8.93%	3.88%	6.97%	8.56%

Source: Uganda Electricity Transmission Company Ltd 2006

4. Utility Initiatives

The sole electricity distribution utility in Uganda is UMEME. Following the energy crisis, UMEME realized the need to sensitise consumers on good energy management for improved demand side energy efficiency. In addition to using the media to highlight how consumers can optimally use their electricity, it introduced the reward and penalty scheme in January 2010.

4.1 Reward and Penalty Scheme for Industrial Users

This scheme was aimed at the industrial sector, which constitutes over 60 per cent of total electricity consumption in the electricity market. Efficiency improvements here would have the biggest impact on overall peak demand. In the scheme, companies that performed well in terms of optimal energy usage would be rewarded with reduced bill payments whereas those that used their energy inefficiently would be penalized with a higher kWh unit cost. The performance measurement was based on the operating power factor. A monthly average power factor above 0.894 would attract a lower cost per kWh while that less than 0.894 would lead to a higher unit cost. The cost per unit on penalty and reward lines was computed according to equations (1) and (2) respectively. The equations were obtained from records at UMEME.

$$B_p = (k - k1/2) + k1 \bullet \tan\varphi \tag{1}$$

$$B_r = (k - k2/2) + k2 \bullet \tan\varphi \tag{2}$$

Where φ is the voltage angle and:

k=184.8: Average tarrif kWh Charge

k1=40: kVArh penalty

k2=20: kVArh Reward

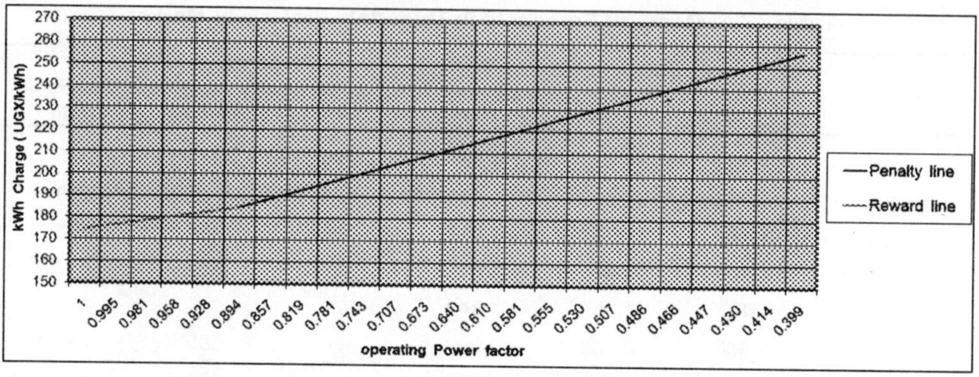

Figure 14.3: Variation of Unit Cost of Electricity with Power Factor (*Source*: UMEME)

The graph in Figure 14.3 shows the variation of unit cost with power factor (pf) giving the reward and penalty lines.

Following the introduction of the reward and penalty scheme, many industrial companies immediately undertook energy audits in order to take advantage of the rewards. It was clear that inefficient operation of industrial equipment and processes incurred heavy cost to the companies every month. The scheme, therefore, provided an unprecedented incentive for the large power consumers to optimally and efficiently use their energy. Many companies then purchased and installed capacitor banks in a bid to improve their operating power factor.

5. Private Sector Initiatives

The contribution of the private sector in promoting energy efficiency in the country's electricity market has been spearheaded by the Private Sector Foundation of Uganda (PSFU). PSFU through its Energy for Rural Transformation (ERT) program provides a grant scheme aimed at improving the capacities of private sector firms in the application of efficient and productive use of electricity. In addition, PSFU promotes capacity for energy professionals in the country through training sponsorships and incorporation of energy efficiency modules in University curricula.

In 2008, PSFU initiated a program of part-financing the recommendations of large companies that carried out energy audits. This financial assistance would be provided in the form of purchase of energy efficient equipment and meeting costs of efficient changes in energy infrastructure. Under the program, PSFU would fully fund energy audits at selected companies and help meet the costs of implementing the recommendations of the audits up to a maximum of USD 25,000. This initiative was targeted at reducing the average peak load by 3.5 MVA. This could be achieved by targeting large industrial companies which not only contribute the largest amount to the peak load, but also are able to afford the considerable cost of buying and installing energy solutions required after the amount contributed by PSFU. The Centre for Research in Energy and Energy Conservation (CREEC) had a Memorandum of Understanding with PSFU to verify the savings accrued. During the preparation of this paper the program was still underway, therefore, no substantiated results could be reported.

6. Conclusion

The paper has highlighted the impact of Uganda's energy crisis on improved energy efficiency in the domestic and commercial sectors. The initiatives by the government, utility and private sectors have contributed to the considerable reduction in the peak load. Furthermore, better energy efficiency has not only enabled companies and homes to save money on their electricity bills but has also reduced the need for load shedding. Energy efficiency has provided a virtual power source through the reduction of the load, energy losses and wastage, especially in large companies. Based on this background, it can be observed that the energy crisis contributed positively to electricity consumers' awareness of the need for optimal and efficient energy usage, and it alerted the government to increased involvement in this process.

Acknowledgements

The authors would like to acknowledge the Ministry of Energy and Mineral Development, Mr. Sylver Hategekimana from UMEME, and Mr. Geofrey Ssebuggwawo from PSFU for providing background information used in this paper.

References

1. Ministry of Energy and Mineral Development, Uganda, 2008. Uganda Energy Balance. http://www.energyandminerals.go.ug/bal.php, accessed February 2011.
2. Uganda Bureau of Statistics (UBOS), 2009. Statistical Abstract.
3. Rugumayo, Albert I. 2008. Renewable Energy Policy Issues in Africa.
4. Ministry of Energy and Mineral Development, 2007. The Renewable Energy Policy for Uganda.

